"In *Brown Faces, White Spaces,* Latasha Morrison masterfully weaves together personal and collective experiences to craft a compelling case for liberation. In a time when so many are trying to redefine or eliminate the call for justice, this book helps readers become deeply rooted in theological truths and equipped with the historical facts needed to confront the systems standing in the way of change. Her writing is thorough, insightful, and challenging. After reading this book, I feel more ready than ever to be a voice for liberation."

—DANIELLE COKE BALFOUR, artist, speaker, entrepreneur, and founder of Oh Happy Dani

"I highly recommend *Brown Faces, White Spaces* by Latasha Morrison. It is a profound exploration of systemic racism in American institutions. Morrison skillfully intertwines historical context with personal narratives, highlighting the long-lasting impact of racial inequities. This is an essential read for anyone committed to understanding and addressing racial justice issues."

—LISA V. FIELDS, founder and president of Jude 3 Project

"In our fractured and polarized times, it seems impossible to write a book about systemic racism that doesn't alienate one faction of the culture wars or the other. Well, Latasha Morrison has done the impossible. With her blend of personal narrative, historical research, and gentle but direct invitation, this trustworthy guide inspires us to imagine a time when racism's power will be broken in every domain of society. Even better, Morrison shows us how we can each speed the arrival of that day."

—DAVID SWANSON, author of *Rediscipling the White Church*

"There are few voices in our midst that can comfort as they convict. My sister Latasha Morrison is certainly one such voice. Through responsibly recounted narratives, she illuminates both past and present realities of the foundations of racial disparity. But she doesn't leave us in despair. Morrison invites us to biblical preparation and action, giving us practical questions to consider and tools to guide and implement. *Brown Faces, White Spaces* is a canvas of both historical and gospel truth upon which Morrison prophetically paints with expertise and hope."

—ASHLEE EILAND, thought leader, Bible teacher, and
author of *Human(Kind)* and *Say Good*

"The truth really shall set us free, and in this book, Latasha Morrison guides us through historical, cultural, and biblical truths—truths that, if we were to take them seriously, would shift the liberation both experienced and felt in the United States. The way Morrison took the time to address several arenas of life is both impressive and important, because racism is found in places that we either ignore or forget about. Her dedication to justice, racial reconciliation, and liberation is clearly displayed throughout this book and is an invitation for us to have a heart for these very things as well."

—PRICELIS PERREAUX-DOMINGUEZ, author of *Being a Sanctuary*,
founder of Full Collective ministry, and
creator of the Sowers Summit

"Injustice does not just happen, and it does not repair itself. To move toward the necessary work of repair by dismantling and resisting the status quo of injustice, we need to be honest about how racism has and continues to remain embedded in systems, policies, and culture. Morrison has given us the gift of her perspective, experience, and research in *Brown Faces, White Spaces*. One day, the status quo of righteousness and justice will roll down like a river. Until that day, this book offers insight and guidance to pick up the mantles left for us to confront injustice and join the important work of resistance."

—MICHELLE FERRIGNO WARREN, activist and
author of *Join the Resistance* and *The Power of Proximity*

"In *Brown Faces, White Spaces*, Latasha Morrison confronts the existence of systemic racism and its social ills. Infused with practical Christian theology, academic scholarship, personal stories, and community experiences, this vital work illustrates how racial reconciliation can be tackled and institutional historical disparities redressed. Steeped in a mindset of cultural humility, Morrison encourages collaborative efforts that advance justice and promote equality within a polarized world."

—CLAUDIA MAY, PhD, author of *Birthing Butterflies* and
When I Fly with Papa

"*Brown Faces, White Spaces* is more than just another narrative about injustice; it's a call to action. It challenges readers to face harsh truths, recognize our shared history of systemic injustice, and engage collectively in creating a more just and equitable society for all. Morrison's approach is insightful and urges readers to consider how they might take transformative action across a wide range of topics where racial injustice persists, including education, healthcare, the justice system, the marketplace, the military, property ownership, entertainment, sports, and the church. Masterfully intertwining personal narratives with historical analysis, Morrison invites readers on a journey that encourages us to love our neighbors in real time as we understand the history that has shaped us."

—DR. TERENCE LESTER, founder of Love Beyond Walls and
author of *I See You, When We Stand,*
and *All God's Children*

"Latasha Morrison is a truth-teller. In *Brown Faces, White Spaces*, she bears witness to the truth as she scrutinizes and dissects the origin stories of nine sectors of U.S. society to reveal the roots of systemic racism. Morrison weaves history with her own personal story to educate our minds and tug at our hearts. She reveals the wound in order to heal the wound. She invites us into the work of liberation through an accessible framework to become peacemakers and active reconcilers."

—INÉS VELÁSQUEZ-MCBRYDE, preacher, reconciler, speaker, and co-lead pastor of The Church We Hope For in Pasadena, California

"I trust Latasha Morrison wholeheartedly, both in who she is as a person and in the words she writes. *Brown Faces, White Spaces* reveals her unwavering commitment to helping people courageously and honestly respond to the racial brokenness and systemic injustice in our world. This book is a road map to help us all reimagine a world where racial diversity is celebrated as a source of strength and every individual is recognized for their inherent value. Through Morrison's striking storytelling and candid narration of history, she extends a compelling invitation for each of us to confront the uncomfortable truths of the past. It's a call to action to forge a future that is characterized by dignity and freedom for all."

—JEANNE STEVENS, founding lead pastor of Soul City Church, Chicago, and bestselling author of *What's Here Now?*

BROWN FACES, WHITE SPACES

BROWN FACES, WHITE SPACES

Confronting Systemic Racism to Bring Healing and Restoration

Latasha Morrison

Foreword by Eugene Cho

Afterword by Dr. Anita Phillips

WaterBrook

Copyright © 2024 by Latasha Morrison
Foreword by Rev. Eugene Cho copyright © 2024 by Penguin Random House LLC.
Afterword by Dr. Anita Phillips copyright © 2024 by Penguin Random House LLC.

Published in the United States by WaterBrook, an imprint of Random House, a division of Penguin Random House LLC.

WATERBROOK and colophon are registered trademarks of Penguin Random House LLC.

Published in association with Yates & Yates, www.yates2.com.

Library of Congress Cataloging-in-Publication Data
Names: Morrison, LaTasha, author.
Title: Brown faces, white spaces: confronting systemic racism
to bring healing and restoration / Latasha Morrison.
Other titles: Confronting systemic racism to bring healing and restoration
Description: First edition. | [Colorado Springs, Colorado] : WaterBrook, [2024] |
Includes bibliographical references.
Identifiers: LCCN 2023046532 | ISBN 9780593444825 (hardback) |
ISBN 9780593444832 (ebook)
Subjects: LCSH: Racism—United States—History. | Minorities—United States—Social
conditions. | United States—Race relations—Religious aspects—Christianity. |
Reconciliation—Religious aspects—Christianity. | Morrison, LaTasha.
Classification: LCC E184.A1 M685 2024 | DDC 305.800973—dc23/eng/20231103
LC record available at https://lccn.loc.gov/2023046532

Printed in the United States of America on acid-free paper

waterbrookmultnomah.com

9 8 7 6 5 4 3 2 1

First Edition

Book design by Sara Bereta

Most WaterBrook books are available at special quantity discounts for bulk purchase for premiums, fundraising, corporate and educational needs by organizations, churches, and businesses. Special books or book excerpts also can be created to fit specific needs. For details, contact specialmarketscms@penguinrandomhouse.com.

To my great-grandparents,
Willie and Gladys Nicholson and Clifton and Lilly Ray.

For all those who survived systemic racism
and those who are still surviving.

Foreword

I remember vividly when I first met Latasha Morrison. I was speaking at a conference in Texas in 2015. It was a huge gathering because, apparently, everything has to be bigger in Texas. It may sound strange to share these details, but she approached me with excitement, thanked me for my ministry, and asked if we could take a picture together.

Of course, I was happy to take a picture with her (I still proudly have it on my phone, by the way), but I think she was genuinely surprised when I reciprocated my gratitude for her work. Even though we had not previously met in person, I knew exactly who she was, because when one seeks to do the work of racial justice and reconciliation in today's context, you eventually "know" others who've also been in the trenches. In this hard, rigorous, and at times lonely work, inevitably, you learn of and about others' efforts.

That's the most important thing I want you to know about Latasha Morrison: Before she became a widely known leader, before she started giving keynote messages throughout the country, before she became a

New York Times bestselling author, before she organically amassed a large social media presence, *Latasha Morrison was doing this work.*

Now, I'm not trying to diminish her aforementioned accomplishments or the substantive work that she continues to pursue through her Be the Bridge organization and community, but the most important thing I can share with you about this book is the credibility of the author.

I need you to know that for Morrison, this isn't just a new book to follow up on the impact of her first book, *Be the Bridge: Pursuing God's Heart for Racial Reconciliation.* This isn't a new talk or initiative that sprang up as part of the wave of experts, gurus, or whatever other elevated phrases we use to describe people, especially with the recent explosion of DEI initiatives where it seemed like so many self-elevated themselves as experts for hire. For Morrison, this book is birthed out of a calling, a deep conviction, and a journey to which she has devoted much of her life as a follower of Jesus.

This is why I'm grateful for Morrison's work in *Brown Faces, White Spaces.* But let me be clear: If you're looking for a quick, light, rah-rah, feel-good, fuzzy, "here are three simple things to do to fix everything" kind of book, well, this isn't quite the book for you. And I'm grateful for this because it's far too tempting to glamorize or romanticize this work. In our incredibly polarized society, another temptation is to err the other way and utilize fear, guilt, and shame to move people to action, which will inevitably fail and only create more resentment and divisiveness.

Let's be honest. Reconciliation and racial justice have become trendy topics. There are gatherings, sermons, classes, podcasts, TikTok videos, and even entire conferences around these subjects. But if we're not careful, it's quite possible and tempting to be more in love with the idea of reconciliation than to engage in the actual work of reconciliation. In other words, we can be enamored by the idea of reconciliation and racial justice until we realize it involves confession, confronting, truth-telling, repenting, dismantling, forgiving, and bridge building.

Furthermore, racial reconciliation, for some, has been relegated to merely personal change or transformation. *Me, myself, and I. My heart. My soul.* No doubt, personal change is absolutely essential. People need to change. But this work can't be solely about personal change. It must also engage structural and societal change through education, health-care, justice, banking and finances, entertainment and storytelling, sports, and so much more. Simultaneously, some people believe we need only systematic change, altogether ignoring the power and importance of personal change.

Our hearts *and* our structures need transformation. Both are essential.

Brown Faces, White Spaces urges us on in that transformative work. This book is pastoral and prophetic. It's personal and communal. It's vulnerable and disruptive. Through it all, the book and its author never relinquish the exhortation to fix our eyes on Christ, the author and perfecter of our faith.

—Rev. Eugene Cho, President of Bread for the World
and author of *Thou Shalt Not Be a Jerk:
A Christian's Guide to Engaging Politics*

Contents

Author's Note

Dear Reader,

I'm so glad you're here, especially given the weight of the topic. It's not easy to pick up a book about racial injustice, particularly when the book examines uncomfortable, often even painful, historical truths. So, thank you for engaging in this conversation with me.

Books like this one—books exposing the artifacts and lingering effects of racism in America—require a lot of humility from both the author and the reader. Both must start from the premise that our personal experiences are not universal. Both must be open to listening, learning, and lamenting as we explore history. Both are obligated to engage the material in search of transformation rather than from an entrenched position of critique. I hope we can do this as we journey through this book together.

Brown Faces, White Spaces explores how Black, Indigenous, and other people of color have intersected historically with systems of oppression in the United States of America, and how the effects of that oppression have an impact on our nation today. It's important to remember that Black, Indigenous, and people of color (BIPOC, as used throughout this book) are not a monolith. We have different experiences within systems, and still, we have a collective story of systemic injustice that connects us to one another. So, as you read these stories, understand there are numerous BIPOC experiences, but there's still a certain connective tissue within them. We call that connective tissue *history*. As you read about the individuals whose stories help illuminate key truths about our nation's ongoing reckoning with our racial history, hopefully you'll see the connective tissue and how it ties into your story, the story of your relatives, or the stories of friends or acquaintances who have been on the giving or receiving end of systemic racial injustice. Maybe your story within this system produced different outcomes—maybe even more positive outcomes. We can celebrate those positive stories while at the same time not denying or deflecting the total impact systemic racism has had on groups of people for centuries.

Please note that systemic racism is a complex issue in the United States, and I didn't have the page count to delve too deeply into each system—the "white spaces"—addressed in this book. In fact, each system represented in these pages could be a book solely on its own. The important thing to remember is that each example of systemic racism—whether in one of the systems depicted in this book or in another system altogether—has a human face. Put another way, systemic racism causes very real harm to very real people, many of whom you know.

As I wrote, I labored over the terminology I used to represent non-white people. I vetted that language with others, both people of color and white people. Sometimes, we disagreed about the use of certain terminology because in the United States we seem to lack a common language and common view of history, even within our own ethnic groups. So know this: When I use the term BIPOC in the book, it is intentional, meant to connect the stories and specific discrimination experienced by Black people, Indigenous people, and people of color.

This term is specific to the United States and centers our experiences and demonstrates solidarity among communities of color. This term emphasizes the continued impact of systemic racism and how it presently oppresses and invalidates the lives of non-white people. But as I already mentioned, this does not mean that all people of color carry the same lived experience, especially when it comes to education, legislation, and systemic oppression, and neither is BIPOC a stand-in term for Black people.

There are also times throughout this book where I use the term Brown, referring to the experiences of Indigenous, Black, Latina/Latino, and Asian Americans. It's an equally permissive term for the shared classification of non-white people, a term that allows us to better frame the broader struggle against years of systemic oppression. And though you might not use these terms in your everyday life, consider the language and how it might draw you into a different understanding of the world around you. Through the lens of a BIPOC or Brown person, America looks very different than it might to white men and women.

Finally, the stories in this book are told from my perspective as an African American woman. Although this book is inclusive, it does not represent every marginalized community. Why? Because as a Black woman, I don't have the perspective needed to share the personal stories of every marginalized community. If you're in another marginalized group, I encourage you to tell your story of being a Brown face in white spaces. If you're a white person, seek to understand the stories of other groups of people and stand in solidarity against oppression.

Now, take a deep breath. In that breath, remember that if you are breathing, you have the agency to bring about change. The issues in this book are layered, painful, and uncomfortable. We didn't cause systemic racism. It's not our fault that unjust systems exist, but it is our collective responsibility not to uphold those unjust systems. And there is plenty of reason to hope. Change is possible if we exercise our shared responsibility to be a part of the solution. We can call communities to a deeper understanding of empathy, love, compassion, and justice. We can build one another up and invest in restoration. We can work toward liberation, just like so many of the people in the pages of this book have done.

Thank you for locking arms with me. Thank you for caring about racial justice. Remember, transformation begins with you.

BROWN
FACES,
WHITE
SPACES

CHAPTER 1

Our Journey Toward
True Emancipation

I

N 1973, I ENTERED THIS WORLD AT CAPE FEAR VALLEY HOSPITAL IN
Fayetteville, North Carolina. I was born fully American, and as a citizen, I'd have the right to free education, to free speech, to property ownership when I reached the age of eighteen, to vote (also when I turned eighteen), and to hold public office one day. But as obvious as all of that might sound (*Aren't all Americans born with those inalienable rights?*), I was the first person in my immediate Morrison family tree to be born under the full protections of the United States Constitution.

Those who know me might be shocked by this statement because I'm not that old. I look even younger than my driver's license says I am—forty-nine years as of the writing of this book. But as we'll see throughout these pages, African Americans born just a generation before me didn't grow up with the same set of rights and protections. And the effects of racism still linger today.

Black and Brown brothers and sisters, I see you nodding.

Some Americans may think of systemic racism as an unfortunate part of history, something that happened "back in the day." It was a fixture in the time of black-and-white television. But many Black and Brown Americans know through firsthand experience that systemic racism still exists today, because the systems were never truly dismantled in our country. How do we know? Because we've heard and lived the stories. We've had our perspectives shaped by both history *and* experience.

The stories of the past, and our experiences in the present, shape who we are and how we move in this world. They continue to shape my expectations, my fears, and my hopes for a better future for my nieces and nephews. I'll share numerous stories and experiences in this book, but let me start with the story of my parents.

My dad was born in North Carolina in a time when state-sanctioned racial apartheid was baked into the state's Jim Crow laws, laws that maintained strict public separation between whites and non-whites. As a young boy in 1952, he was shut out of the better schools in and around his hometown of Fayetteville and sent to Black-only schools in Black-only redlined districts drawn by white legislators. The United States Supreme Court had long since declared in the 1896 case of *Plessy v. Ferguson* that segregation laws were enforceable, so long as the facilities provided to ethnic minorities were "separate but equal." Yet the schools my dad attended were anything but equal. The facilities were run-down and understaffed, and the teachers—most of whom were Black—were underpaid. Students were not given current textbooks or other educational materials. These realities would not change for many schools in the American South, even after the 1954 Supreme Court ruling in *Brown v. Board of Education* ended school segregation. (See chapter 2 for more information on this.)

My mom was not a stranger to discrimination and systemic racism either, though her experience was very different from my dad's. She was a military kid, and her dad—my grandfather, whom I discuss in chapters 2 and 6—moved from one base to another. This gave her an international educational experience in military schools, which were mostly desegregated.

When she was in high school, her class was the first to integrate at

Seventy-First High School in Fayetteville, North Carolina, in 1968. Though integration wasn't easy, my mom navigated it, helped in part by the education she'd received in her earlier years.

Though my mom had better educational experiences than my dad, her family still felt the brunt of systemic racism. Many men of color fought bravely for their country in World War II, the Korean War, and the Vietnam War, and yet a disproportionate number of them died for their country, often with little recognition. Though the military was desegregated in 1948 by President Harry S. Truman, equal pay for Black and Brown military members was little more than a pipe dream well into the 1980s and 1990s. Non-white service members were often given less desirable posts, which meant lower wages. Men of color didn't advance through the military ranks as quickly (or as far) as their white counterparts either. So, my mom and her family endured a military environment that treated men like my grandfather as if they were second-class service members, both in pay and in their assignments.

The stories of my immediate family's experience of racism were not the only thing that shaped me. Years ago, my aunt Len shared a story about my great-uncle Willie Junior (my mother's uncle), who passed away before I had the chance to know him. As a young man, he migrated to New York City sometime in the 1950s to escape the racial terror of Jim Crow laws. He'd had enough of pretending to be docile even when being called "boy"—or worse—by white people, so he was one of thousands who made the move in hopes of finding a better way of life and job opportunities beyond sharecropping or serving as a house servant. However, much to his dismay, he was greeted in northern states with what some called "James Crow" laws—laws that, while not as draconian as the Jim Crow segregation laws in the South, still disadvantaged non-white people. So, imagine the rage he must have felt when he realized the conditions in the North were not that much better. Imagine his anger when he realized white systems are the same, no matter where you go.

After living in the North for some time, my great-uncle, whom we affectionally called Uncle Brother, returned home to visit my great-grandfather Willie Nicholson, an illiterate Southern Black man who worked as a country sharecropper, port laborer, and railroad hand in an effort to create a better way for his children. My great-grandfather endured insults, being called every name in the book. I'm sure he took a beating or two along the way. He was trained not to look into the eyes of a white man, not to walk on the same side of the sidewalk, and to call every white person "mister" or "missus," regardless of their age, though my great-grandfather was a landowner. He had inherited twenty acres of farmland from his mom, who had received a portion of the land where her mother, Sally McQueen, was enslaved.

Over the years, my great-uncle had watched as his father (my great-grandfather) fought to retain ownership of his land. He saw white people pull out forged deeds for the property, hoping to steal it from his father. My great-uncle discovered that his father had to hire a lawyer so he wouldn't lose the land. The system was stacked against Black men, and my great-uncle knew it. So, while visiting his father, my great-uncle heard him call a white gas station attendant "sir," and he lost it. When they climbed back in the car, he exploded, telling my great-grandfather to stop being so polite to all the white men who'd mistreated him for so many years.

As the family story goes, my great-uncle tore into his father. "They ain't no sirs or misters!" he yelled. It's said that my great-grandfather didn't yell back but simply replied that a Black man living in the South has to make some concessions to get along and survive. That was that.

My great-grandfather learned to put on a polite face and call the white men of his community "sir" as his small concession for survival. By doing so, he'd gotten into less trouble than many of his other Black friends, and he'd enjoyed a little more prosperity too.

Times have changed—or at least they've been rebranded. Schools celebrate Black History Month. (Though as of the writing of this book, some public schools restrict the teaching of Black history, claiming that it's "woke" or Marxist.) Companies have diversity and inclusion committees. But even so, as you'll see throughout this book, there are still many spaces where people of color are silenced, underrepresented, and underserved. You'll meet a Black military member who was told he was too intimidating, that he should tone it down. You'll meet a professional athlete who was blackballed by the National Football League for standing against racism. You'll read about people of color who were arrested for sitting in a restaurant. You'll see the way systems of racism are woven into the modern fabric of American life. As a result, even in a modern America where slavery and Jim Crow have been abolished, many BIPOC continue to do just what my great-grandfather did—they go along to get along.

CREATED EQUALLY, TREATED DIFFERENTLY

The message of history as it has played out through American systems is clear: Though "all men are created equal," they're not all treated as equals. As we'll see in this book, BIPOC—Black, Indigenous, and people of color—have been treated differently in systems created by white men: education, the military, commerce, and other societal spaces. The unfortunate truth is that the stories illustrating these forms of systemic racism are rarely taught in our educational system. Why? Maybe it's because they cause too much shame for white people who've perpetuated the systems and for Brown people who've been subjected to those systems. Maybe it's because there are men and women in power who'd just as soon maintain the status quo to retain power. Maybe it's because we believe the lie that to move forward, we must stop dwelling on the past. Whatever the reason, the truth about our American systems has too often been swept under the rug.

To solve any social issue, we must take a holistic view of the problem. If there were a food shortage, we would look at what caused the shortage and how we might prevent it from happening in the future. Ignoring the problem wouldn't cure the food shortage, and simply talking about it wouldn't fill people's bellies. The same is true about issues of race. If we don't talk openly about the historical *and* current reality of racial bias and inequity, and if we don't act based on those conversations, we'll continue to suffer the effects across all segments of American society.

So let's talk openly about the unfortunate truth that the racist systems of the past continue to shape the systems of today. They shape the opportunities people of color receive, the ways we're viewed, and the ways we are treated by society. Every Black and Brown person I know has suffered some kind of discrimination, whether in a job interview, while applying for a loan, at a traffic stop, at a polling place, or at a hospital. At some point, each of us has felt like an outsider in our own country. This is precisely why I wrote this book.

Looking at America's history, there can be no doubt: Black and Brown people have found themselves on the outside looking in, making concessions to survive. Even today, many of us modify our behavior to fly under the radar, to make less noise so we won't be the targets of discrimination.

When we explore the Scriptures, as we'll do throughout this book, it's clear: God hates any form of partiality (James 2:1–13). And racism is nothing more than partiality based on skin color. God wants to root this out and tear down the structures and systems that perpetuate racism and racial partiality. He wants his people to prepare their hearts and dedicate themselves to the liberation of people and systems. So why haven't we?

In this book, we'll ask that question while looking at various systems of American society—education, economic, military, entertainment, judicial, religious, and others. We'll ask questions like:

What is the truth inherent in this system of power?
What role have people of peace played in paving the pathway to repair?
How might we create systems for all to flourish?

We'll also glean wisdom from the Bible, considering how it might ask us to dismantle racially inequitable systems. As we do, we'll examine how to prepare for change, how to dedicate ourselves and our systems to equity, and how that preparation and dedication will lead to true liberation for people of color today.

Perhaps you are wondering, when I use the term *liberation,* what do I mean? Good question.

LIBERATION FROM A CHRISTIAN PERSPECTIVE

I approach liberation from a Christian perspective. Gustavo Gutiérrez, a Peruvian priest and one of the fathers of liberation theology,[1] wrote several books that influenced Black theologians, who in turn influenced the preachers I've listened to all my life. If we believe that God created all people with equal dignity, opportunity, and agency, shouldn't we dismantle the systems that are opposed to this freedom? This was the message I heard from my earliest days in church.

If you grew up in a Black church, maybe you've heard numerous sermons on the Exodus account. Though my parents weren't regular churchgoers, I attended services with my grandparents frequently. There, I heard the stories of liberation. The people of God—the Israelites—were enslaved by the Egyptians, just as African Americans were enslaved in the seventeenth, eighteenth, and nineteenth centuries. For more than four hundred years (see Exodus 12:40–41), they labored under their oppressors, contributing to the wealth, infrastructure, and power of Egypt, just as my ancestors had for white Americans. But God heard their cries and chose Moses, an Israelite raised as an Egyptian, to free his people.

Maybe you know the rest of the story. God sent Moses to pronounce a series of plagues on Egypt, each time informing Pharaoh that the plague could be avoided if he would simply liberate the Israelites from slavery and oppression. Since Pharaoh refused, he and his people suffered the consequences of nine plagues (see Exodus 7–10). After the ninth plague—a plague of total darkness covering the land—Moses announced the tenth and final plague:

> "This is what the LORD says: 'About midnight I will go throughout Egypt. Every firstborn son in Egypt will die, from the firstborn son of Pharaoh, who sits on the throne, to the firstborn son of the female slave, who is at her hand mill, and all the firstborn of the cattle as well. There will be loud wailing throughout Egypt—worse than there has ever been or ever will be again. But among the Israelites not a dog will bark at any person or animal.' Then you will know that the LORD makes a distinction between Egypt and Israel. All these officials of yours will come to me, bowing down before me and saying, 'Go, you and all the people who follow you!' After that I will leave." Then Moses, hot with anger, left Pharaoh. (11:4–8)

Unlike with the other plagues, God issued special instructions to his people for this final plague. They were to clean their houses of all leaven on the first day of the month (see 12:15) and prepare a sacrificial lamb. On the fourteenth day of the month, each family was to sacrifice the lamb and dedicate their house to the Lord by painting the blood of the lamb on their doorposts (see 12:6–7). On the Passover night, as the Israelites ate their first liberation meal, the angel of death passed over the land of Egypt, bringing death and destruction to the oppressor while sparing the houses of Israelites who had prepared and dedicated themselves to their coming liberation.

On the following day, Pharaoh, who'd lost his own son in the plague, liberated the Israelites. This is a reminder to people of color today that just as the Israelites were liberated from systems of injustice, we can trust that God will do the same for us.

This theology of liberation also comes from Jesus himself. Jesus, we were taught, is the Savior, Redeemer, and Deliverer of all. I still hold to that truth. Through his death and resurrection, we are saved from our sin and restored to right relationship with God. And a natural outcome of that divine act of reconciliation is the liberation of humanity from *every* sin-filled system of oppression. That's why, when Jesus started his earthly ministry, he went into the synagogue and read from the prophet Isaiah:

> The Spirit of the Lord is on me,
>> because he has anointed me
>> to proclaim good news to the poor.
> He has sent me to proclaim freedom for the prisoners
>> and recovery of sight for the blind,
> to set the oppressed free,
>> to proclaim the year of the Lord's favor. (Luke 4:18–19)

That's also why, in the gospel of Matthew, he preached a counter cultural sermon, one in which he taught that the poor in spirit, the mourners, the meek, those who hunger and thirst for righteousness, those who are merciful, the pure in heart, the peacemakers, and the persecuted would all be liberated from the troubles of the earth and would take their rightful place in heaven with God (see Matthew 5:3–12). Later, in that same gospel, Jesus preached that those who liberate the hungry, thirsty, and oppressed are serving God himself. "Truly I tell you, whatever you did for one of the least of these brothers and sisters of mine, you did for me," Jesus said (25:40).

Jesus practiced what he preached. Over and over again, he liberated people from sickness, demonic possession, and religious oppression. In the ultimate act of liberation, he died, was buried, and was resurrected, breaking the bondage of sin and the chains of death.

As our congregation listened to those sermons, we came to understand that liberation was a primary theme of the Scriptures. The liberation of Christ gave us hope that we wouldn't always live in oppressive structures, that one day Christ would return and tear down every unjust system. We were also taught that we were agents of liberation, and so we were to be about the work of liberation. But that liberation doesn't happen overnight. Liberation requires preparation and dedication, a truth we also see throughout the Scriptures, both in the spiritual and physical contexts.

In my adult years, I've come to recognize other passages of Scripture as passages of liberation. For instance, in his letter to the Romans, Paul wrote about Christ's return to liberate his people from sin and death. In Romans 13:1–10, he encouraged the believers to be honest, to submit to governing authorities, to love one another, and to obey the commandments. He continued, calling the people to dedicate themselves to purity:

> The night is nearly over; the day is almost here. So let us put aside the deeds of darkness and put on the armor of light. Let us behave decently, as in the daytime, not in carousing and drunkenness, not in sexual immorality and debauchery, not in dissension and jealousy. Rather, clothe yourselves with the Lord Jesus Christ, and do not think about how to gratify the desires of the flesh. (verses 12–14)

Paul encouraged the people of God to prepare their hearts—*put aside the deeds of darkness and put on the armor of light*—and dedicate their lives. Why? Because liberation and salvation were coming. As Paul wrote, "Our salvation is nearer now than when we first believed" (verse 11).

Paul's message in the thirteenth chapter of Romans sums up God's plan of liberation from sin. We prepare our hearts, dedicate them to Christ, and as we do, we move closer to the spiritual liberation promised to us. But this message of preparation, dedication, and liberation can also be applied to the everyday liberation of Brown people from structures of racial discrimination and oppression.

Preparation, Dedication, and Liberation:
A Simple Framework

I am grateful you picked up this book. I've dedicated my life to the work of biblically based racial reconciliation, which is why I started Be the Bridge, an organization committed to building bridges between white communities and BIPOC communities. It's also why I wrote my first book, *Be the Bridge: Pursuing God's Heart for Racial Reconciliation,* and it's why I travel the country teaching others how to be bridge builders in a world that often leaves people of color on the outside of society looking in. The fact that you'd join in this journey means you want to be part of the solution for ending systemic racism in this country. That's a *really big deal.*

Those who've taken up the call to be bridge builders in a world of ethnic division know that some form of discrimination has seeped into every segment of society. In this book, we will examine nine sectors of American life, sectors that have traditionally been seen by BIPOC as "white spaces." In each chapter, I'll share a current story of systemic inequity or disparity, and I'll trace it back to its historical roots. In most chapters, we'll also look at what it means to recognize and confess the truth about inequities in the system (preparation), commit ourselves to changing the system (dedication), and move into true freedom as a society (liberation).

These days, there's a lot of baggage associated with the word *liberation.* I think that's a crying shame. Many people associate the word with woke Marxists or liberal Catholic theologians. But when I use the term, I'm not associating it with a political ideology. I use the term in much the same way the Israelites who were liberated from Egypt by Moses might have. I use it in the same way the lepers who were liberated from their sickness by Jesus might have used it. I use the term in the same way most of the Christian church uses it to talk about liberation from sin and death. Liberation is a spiritual principle that is relevant to our daily circumstances. It is our process of everyday sanctification.

Many systems of American society have oppressed Black and Brown people for far too long. Though we're no longer enslaved, though Jim Crow laws have been eradicated, we're not completely free from the effects of racism. If we're going to change that reality, we must come together—white and BIPOC communities alike—and work toward true, holistic, Christian liberation. So, let's examine how our preparation and dedication can lead to liberation of these systems. Let's ask how we can reform historically white spaces and create systems that work for the good of all. Let's listen, learn, and work together as we strive for racial equity in our communities and our nation.

Finally, here's a quick word on how to use this book. This isn't a book to be read quickly and tossed aside. Instead, this book is meant to be read with reflection and consideration for how you can be part of the solution. That's why I've included a "Questions for Reflection" section at the end of each chapter. Please don't breeze by these. Instead, pause and consider them. These questions will help you take a closer look at the racial inequities in systems you may have overlooked. They'll help you identify areas where you can get involved, places where you can make a difference. Engage thoughtfully with the stories of those who've chosen to act in liberating ways in the "Voice(s) of Liberation" sections at the end of chapters 2 through 10, considering how they might inspire you to action. Finally, if you'd like to meditate more on the chapter's topic, turn to the collection of prayers at the end of this book and ask God to open your eyes to what you might need to see.

I believe it's possible to root out the racism in our country and to create better, more equitable and just systems. But it has to start with individuals aiming to make a difference in their communities. If enough of us engage this work, I believe we'll see change in our lifetime. I'm writing this book because I believe in our power to change things. I hope that's why you're reading this book.

Are you ready to work toward true equality, true liberation in your community? Are you ready to reflect, meditate, and act? If so, let's get started.

QUESTIONS FOR REFLECTION

Before we move on, let's pause and consider the documents that lay the basis for our society. In the United States Declaration of Independence we read, "We hold these truths to be self-evident, that all men are created equal, that they are endowed by their Creator with certain unalienable Rights, that among these are Life, Liberty and the pursuit of Happiness."[2] What's more, the Constitution directs us to "establish Justice . . . and secure the Blessings of Liberty."[3] Considering these words, ask yourself:

1. In what ways have you witnessed people, organizations, or governmental bodies establishing justice for all citizens?

2. In what ways do you see American institutions missing the mark of establishing justice for all? List specific examples.

3. List the ways in which you've been involved in advancing justice in your own community. If you can't name any ways, be honest about that.

Now, before you turn the page, here's a brief meditation: Take a deep breath in, and as you do, say these words: *Liberty is a blessing*. As you exhale, say this: *Liberty is for all*. It is true liberation we all deserve.

CHAPTER 2

Learning Our Lessons

EDUCATION

B Y THE TIME I ENTERED MIDDLE SCHOOL, EVERYONE WAS TALKING about college. My teachers—most of whom were white—told us how important it was to make good grades so we could get into the universities of our choice, and my friends talked about whether they'd apply for college and how they'd manage to pay for it. My grandmother impressed upon me the importance of college, and as I looked around my community, I noticed that most of the folks who were really successful in business—like, able-to-retire successful—had college degrees or military experience. Granted, most of these successful individuals weren't from BIPOC communities, but a college degree seemed to be the ticket to success, particularly in a white-dominated society that placed a heavy emphasis on education. And so I set my sights on college.

During those middle school years, curious as I was to understand more about college, I asked my maternal grandmother if and where she'd gone to school. To my surprise, she told me that neither she nor my grandfather, Troy McDuffie, Sr., had graduated from high school. Most African Americans living in rural North Carolina—particularly

those born in the 1930s, like my grandparents—didn't have the resources or access to attend school past the tenth grade.

It's not that they didn't want to finish high school, but rather, racial
segregation and Jim Crow laws kept many non-white people—
particularly those in the Black community—from receiving an education equal to that of white people, which put them at a distinct
disadvantage. Educational opportunities were also limited for those in
poor rural communities, just as they are today, and even more so for
Black and Brown people. Back then, even if a non-white person could
graduate from high school and get accepted into a college, many of
those colleges were segregated. The Historically Black Colleges and
Universities (HBCUs) that served the Black population were typically
underfunded and short-staffed. This historical and cultural reality
forced my grandmother and grandfather to pursue success outside the
formal education system.

They found a way to overcome their lack of formal education
through my grandfather's career in the military, his willingness to take
business risks in later years, and my grandmother's willingness to help
my grandfather in business. It was hard work, but they more than
survived—they thrived.

Still, their lack of a high school diploma was a shocking revelation.
I'd always assumed my grandmother was high school educated. She
had the best penmanship of anyone I'd ever met, was knowledgeable
about world events, and kept the books for my grandfather's businesses. My grandfather Troy was equally capable. After his retirement
from the military, he used his savings and pension to open two automo-
tive stores in North Carolina—a transmission shop and a shop where
they customized vans for wheelchair lifts. He had a natural talent for
business, and his stores did well. My grandparents weren't rich by any
stretch of the imagination, but they were so well off that I never questioned whether they were high school graduates.

Since my grandparents knew the value of the education they

couldn't get, they made sure their children graduated from high school, though neither of my parents went to college. My parents, in turn, impressed on me the power of an education. I understood the value of access to equal-opportunity education and was the first person on my father's side and the second on my mother's side to attend college. That's how I landed at East Carolina University, where in 1995, I graduated with my bachelor's degree. I continued my education, and in 2013, I received a master's degree in business leadership from Liberty University (an ironic event, as you'll discover later). I'm currently furthering my education in seminary.

In a sense, I was lucky. Although North Carolina schools weren't fully desegregated until 1971—just two years before I was born—I lived in a time and place that allowed me, a Black woman, to pursue higher education. Still, there were challenges. My teachers, administrators, and the older students were products of a time when segregation was the norm, and some of those old segregationist ideas were still hanging around—namely, that Black people weren't as smart or that we were slower learners. But the fact that I was able to pursue a diploma in an integrated environment and that I was able to attend an integrated college was something I didn't take for granted.

Looking back, I'm left with a simple question: Why was the education system segregated for so long, especially after the passage of the Thirteenth Amendment in 1865, which abolished slavery, and the Fourteenth Amendment in 1868, which supposedly ensured equal legal rights to all Americans? The answer is simple, even if it's difficult to hear.

When the United States was founded, racism was institutionalized. Enslaved people would be counted as three-fifths of a human for the purpose of determining the number of representatives each state would have in the House of Representatives. Likewise, Native Americans were treated as non-Americans.[1] This institutionalized view of people of color was like leaven, working its way through every governmental system. In the wake of emancipation, white politicians created a sort of caste system—and there's almost nowhere that caste system was more evident than in the education sector of the United States.

SEPARATE BUT EQUAL:
THE LEGAL DOCTRINE THAT CEMENTED CASTE

How did this caste system become a fixture of American society? To answer that question, we must go all the way back to a Louisiana railcar a few years after Reconstruction.

In 1890, Louisiana politicians passed the Louisiana Railway Accommodations Act (popularly known as the Separate Car Act), a law requiring that railroad cars be segregated. Section 2 of the act states, "Any passenger insisting on going into a coach or compartment to which by race he does not belong, shall be liable to a fine of twenty-five dollars or in lieu thereof to imprisonment for a period of not more than twenty days in the parish prison."[2]

As you might imagine, people of color didn't take kindly to the act, which was passed by a white legislature and signed by a white governor. A group consisting of Black, free people of color, and white residents of New Orleans formed the Comité des Citoyens (Citizens' Committee), and through peaceful protest, they set out to change the law.

The plan, developed by two attorneys—Louis A. Martinet, who was Creole, and Albion W. Tourgée, who was white—was a long shot.[3] They were looking for a representative whose African American lineage was not discernable and who could pass as white. (Homer Plessy's team would later argue that he was "seven eighths Caucasian and one eighth African blood" and that "the mixture of colored blood was not discernible in him, and that he was entitled to every recognition, right, privilege and immunity secured to citizens of the United States of the white race.")[4] They intended to have that person purchase a first-class ticket, which would put him in the same car as white passengers; then, after the railroad reported the passenger, who'd be arrested by the authorities, he would appeal the law. Because the Separate Car Act didn't clearly define "race," it would force the railcar workers to make a judgment call about the race of passengers on a case-by-case basis. And since a person who was only one-eighth African ancestry might not even know they were Black, how could a railroad worker make that determination?

The group put their plan into action. Daniel Desdunes, a Black man who could pass as white, purchased a first-class ticket on the Louisville & Nashville train line on February 24, 1892, to travel from New Orleans, Louisiana, to Mobile, Alabama. He was arrested for sitting in the whites-only car. However, the charges were later dropped because the Louisiana Supreme Court determined that the Separate Car Act did not apply to railroad trips across state lines.[5]

This failed effort did not stop the Citizens' Committee. In June 1892, they tried again. Homer Plessy bought a first-class railroad ticket from New Orleans to Covington, Louisiana. After sitting in the whites-only railcar, he was arrested and taken to the Orleans parish jail. He made bail and awaited trial.

Plessy's attorneys swung into action, claiming the laws were unconstitutional because they violated the Thirteenth and Fourteenth Amendments, which provided that all citizens of the United States were entitled to equal protection under the law, regardless of their skin color. Neither the trial court nor the Louisiana Supreme Court were persuaded by Plessy's arguments, though, so in 1893, the case made its way to the Supreme Court of the United States.[6]

The Supreme Court wasn't persuaded either. The justices ruled against Plessy by a margin of seven votes to one (with one judge who abstained from voting). In that ruling, the majority concluded that

the object of the [Fourteenth] amendment was undoubtedly to enforce the absolute equality of the two races before the law, but, in the nature of things, it could not have been intended to abolish distinctions based upon color, or to enforce social, as distinguished from political, equality, or a commingling of the two races upon terms unsatisfactory to either.[7]

If that weren't bad enough, the court continued,

We consider the underlying fallacy of the plaintiff's argument to consist in the assumption that the enforced separation of the two races stamps the colored race with a badge of inferiority. If this be so, it is not by reason of anything found in the act, but solely because the colored race chooses to put that construction upon it.[8]

Yeah. That happened.

The majority of the Supreme Court justices declared that segregation was legal so long as the accommodations for Black people were "equal." There was only one dissenting opinion. Justice John Marshall Harlan argued, "There is no caste here. Our Constitution is color-blind, and neither knows nor tolerates classes among citizens. In respect of civil rights, all citizens are equal before the law."[9] Harlan's was a voice crying out in the wilderness, urging his fellow justices toward a little common sense. Why? Justice Harlan knew the majority's opinion would cement a racial caste system in America, and as history shows, that's exactly what happened.

How "Separate but Equal" Applied to the Education System

Black and Brown people weren't fooled. They knew that separate spaces could never truly be equal. My grandparents and their parents experienced this firsthand. Separate seating areas in buses, trains, and terminals weren't equal; whites got the premium seats. African Americans were kept from living in whites-only subdivisions, which were often subsidized by the Federal Housing Administration (FHA); conversely, the FHA often refused to insure mortgages in African American neighborhoods, which made home ownership by Black people difficult.[10] (This kind of outright discrimination would continue until the passage of the Fair Housing Act in 1968.) While white people were offered gender-specific public restrooms, non-white people usually shared one bathroom, which was often unkept, inoperable, and lacked essentials such as toilet paper.

Worst of all, educational spaces serving people of color didn't have funding access to books, or instruction equal to that of white schools. In 1930, Charles Hamilton Houston, a member of the National Association for the Advancement of Colored People (NAACP) and a graduate of Harvard Law School (which has admitted Black students since the 1847 admission of Beverly Garnett Williams), began his assault on the unjust and un-American laws that hurt people of color. Houston and the attorneys at the NAACP won early challenges to segregationist education systems.

The NAACP had been founded in February 1909 by Black and white activists like W.E.B. Du Bois, Ida B. Wells, and Henry Moskowitz to provide a voice for those forsaken by the justice system. In 1938, Houston and his team took a case to the United States Supreme Court, which ruled that the state could not constitutionally refuse Black students admission to the University of Missouri School of Law.[11] In later cases, the NAACP successfully argued that "equal" meant students must receive the same financial and educational resources they'd receive if they were white. The 1946 *Mendez v. Westminster* ruling stated that segregation of Mexican American students to separate schools was unconstitutional, a decision that was upheld by a United States Court of Appeals.[12] Following the decision, the governor of California, Earl Warren (later chief justice of the Supreme Court), signed a law ending school segregation. These victories built the foundation for one of the most important cases in United States history, especially when it relates to people of color and education.

In 1952, the United States Supreme Court began hearing cases from

Kansas, South Carolina, Virginia, Delaware, and Washington, D.C., each of which dealt with the racial segregation of public schools. In those cases, known collectively as *Brown v. Board of Education of Topeka,* Black parents—including Oliver Brown, who filed a suit on behalf of his daughter, Linda Brown—argued that segregation was unconstitutional. However, using *Plessy v. Ferguson*'s "separate but equal" doctrine, the states maintained segregation in the public schools.[13] The question presented to the Supreme Court was straightforward: Did the "separate but equal" doctrine allow states to deprive Black students of educational opportunities alongside white students, or was this kind of segregation innately unconstitutional?

The Supreme Court's opinion in *Brown,* written by Chief Justice Earl Warren in 1954, was a significant marker for racial equality. The court found that maintaining separate educational facilities and systems for Black and white students was inherently unequal and a violation of the Fourteenth Amendment. Because school systems were based on geographically racially segregated communities, the schools were products of those communities. Since Black communities tended to be less affluent and underserved precisely because of segregationist laws, the schools that served this population would be underserved too. The court ruled that schools must be integrated "with all deliberate speed."[14]

WHITE REACTIONS TO *BROWN*

Many hoped that desegregation, especially by way of busing kids from predominately Black communities to historically white communities, would level the playing field. But it didn't happen. (As we'll see later, it still hasn't happened across the board.)

Some schools rejected the *Brown* decision outright, and some Black students who attempted to integrate were met with white terrorism. For instance, the governor of Arkansas, Orval E. Faubus, used the National Guard to block nine Black students from entering Little Rock's Central High School. The Little Rock Nine, as they were called, were kept from enrollment until a federal court ordered the removal of the National Guard.[15] Little Rock police officers then escorted the students into the high school through a mob of white protestors on September 23, 1957. Two days later, trying to maintain the peace, President Dwight D. Eisenhower sent members of the 101st Airborne Division (US Army) to stand watch over the school.[16] Lest you think this is ancient history, as of the writing of this book, eight of those former students are still alive and in their eighties.

It wasn't just Arkansas. Across the South, many local governments and school systems resisted integration or adopted anti-integration policies. The 84th United States Congress did too. In 1956, Congress introduced the Declaration of Constitutional Principles, which was known by many as the "Southern Manifesto."[17] The manifesto stated,

> This unwarranted exercise of power by the Court, contrary to the Constitution, is creating chaos and confusion in the States principally affected. It is destroying the amicable relations between the white and Negro races that have been created through 90 years of patient effort by the good people of both races. It has planted hatred and suspicion where there has been heretofore friendship and understanding.[18]

The court had planted hatred and suspicion between white people and Black folks? I guess it had nothing to do with the decades of slavery, legalized beatings, lynchings, and mistreatment under Jim Crow laws. The manifesto was signed by eighty-two United States representatives and nineteen senators.

Promoting the Southern Manifesto wasn't the only thing that political leaders across the South were doing in response to *Brown*. Many, including Virginia senator Harry F. Byrd, who'd signed the Southern

Manifesto, called for "Massive Resistance."[19] In Virginia, this resistance included the creation of a Pupil Placement Board, which removed the authority of superintendents to determine how the schools in their district would integrate. Instead, a board of three men appointed by the governor would determine which students would attend which schools.[20] You can imagine how well this turned out for BIPOC students. This special kind of craziness was disrupted by the federal courts again and again, until the board was disbanded in 1959.

In addition, Massive Resistance laws attempted to defund Virginia schools that moved toward integration. This series of laws led the Prince Edward County school system to refuse to levy taxes for the 1959–60 school year, leading to the closure of all its public schools for the foreseeable future. County families were told to send their children to private schools, which were obviously segregated. Funds were directed to those schools through state tuition grants and county tax credits, and the schools were operated by a private group of citizens.[21] It seemed the people of Prince Edward County had found a way around the *Brown* ruling.

But the American BIPOC communities are resilient. We do not suffer injustice quietly.

In 1962, a group of Black students, including Cocheyse Griffin, sued the school board of Prince Edward County (*Griffin v. Board of Supervisors*), claiming that the school closures were simply a way to get around integration laws. The Supreme Court of Appeals of Virginia ruled in favor of the county,[22] finding that the county had the right to close the public schools and fund whites-only private schools—a ruling that blows my modern Black mind. Thankfully, the United States Supreme Court reviewed the decision in 1964. In considering the case *Griffin v. School Board*,[23] the Supreme Court found that the decision to close the schools affected the Black children of Prince Edward County more negatively than the white children because white children were allowed to attend the segregated private schools. Because the closing of the Prince Edward County schools was meant to circumvent integration, the court found the action to be a blatant violation of the Constitution. The schools were reopened after the ruling.

Of course, some took the Supreme Court's order in *Brown* seriously. In 1960, six-year-old Ruby Bridges was the first Black child to enter William Frantz Elementary School in New Orleans. This led to a massive outcry in the community and among the teachers, all but one of whom refused to teach young Ruby. The outlier? Barbara Henry, a white teacher who chose liberation over discrimination. For the first year, she taught Ruby one-on-one because the white students refused to be educated in the same room with the young girl.[24]

Sadly, Henry—a white teacher with a conscience—was the exception, not the rule. Across the South, many schools continued to resist integration, including the schools my grandparents and parents attended in North Carolina. Much of this resistance continued into the seventies and eighties. A few school districts would hold out even longer. In fact, the school district in Cleveland, Mississippi, didn't fully desegregate until 2017.

Cleveland, a town with approximately twelve thousand citizens, maintained two high schools—Cleveland High School, which was approximately 47 percent white and 45 percent Black, and East Side High School, which was almost entirely Black.[25] (It is worth noting that, according to the most recent census data, whites comprised the minority population, making up less than 40 percent of the population;[26] virtually all white high school students attended Cleveland High.) East Side didn't have the same amenities that Cleveland High School had, including a softball field and an adequate weight room for athletes. According to former students of East Side, they did not have science textbooks they could take home, and they didn't have lockers. In an interview with the *Atlantic*, one student at East Side claimed he didn't receive ACT preparation.[27] After years of legal struggle, the community finally relented, and in 2017, the two high schools consolidated. According to that same article,

An investigator hired by the Justice Department in 2009 found that the quality of Cleveland's all black—or mostly black—schools was "not comparable to [the quality at] those with majority white enrollments," noting lighting that failed to meet minimum standards and buildings that were of "substantially poorer quality."[28]

If you're from Cleveland, Mississippi, there's a good chance you grew up in a segregated school system. In fact, if my math serves me, the class of 2021 was the first class to experience a fully desegregated high school experience. What does that mean? It means generations of BIPOC students were robbed of amenities, opportunities, and equitable treatment. But it also means that scores of Black and white students missed out on vibrant relationships and experiences with one another, experiences that might have led to greater understanding, empathy, and ultimately, greater liberation.

The Unintended Consequences of Brown

The *Brown v. Board of Education of Topeka* ruling did not fully overturn *Plessy v. Ferguson*. Pools, golf courses, cemeteries, doctors' offices, movie theaters, public transportation, and restaurants would remain racially segregated for another decade. In addition, when the educational system was integrated, the result included some unintended consequences. Though in theory *Brown* provided Black students with the same opportunities as white students, this was not the reality my dad and others experienced.

Under the *Brown* ruling, with no need for separate educational systems for Black and white students, some schools had to close. Most of these were predominantly Black, like the ones my dad had attended a few years earlier, forcing Black students and their families to rely on busing to get to previously all-white schools. As you can imagine, this made education even more difficult for Black students. In this newly integrated environment, BIPOC faces in white spaces weren't given an opportunity to thrive. They were bullied, abused, treated as inferior, and discriminated against in the classroom.

But students weren't the only ones who suffered. As schools closed, many highly experienced and credentialed Black and Brown educators had their positions eliminated by white superintendents responsible for integrating the schools.[29] In fact, shortly after the *Brown* decision, the school district in Moberly, Missouri, closed a Black school, and eleven Black teachers—including one with a PhD—found themselves without jobs, while some less qualified white teachers kept their jobs. According to reporter Madeline Will, "Seven of the dismissed black teachers sued the school district, claiming they lost their jobs because of their race. The courts sided with the district, and the Supreme Court declined to hear the case."[30]

What does the history of race relations in the American education system show us? First, it reveals that those in power will try to create laws to protect their power instead of righting historical wrongs. But it also shows us something even more fundamental: Even after the *Brown* ruling in 1954, educational spaces continued to be dominated by white voices to the detriment of their Brown students. Truly, many people of color have been educated in white spaces. With the closing of those schools, many non-white students lost advocates and role models. They were often put in classrooms with white teachers whose prejudices kept them from believing in their Brown students' true potential.

In her article for *Education Week,* Will also explained that, prior to desegregation, in seventeen states with segregated school systems, 35 to 50 percent of the teachers were Black.[31] As of the writing of her article in 2019, statistics show that only 7 percent of public school teachers and 11 percent of public school principals today are Black.[32]

According to data reported by the National Center for Education Statistics, in the 2017–18 school year, more than 79 percent of public school teachers were white. Just over 9 percent were Hispanic. Less than 7 percent were Black, and 2 percent were Asian.[33] What does that mean for BIPOC students? It means many of us grew up without advocates who understood us and empathized with us. It means many of my BIPOC friends believed they were intellectually inferior and didn't know whether they could make it in a white-dominated world. Though there might be many reasons why the American education system is a white space, intellectual honesty requires us to look at our history. It requires us to admit that so much of the inequity and disparity in our present system is a product of our past.

EDUCATIONAL SEGREGATION THROUGH THE LENS OF CHRISTIAN FAITH

In the United States, white politicians, white school board members, and white citizens have perpetuated discriminatory systems that kept people of color in disadvantaged educational systems, often while claiming to hold Christian values. Look no further than Jerry Falwell, the preacher whose motivation for starting a private Christian K–12 school system (and later Liberty University, where I received my master's degree of business leadership) was, in part, based on segregationist ideology. In a sermon preached four years after the *Brown* decision, he said,

> If Chief Justice Warren and his associates had known God's word and had desired to do the Lord's will, I am quite confident that the 1954 decision would never have been made. . . . The facilities should be separate. When God has drawn a line of distinction, we should not attempt to cross that line.[34]

But God didn't draw lines of distinction between men and women of different ethnicities. He didn't create certain ethnicities to hold power and certain ethnicities to be subservient. He created us to be members of a diverse family. Falwell should have known as much. (He later admitted his own racism, stating, "I never once considered myself a racist. Yet, looking back, I have to admit that I was one.")[35] After all, he would have been familiar with the writings of the apostle Paul.

Paul, a man who'd been so proud of his Jewish identity before becoming a follower of Jesus, wrote in his letter to the church in Galatia,

> In Christ Jesus you are all children of God through faith, for all of you who were baptized into Christ have clothed yourselves with Christ. There is neither Jew nor Gentile, neither slave nor free, nor is there male and female, for you are all one in Christ Jesus. (Galatians 3:26–28)

This truth wasn't just something the early church leaders preached. They acted on it.

In the earliest days of Christianity, people from all over the known world were converting. Greek Jews and Hebraic Jews joined the growing church each day. It wouldn't be long before Gentiles started coming into the church too. With the influx of people, there were sure to be disagreements based on ethnicity.

We see the first symptoms of the church fracturing based on ethnicity in the book of Acts. There, the writer, Luke, recorded, "In those days when the number of disciples was increasing, the Hellenistic Jews among them complained against the Hebraic Jews because their widows were being overlooked in the daily distribution of food" (6:1). Those holding power in the church—those of Hebrew descent—were providing certain services to their own widows while denying those same services to the Greek-speaking Jews. But the disciples, whose Pentecost experience showed them God's desire that all people be included in God's family, knew that this sort of systemic discrimination was unjust.

The Twelve gathered all the disciples together and said, "It would not be right for us to neglect the ministry of the word of God in order to wait on tables. Brothers and sisters, choose seven men from among you who are known to be full of the Spirit and wisdom. We will turn this responsibility over to them and will give our attention to prayer and the ministry of the word." (6:2–4)

Men of God, including Stephen, a Greek-speaking Jew who would be the first martyr of the church, were chosen for the task. The result? Luke recorded, "The word of God spread. The number of disciples in Jerusalem increased rapidly, and a large number of priests became obedient to the faith" (6:7).

There is no clear indication that the church in Jerusalem grew because men of God put an end to the discrimination in the distribution of food to early church members, but it only makes sense that this would be the case. The apostles understood the necessity of embodying what they preached: All of us are made in the image of God and deserve to be treated with dignity and respect in everything, even providing equal access to meals. So the early church leaders shared power—appointing some Hellenistic Jews as deacons—and resources between Hebrews and Hellenists. Put another way, they honored Greek faces in Hebrew spaces.

Likewise, as people of faith, we can provide services, including educational services, to everyone equitably, without discrimination. We can share power with those who've been excluded from the decision-making. But if we're going to make changes in the system to create liberation for people of color, we must first acknowledge the historical truths (preparation) and dedicate ourselves to righting the historical wrongs.

Preparation Looks Like a Complete Education

My parents were born into a "separate but equal" world, a world before the *Brown v. Board of Education* ruling. This system shaped them, just as it shaped their parents. But it shaped me, too, together with the many students who still navigate spaces where teacher ethnicity is majority white, where functional segregation persists, and where badges of racism continue to exist.

If we're going to seek biblical liberation of BIPOC communities from that system, we can't ignore or whitewash our uncomfortable history. We cannot heal what we continue to conceal. Healing requires revealing, just as the disciples revealed the inequities in the early church. If we're going to reform the education system, we have to tell the whole truth, even the parts we wish we could ignore. Then we must do something about it.

If we're going to prepare the way for a more just and equitable system, our students—all of them—need to understand how today's system continues to give advantages to white students while putting people of color at a disadvantage. We can help them understand that this past reality has led to current educational deficiencies and economic disparities between ethnic groups. (Just take Cleveland, Mississippi, as your example.)

Preparation involves more than just looking at history and personal stories. It requires us to listen to the experts about contemporary realities too. For instance, as reported by Edwin Rios in a 2022 article for the *Guardian,*

> More than a third of students in the US attended racially segregated schools—schools in which more than three-quarters of students were accounted for by one race or ethnicity, according to an analysis of 2020–21 Common Core education data by the US Government Accountability Office. What's more, more than

one in 10 students—14%—attended schools where 90% of students were of one race or ethnicity.[36]

In that same article, Rios noted that a study six years earlier indicated a "stark increase in the percentage of poor, Black and Latino students attending predominantly poor and minority schools over the course of a decade and a half."[37]

Research further suggests that when Black students are integrated into better school systems with more integrated teacher populations, they do better—*no surprise.* They're more likely to graduate from high school and enroll in college when they have at least one Black teacher in elementary school.[38] Black students are also more likely to excel academically and are less likely to receive suspensions, expulsions, or detentions when they have Black teachers.[39] But as Rich Milner of Vanderbilt University noted, "With the decline of [Black] teachers post *Brown,* we see that [Black] students are often underserved and are not supported in ways that would be advantageous to their academic and social success."[40]

I could share pages of statistics indicating how students of color experience inequity and racism in the educational system, including the fact that they're without adequate BIPOC role models and advocates in the classroom. But statistics only tell part of the story.

In many white educational spaces, particularly in the American South, students of color have been met with racist naming conventions, mascots, and symbols. In a 2020 article for FiveThirtyEight—Nate Silver's ABC News–affiliated website best known for its political polling—Hope Allchin noted, "There are currently 1,232 high schools with Native American team names, according to my analysis of data from MascotDB. That includes 411 Indians and 107 Chiefs or Chieftains, and there are still 45 schools that bear the former name of the Washington Football Team."[41] (In case you don't follow football, that team's former name was the "Redskins.")

In a 2019 dissertation entitled "The Rebel Made Me Do It: Mascots, Race, and the Lost Cause," Patrick Smith of the University of Southern Mississippi, using research gleaned from a journal article by H. E. Gulley, noted that "there are 162 occurrences of Rebels in forty-one states and 161 cities."[42] Guess which states had the highest concentration of Rebel mascots? Louisiana led the way with fifteen, followed by Mississippi with thirteen, Alabama with twelve, Tennessee with ten, and Georgia and Texas each with nine. Notably, "the eleven states of the former Confederacy collectively have 86 or 53% of all Rebel mascots. If Missouri and Kentucky are included with this group, as they are sometimes, these thirteen states account for 97 or 60% of all Rebels."[43] Many schools used the Confederate flag as a symbol until the late 1990s and early 2000s, and at the time Smith wrote his dissertation, at least one school—a private school established in 1968 for white flight—still displayed the Confederate flag as a banner of school spirit.[44] Can you imagine being a BIPOC face in a space that had no non-white teacher representation, was named after a Confederate character, and flew a rebel flag at pep rallies? When this happens in public schools, shouldn't we consider this a form of state-sanctioned harassment?

To prepare the system for change, we must study the facts, statistics, and stories that reveal the ways our shared spaces need to be reformed to right historical wrongs. Once we determine where educational reform is needed, we must dedicate ourselves to the liberation of BIPOC faces in educational spaces.

When Dedication Leads to Educational Liberation

School segregation is not a thing of the past. As Tiffany Cusaac-Smith reported in an article for *USA Today,* modern school segregation is driven by housing decisions, school secession, and historic discriminatory practices, including redlining—the process of refusing loans or mortgage insurance for BIPOC who wish to live in certain areas.[45]

What can we do to advocate for equity and inclusion in education? If you have kids, you might consider sending them to your local public school instead of a private school where the children all look the same. You might join a local school board or enter the school system as a teacher or volunteer, serving as an advocate for non-white students. But even if you do neither of these things, you can use your voice to speak out against injustice in our local school systems.

Consider the story of Southside High School in Fort Smith, Arkansas. I've talked to one student who attended the school in the late 1990s. The Rebel was their mascot, and in the entrance to the school, a massive wooden statue of Johnny Reb—a fictional Confederate soldier—greeted the students each morning. During pep rallies, the principal played the school's fight song, "Dixie," on the harmonica, and the band played the same song after every touchdown on Friday nights. "Dixie" was played especially loudly, he said, when the Rebels competed against their crosstown rivals, the Northside Grizzlies, who had a majority BIPOC population. And though the Confederate flag had been removed from official use a few years before he began attending high school, he could still find it flying in the parking lot at any high school sporting event.

Times changed, though, and twenty years after he graduated, the people of Fort Smith began to acknowledge the problems with the mascot and song. Luke Pruitt, a proud graduate of Southside High School in 2003, determined to take on the racist symbols and song. He did a historical deep dive and then shared his findings in an online article, "To a Town Divided: The History of the Southside Rebel."

Pruitt began with the United States Supreme Court's ruling in *Brown v. Board of Education of Topeka*, how it led to backlash across the South, including in Fort Smith. Pruitt shared that in 1956, the Fort Smith School Board decided to comply with the law.[46] Was that compliance only technical?

In July 1961, Fort Smith opened a new public high school. Fort

Smith High School became known as Northside High School,[47] and Southside High School was officially under construction, opening its doors in 1963.[48] How were the district lines drawn for these two schools? While Northside served a more eclectic group of students, the vast majority of Southside served a majority white student population.

So how did Fort Smith's Southside High School choose its mascot, fight song, and school flag? Pruitt explained that during the first week of classes at Southside, the local newspaper published a photo of Alabama students celebrating Governor George Wallace's fight against desegregation. The caption under the photo read: "Cause to Celebrate: A group of high schoolers wave confederate flag and sing Dixie as they whoop it up on a porch across the street from Tuskogee, Ala. High School which was scheduled to open on an integrated basis Monday. The kids had just gotten word that Gov. George Wallace ordered a one week postponement. School officials broke up the celebration promptly."[49] As Pruitt described, "The next day, the Southside student body voted on a mascot, and the Southside Rebels played their first football game that Friday."

The mascot, fight song, and school flag symbolized white power. Decades later, Pruitt, along with others in the community, acknowledged that historical truth, and they dedicated themselves to removing the symbols of racism from Southside.

Another factor that led to liberation within the school system was that the town heard from Black citizens, including a local lawyer, Eddie Walker, whose three children attended the school. He said the mascot and theme song "has a lot of negative symbolism for me."[50]

With this much history, you'd think that the decision in 2015 to get rid of the lingering racist badges would be a no-brainer, but change would not come without a fight. The principal of the school, who'd banned the use of the Confederate flag in 1990, opposed changing the mascot, claiming it would cost too much money to rebrand the school.[51] A local lawyer sued the school board in an effort to block the mascot change. In a later article, the attorney is quoted as stating that Abraham Lincoln was a white supremacist. Then he doubled down, stating, "I'm tired of folks on the other side of this issue bashing true heroes like Robert E. Lee and then acting like Abraham Lincoln is some kind of icon."[52]

True heroes like Robert E. Lee? Really?

At the end of the day, the school board studied the issues and listened to the people (preparation). It was this preparation that strengthened its resolve to do the right thing (dedication). A portion of the board minutes recommending the change before the full school board vote states,

> Giving great consideration to the continuing impact of perceived symbols of racism on the community, state and nation, the Fort Smith Public School Board committee members discussed changing the Southside High School mascot and discontinuing the "Dixie" fight song. Symbols associated with Southside High School have been a topic of discussion with the FSPS Board of Education since a resolution to study the use of these symbols passed in 1989.[53]

After unanimous approval of the motion, on July 27, 2015, after hearing from the community—and more than twenty-five years after first resolving to study the symbols—the school board engaged in a true act of liberation, freeing Black and Brown people in the community from living under constant reminders of the school's racially divisive past.

This is what it means to be a voice of liberation in education. You don't have to change your career path or volunteer every free hour at a local school. Instead, you can do the hard work of discovering where the historic effects of racism still linger in your public schools—redlining and racist signaling through fight songs and mascots being just some of those effects. You can acknowledge them publicly and use your voice to call for liberation. You can gather people to do the work with you. If the group is large enough, educated enough, and clear in its call for change, you can bring liberation.

BE A VOICE OF LIBERATION

Perhaps you live in a community with its own history of disparity in the administration of education—a history that may not be as blatant as that of Fort Smith, Arkansas, or Cleveland, Mississippi. It may take some digging and a great deal of listening to discover the ways your local education system might need to reform. As you research the history, take time to listen to the BIPOC communities. Prepare yourself to be a voice of change. Then when you identify the places your local education system needs to be freed from white supremacy, act as a liberator.

Equal education will only come from truly equitable spaces.

QUESTIONS FOR REFLECTION

1. How would you describe the impact of racial segregation in education in your community? In your state?

2. Discuss the education disparities in your city and state. How have you or your family navigated these disparities?

3. If you were to reimagine the education system in your area, how would you make it more equitable for all?

Voice of Liberation: Gloria Clark

GLORIA CLARK IS A BE THE BRIDGE MEMBER AND LEADER WHO identifies as Native American (a member of the Haliwa-Saponi tribe) and African American. She's been a teacher and a principal and has served in several different states and districts, including Delaware and Washington, D.C.

For years, Gloria served in a predominantly white school district, and she understands how the majority population so often rejects change or limits BIPOC expression. "Developing villages of support within white spaces," Gloria says, "is key for [student of color] survival."

That's why she became an advocate for students who were told they could not wear Black Lives Matter attire or carry BLM paraphernalia, despite the fact that white students were allowed to wear clothing with political messages. It's also why she's led several book clubs in her school and community to educate people on the basics of racialized problems. She has elevated the voices of students and parents who lament the lack of BIPOC teachers, and she advocates for them with the administrators. Gloria has also helped raise awareness to the collective trauma students of color have dealt with as a result of police brutality. Through her advocacy, she liberated students of color, allowing them to be seen and heard.

Over the years, Gloria felt called to make a difference elsewhere. She left the school and began pursuing liberation for a different sort of student, the students who find themselves on the wrong side of the justice system (another white space, as we'll discuss in chapter 4). Believing no student should be left behind, she started working with the Cobb County Juvenile Court Programs, where she became the curriculum coordinator. There, she helps ensure that students have educational opportunities so that they can come out prepared to change.

CHAPTER 3

An Inequitable Prescription

HEALTHCARE

W HEN AMERICA GETS A COLD, BLACK PEOPLE GET PNEUMONIA. IT'S a common expression, one I heard from my elder family members growing up. But it made me curious. When did all of America get a cold, and how would Black folks like me get pneumonia from it? These were the questions I had in my younger years before I understood that it was simply a metaphor meant to convey a painful truth: Historically, hard times tend to hit African Americans and other people of color harder than white Americans.

That's exactly what happened during the Great Depression, when people of color were the first to lose their jobs and received less assistance from the government,[1] and more recently during the Great Recession. According to scholars at the University of New Mexico, "Between 2005 and 2009, Hispanic households lost 66 percent of their wealth and black households lost 53 percent, while white households lost only 16 percent."[2] It happened again in 2020, during the greatest healthcare crisis of my lifetime.

Like me, you probably remember where you were when you heard the news that a pandemic had erupted. I was on a book tour when I heard a new virus was heading to the States, but there seemed to be little preparation. I had just returned from an event in Boston and New Hampshire when the nation went into lockdown. As I watched the news unfold, I was sure it would be only a matter of time before Brown people began to experience the effects in ways that were much more pronounced than our white counterparts. I was not surprised when that's exactly what happened.

In a study entitled, "The Disproportionate Impact of COVID-19 on African Americans," released in December 2020, Maritza Vasquez Reyes explained that although 213,876 COVID patients died (as of the writing of the study), an examination of the data indicates that non-white patients were "disproportionally affected by the pandemic."[3] (More recent studies show, however, that though Black patients were more likely to die from the pandemic until fall 2021, the script has flipped. White patients are now more likely to die from the virus, though only by a marginal amount.)[4]

As an example of the disparity, Reyes indicated that in Kansas, as of June 27, 2020, only 4,854 COVID tests out of 94,780 were given to Black residents.[5] At first glance, this might make sense because about 5 percent of the tests were distributed to a group that makes up somewhere between 5 and 6 percent of the state's population.[6] Still, there seemed to be a disconnect. At the time of the study, Black Kansans made up a disproportionate number of the state's deaths—almost one-third.

Reyes further wrote that, according to American Public Media, through July 21, 2020,

Approximately 97.9 out of every 100,000 African Americans have died from COVID-19, a mortality rate that is a third higher than that for Latinos (64.7 per 100,000), and more than double than that for whites (46.6 per 100,000) and Asians (40.4 per 100,000).[7]

Black people didn't experience the worst of it either. A study by Princeton University, discussed in a 2021 article by Riis L. Williams, shows that Native Americans experienced substantially higher rates of COVID-19 mortality compared to other ethnic groups.[8] Reviewing the data, Williams wrote, "[Native Americans] living on reservations seem especially vulnerable to the virus, due to high rates of poverty, crowded living conditions and limited access to high-quality medical facilities." As a result, the COVID-19 mortality for the sample of Native Americans examined in the study was 2.8 times higher than that of the white group.[9]

These disparities extended beyond the United States. Across the globe, vaccines were less likely to be distributed to the Global South. As of September 2021, less than 1 percent of people from those countries—countries with mostly Black and Brown citizens—were fully vaccinated a stark contrast to vaccination rates of 60 percent and higher in most wealthier countries.[10]

The statistics are bad enough, but in 2021, things got personal. I found myself on the phone with a doctor who was treating my dad for the virus. He ran through a battery of questions: "Is there a family history of heart disease? What about respiratory issues? Was he a smoker?"

"He wasn't a smoker," I explained. "He was in relatively good health."

There was a pause on the other end of the phone.

Concerned that there might be a disparity in the ways Brown and white COVID patients were treated, I suddenly felt the need to humanize my father. "My dad served in the military," I said, thinking that maybe his status as a veteran would make him easier to identify with. I explained that he was beloved by his family and that he had close friends who loved him. I told him my dad wanted to live. He worked out five to six times a week and had no preexisting conditions. I then asked the doctor to do everything in his power to save him.

I hung up the phone, hoping I'd shared enough to erase any unconscious bias the doctor may have had, even though I had no reason to believe the doctor wouldn't do everything in his power to save my dad.

My dad didn't make it. I know it wasn't because the doctor didn't try his hardest to save him. Still, I wonder, would the outcome have been different if he had been white? Maybe that's not fair. But this is how many Black and Brown people think, because we know the history of the medical community's treatment of people of color. And that's a hard history to shake.

A Troubling Medical History

From the earliest days of American history, Black and Brown people have been marginalized, ignored, or used as subjects of experimentation for the sake of medical progress by white doctors. In fact, entire fields of medicine—including the development of instruments and tools that went along with those new fields—arose from this. It sounds unbelievable, doesn't it?

Well, believe it.

Anarcha Westcott was born into slavery on an Alabama plantation in 1828. After becoming pregnant at the young age of seventeen, she suffered through three days of painful labor before the plantation owner finally sent for a doctor—James Marion Sims.[11]

By all accounts, Sims was known as a well-to-do physician from South Carolina, and at the time of his visit to Anarcha's plantation, he was well regarded. But it wasn't always that way. After a two-year university stint and some introductory medical work, Sims enrolled in Jefferson Medical College,[12] graduating in 1835 as "a lackluster student who showed little ambition after receiving his medical degree."[13] Sims opened his first practice in his hometown of Lancaster, South Carolina. After his first two patients died, he packed up his belongings and moved to Mount Meigs, Alabama, where he met his wife. He then opened a practice for plantation owners about ten miles away in Macon County, Alabama, in 1838.[14]

In 1840, Sims moved to Montgomery, Alabama, where he expanded

and created a large surgical practice. Sims began treating enslaved people and developed a reputation as a capable doctor, particularly as it
related to women's health. He was respected in the community, at least
by the plantation owners, who needed the doctors to preserve their
property—Black people—and expand their wealth, which meant ensuring the birth of healthy Black babies. Take a moment to consider
this reality of the times, a reality that's difficult for me to write as a
Black woman: When people are treated as property, each person increases the wealth of the slave owner. And so, the reproduction of
those people also increases a slaveholder's wealth. Prior to the abolition of slavery, plantation owners had a vested interest in ensuring
their African American women reproduced, especially after 1808, when
slave importation was outlawed. So, in 1845, Sims was called on to de-
liver Anarcha's baby.[15]

Monica Cronin, in a research article about the legacy of Sims,
quoted from his autobiography, *The Story of My Life*, about the delivery
through the use of forceps on Anarcha's twisted body.

The baby's head, [Sims] wrote, "was so impacted in the pelvis
that the labor pains had almost ceased." Forceps could be dangerous to both mother and baby, potentially resulting in haem-
orrhage, or injury to the fetus, particularly in inexperienced
hands, but there was little choice. Anarcha survived this labour,
but the doctor . . . did not record the fate of the baby. As a result
of the complicated labour Anarcha sustained several fistulae.
This was the first case of obstetric fistula Sims had seen, and he
recorded her condition as "hopelessly incurable."[16]

Others note that Sims attempted other experiments on enslaved
women and their children. It has been reported that Sims treated enslaved infants suffering from neonatal tetanus by trying to pry the
bones of their skull into alignment with the point of a shoemaker's awl,

a tool normally used to punch holes in leather.[17] (I'm no doctor, but I don't think it takes a medical degree to see how inhumane the practice is.) When the children died, Sims blamed "slave mothers and nurses for infant suffering, especially through their ignorance."[18]

Anarcha's fistula—a painful condition often caused by long labors that damage the vaginal wall—did not heal, and it was debilitating. In that era, there was no surgical procedure for repairing it. Still, Sims agreed to treat her, which is to say *experiment* on her. And that's how the study of modern gynecology began.

Anarcha was not the only patient to endure this horrific treatment. Since African Americans were seen as less than human, no one thought twice about Dr. Sims experimenting on Black bodies. He created specialized tools for gynecological examinations and surgeries, testing them first on Black women. Because of the nature of his procedures and the use of experimental tools, many of the surgeries were unsuccessful. For instance, Anarcha endured twenty-nine failed surgeries before one was successful.[19] Do you think those surgeries were carried out in a humane way? Not a chance.

It's been noted that Sims did not use anesthesia on his Black patients, even though it had been in use for years. However, Sims himself indicated he used anesthesia on at least one "young, beautiful, rich, [and] accomplished" white woman.[20] Why not use the same anesthesia on enslaved women, then?

According to his own records, Sims completed his experimental surgeries on at least twelve women,[21] though we know the names of only three—Anarcha, Betsey, and Lucy. One can only imagine the torture these women endured as the subjects of this man's experimentation, to say nothing of the lack of dignity or compassion he showed them.

Still, his experiments yielded results. Sims discovered treatments and developed tools, some of which are still used today. Those accomplishments, despite being achieved at the expense of Black women made in God's very image, won him recognition as the "father of gyne-cology." Paintings, medical facilities, dormitories, and statues have been erected in honor of Sims over the years, including one women's dormitory on the University of South Carolina campus. One of those memorials, a bust of Sims himself, stands on the grounds of the South Carolina State House.

At Sims's funeral in 1883, Dr. William Waring Johnston, a promi-nent obstetrician, stated in his eulogy, "Who can tell how many more years the progress of the art might have been delayed, if the humble negro servitors had not brought their willing sufferings and patient en-durance."[22] However, as stated by Dr. Deirdre Cooper Owens, profes-sor in the history of medicine at the University of Nebraska-Lincoln, "Contrary to Johnston's assertion, however, these sick black women, representing both Sims's slave patients and his nurses, were experi-mented and operated on because their masters permitted them to be, not because of their autonomy."[23]

But not all the Sims memorials have been left undisturbed. In 2005, the University of Alabama at Birmingham removed a painting that her-alded Sims as one of the "Medical Giants of Alabama."[24] A statue of Sims that stood in Central Park directly across from the New York Academy of Medicine was removed in 2018 when the city of New York finally listened to activists and scholars. In April of that year, Mayor Bill de Blasio ordered the removal of the statue after the Manhattan Com-munity Board determined, "In light of the horrific and inhumane prac-tices of the aforementioned James Marion Sims, [the committee] advocates the immediate and permanent removal of the James Marion Sims statue from Central Park by a vote of 25 in favor of 0 opposed 0 abstentions."[25]

The removal of these memorials marks a season of change. It hon-ors those who have been harmed by the person's unjust ideologies. Re-moval rejects the whitewashing of history. Removal shifts the narrative, embraces the whole of the person's life story. But the removal of memorials alone will not bring liberation to people affected by a medical system that has exploited people of color for so many years.

RACISM AS A HEALTH CRISIS

Maybe you're thinking: *That was then, and this is now. Things have changed; the playing field has been leveled.* Though that might be true with respect to the kind of human experimentation done by Sims and the doctors of his era, the American healthcare system continues to be inequitable. Those disparities haven't entirely disappeared, even with advancements in civil rights.

According to a report by the Commonwealth Fund, "the United States ranks last overall, despite spending far more of its gross domestic product on health care. The U.S. ranks last on access to care, administrative efficiency, equity, and health care outcomes, but second on measures of care process."[26] Dr. Robert Pearl—a doctor and professor at Stanford University—examined some of the reasons for our failing healthcare system. In a 2015 article for *Forbes,* "Why Health Care Is Different If You're Black, Latino or Poor," he wrote,

> One reason the U.S. ranks so poorly globally is that health outcomes for certain racial, ethnic and socioeconomic groups fare so poorly domestically. African-Americans, Latinos and the economically disadvantaged experience poorer health care access and lower quality of care than white Americans. And in most measures, that gap is growing.[27]

In fact, the Robert Wood Johnson Foundation "estimates Latinos and African-Americans experience 30 to 40 percent poorer health outcomes than white Americans."[28]

The American Bar Association (ABA) has also recognized the disparity in healthcare across ethnicities. In an ABA article titled "Implicit

Bias and Racial Disparities in Health Care," Khiara M. Bridges, a professor of law and anthropology at Boston University, noted that people of color receive "inferior care" and "are less likely than white persons to be given appropriate cardiac care, to receive kidney dialysis or transplants, and to receive the best treatments for stroke, cancer, or AIDS."[29] When they do receive care, Bridges observed, they are more likely than white people to receive life-altering treatments such as amputations.

KFF (formerly known as the Kaiser Family Foundation), a nonprofit organization focusing on national health issues in the United States, also noted that our Black, Native American, and Alaska Native brothers and sisters have worse health outcomes when compared to our white brothers and sisters. For instance, among BIPOC communities, infant mortality rates and rates of HIV and AIDS diagnoses are higher, while average life expectancy is lower.[30] In fact, the Centers for Disease Control and Prevention (CDC) reports that infant mortality rates for Black people and Native Pacific Islanders are twice as high as those of white people.[31] (Only Asian Americans had lower infant mortality rates than white people.) The death rate from breast cancer for African American women is 40 percent higher than for white women, and among women under the age of fifty, the mortality rate for Black women is double.[32]

Not only is there discrimination in the ways we treat diseases, there's also discrimination in the ways we talk about them. Take COVID, for instance. Some in America blamed Asians and Asian Americans for the outbreak of the virus.

This kind of discriminatory storytelling is nothing new. In fact, in the early twentieth century, Chinese immigrants were blamed for spreading certain illnesses like the bubonic plague and smallpox.[33] Now, with the new wave of pandemic blame-shifting, people of Asian descent are again in the crosshairs. Mika Roland, a Japanese immigrant who serves as a hospice nurse and works with Be the Bridge, shared that during the COVID-19 outbreak, certain hospice patients refused to allow her to be their nurse due to their fear that Asian people carried the virus. They harbored this prejudice even as they were dying.

Breaking Free of Medical Apartheid

Students of history will remember South Africa's apartheid, a policy of legal segregation that existed well into the 1990s. *Apartheid* is an Afrikaans word meaning "apartness." In modern America, we're suffering under a kind of medical apartheid, a system in which Black people are treated differently than white people when it comes to medical care. Just in case you question whether the majority of Black people have experienced some form of medical apartheid, let me assure you: We have.

My cousin Larry recently had surgery to remove a cancerous mass in his colon. Patients who have this kind of surgical procedure are not usually released from hospital care until they have a bowel movement. However, he was released early—before achieving that indicator of a successful procedure. As a result, complications arose, which required him to be readmitted. Had he not returned to the hospital—a temptation for many non-white people who've had negative healthcare experiences—his complications could have resulted in severe sickness or death. Since this is a known issue with this surgery, any doctor or nurse would typically be aware of this as step one to recovery.

Was the treatment based on racial disparity? I honestly don't know. Maybe it was just sloppy medical work. But this is the kind of negligence many people of color endure on a regular basis. Based on statistics and expert opinions, unconscious racial bias often plays a role.[34]

How can we liberate people of color in the healthcare industry? We can start by looking at Jesus, the Great Physician, who sees all of us through the lens of compassion.

When we look at Jesus's ministry, we see that he healed all kinds of people without regard to ethnicity or gender. He healed an outcast, a woman who'd been plagued by a demon for eighteen years (see Luke 13:10–13). He healed the servant of a Roman centurion, a man with great power and authority (see Matthew 8:5–13). He healed a Gentile who was possessed by demons (see Mark 5:1–13). He healed a man who was paralyzed and likely had no status in society, and who had to be carried to Jesus by his friends (see Mark 2:1–12). He healed people with leprosy, untouchables that society was afraid of (see Matthew 8:1–4). Rich and poor, man and woman, Jew and Gentile, he healed them all, making no distinction among them. He didn't come to separate the sick by class. He came to liberate all people from disease.

As Christians, our primary objective is to look and act like Jesus, and that's true in all walks of life, including the ways we administer healthcare. We're supposed to bring liberation to the sickest of society, without regard to skin color. So let's look at what liberation from medical apartheid might mean in the United States.

PREPARATION FOR MEDICAL LIBERATION

As a Black woman living in America, I prepare my heart to deal with that history and face those statistical disparities regularly. I prepare myself to be treated differently by healthcare professionals and to advocate for myself and my family members by asking a lot of questions. I also prepare myself to listen to my friends of color who find themselves on the short end of the medical stick—particularly those who are less affluent and don't have great health insurance—without losing my freaking mind. If you're a middle-class white person, can you imagine how that must feel?

There are other things people of color can do in preparation for healthcare liberation. Request copies of your medical charts and keep them updated after your doctor visits. You might even use online software to keep all your medical charts updated and backed up in the cloud. This keeps your doctors accountable and helps you better understand trends in your health. Consider going to appointments with an advocate, someone who can help you stand up for your own rights. And maybe you can be that person for someone else. Don't leave the office until *all* your questions are answered.

Whether you're Brown or white, in order to be more aware of the inherent bias within the medical system, you might choose to further educate yourself. Consider picking up *Medical Apartheid* by Harriet Washington, which examines the history of medical mistreatment of Black people. I encourage you to pore over the endnotes for this chapter and read the associated articles, studies, and reports. Then, after taking in the history and statistics, ask yourself some really hard questions:

How would I feel if I learned my ancestors were used as medical experiments without their permission?

What would I do if I were treated like a second-class citizen at the emergency room or during a visit to the oncologist?

What if a doctor pressed for an amputation or hysterectomy, even if I knew there were other options for patients with different skin color than me?

If you're white, put yourself in the shoes of a BIPOC patient and consider how the history of the medical community might affect your ability to trust the American healthcare system.

Dedication to Medical Liberation

In my work as a bridge builder, I've spoken with several Brown professionals within the medical industry, many of whom have dedicated their lives to bringing change. My cousin Qiana, for instance, serves as a nurse in Lumberton, North Carolina, which is located in Robeson County, one of the poorest counties in the country at the time this book was written.[35] Lumberton has a high concentration of BIPOC, with approximately 60 percent of the population identifying as non-white.[36] In the surrounding county, the diversity numbers are even more stark. In 2022, approximately 41.9 percent of the Robeson County population identified as Native American, with over 23 percent Black, approximately 9 percent Hispanic, and 30.1 percent white.[37] (The remaining residents consider themselves non-white.)

As a patient, an advocate, and a medical caregiver, Qiana has experience with the healthcare system. If you ask her, she'll tell you that her county lacks the resources to provide meaningful mental healthcare. Most mental healthcare facilities in the town have closed, and at the hospital where she works, there isn't a psychologist on staff. Instead, the hospital relies on telemedicine to provide for mental healthcare. This might not seem like a big deal, particularly to those who view hospitals as places to primarily tend to physical needs. But this gap in the medical system of Lumberton undoubtedly affects the community. Put another way, unhealthy people create an unhealthy community.

Qiana's experience supports the research regarding levels of care afforded to BIPOC patients versus the level of care afforded to white patients. She's seen non-white patients' pain dismissed by white medical professionals, while the pain of white people is taken seriously. She says a racial bias is ingrained in the culture of the medical field, though most don't realize it.

She shared, "It would take a lot of education and patients and advocates calling it out for change to begin."

Qiana had to advocate for her mom as well. When her mom was in the hospital, her symptoms and chart clearly indicated her blood was infected, a potentially life-threatening condition. Still, the hospital released her, and when Qiana discovered it, she jumped through all the right hoops to have her mom readmitted so she wouldn't die. As Qiana explained, any knowledgeable doctor or nurse should have been able to look at her mom's charts and know she shouldn't have been released, but Qiana believes there's a disparity between how closely doctors look after the health of white people and how they look after the health of African Americans. Maybe you're skeptical, or maybe you wonder why this is the case. This is the same question people have been asking for decades.

Unfortunately, you don't unravel centuries of racial discrimination in a few decades. No one drops a racial bias at the door. It shows up in the boardroom, operating room, classroom, or any other room. Racial biases even follow people into the racial justice space. We must all examine our racial biases and work hard not to give in to them.

DR. FOLUSO FAKOREDE: A LIBERATION STORY

While researching this book, I stumbled across a stunning story of liberation in the healthcare industry. In 2015, Dr. Foluso Fakorede, an African American vascular surgeon, found himself without a job. After a billing dispute with his clinic in Tennessee, one in which he charged the clinic with claiming improper expenses, Dr. Fakorede was terminated. In the wake of that termination, Dr. Fakorede, a Nigerian native who'd moved to New Jersey as a teenager, decided to head south. He wanted to understand the status of healthcare in the Mississippi Delta.[38] What he found was appalling.

He spent days driving across the fertile farmland of the South, and as he made stops along the way, he noted a number of Black amputees living in the area. As a vascular surgeon, he knew these amputations resulted from an elevated regional incidence of diabetes—Mississippi has some of the highest rates of type 2 diabetes in the country—which decreased blood flow to extremities, led to gangrene in those extremities, and if untreated, could ultimately lead to death.[39] Dr. Fakorede also knew that African Americans were more likely to develop diabetes than those of other ethnicities, and this is especially pronounced in rural communities like the Delta.[40] They were more than twice as likely to die and their average lifespan is decreased by three years. This was, in part, due to genetics, but the sugary and fatty Delta diet played a factor too.[41] Dr. Fakorede realized that moving to the Mississippi Delta would give him the opportunity to bring liberation to a population who desperately needed the better health outcomes that result from treating amputation as a last resort, not a first. So he made a decision: He wouldn't seek better pay and a more prestigious job elsewhere. He'd open a practice in the Delta in hopes of serving a historically marginalized community.

Dr. Fakorede leased a space in Cleveland, Mississippi, in a region where there was no diabetes specialist within one hundred miles. When he began to examine his new patients, he found evidence of arterial disease that blocked blood flow to their lower legs and feet.[42] Dr. Fakorede knew that if he could improve the blood flow of his patients, he could decrease the rate of amputations, which could lead to increased lifespans for his predominately Black patient base. Talk about liberation!

However, it wasn't easy. He struggled to get funding and referrals. According to an article about Dr. Fakorede, he also discovered that "general surgeons have a financial incentive to amputate; they don't get paid to operate if they recommend saving a limb."[43] Still, he pressed on and fought the system. After obtaining surgical privileges at the local hospital, he set to work repairing his patients' arterial blood flow to their extremities. By 2019, Dr. Fakorede claimed he had reduced major amputations by 88 percent, from fifty-six the previous year down to seven.[44]

POLICIES OF LIBERATION

Compare this story of true liberation to the story of James Marion Sims. Sims exploited Black women to advance medicine. Dr. Fakorede uses advanced medicine to liberate people of color who haven't received the best treatment historically.

Though not many of us are surgeons like Dr. Fakorede, and we may not have the nursing skills of Qiana McDuffie, we can do our part to deconstruct systems of medical apartheid. We can tell the truth about the history of racial disparity in the American healthcare system. We can share the stories of people like Dr. Fakorede and his staff, stories of healthcare professionals who aim to liberate people of color from the disparities of a historically discriminatory system. We can speak out against those who would disparage our Asian friends and blame them for a pandemic. We can protest memorials to those who advanced systems of medical apartheid, and we can file petitions to have those memorials removed. Finally, we can advocate with our Brown neighbors for policy reforms that would bring better healthcare outcomes.

What kind of policies? One is particularly near and dear to my heart, but before I present the policy to you, here's a story.

My grandmother on my father's side—we called her Grannie—worked at a large manufacturing plant and was able to live just above the poverty line. Over the years, she and my pop-pop scraped together enough money to buy their home, though she was a far cry from the middle class. But in her later years after my pop-pop's death, she developed heart issues and had to have a bypass operation. After the surgery, the doctors prescribed medicine, which she couldn't afford because of the limitations of her healthcare coverage. Because she owned her home, she was considered too wealthy to receive Medicaid coverage. Here was a woman who wasn't granted the right to vote until she was in her thirties, who suffered the worst of Jim Crow, who had relatively little income and no real retirement to speak of, and yet she was kept from receiving coverage for necessary medication because she owned a home. Grannie's quality of care was hindered by her socioeconomic status, which was, historically speaking, affected by her ethnicity.

If your state hasn't adopted the Affordable Care Act's Medicaid expansion (ten states, including my home state of Georgia, have not), advocate for it. The Medicaid expansion gave states the ability to provide coverage to those who earn up to 138 percent of the federal poverty level, benefiting the millions of workers who, despite holding gainful employment, still exist below, at, or near the poverty line.[45] Many of these workers are people of color—just like my grandmother—whose health and economic opportunity have been disproportionately affected by our nation's history of discrimination. Medicaid expansion, if adopted by those ten states, would give more opportunity to more Americans to live longer, healthier lives.

There are other ways to dedicate yourself to liberating people of color from the healthcare disparities, so get involved. Work to eliminate systems of medical apartheid. Then, when the next cold breaks out in America, maybe we'll see more resilient BIPOC communities that are able to protect themselves from getting pneumonia.

QUESTIONS FOR REFLECTION

1. How would you rate your personal level of trust in the medical community? How does your family's experience, and your own, influence this?

2. To what extent might your ethnicity be connected to your experiences and perspective, and why?

3. Why do you think the United States ranks so low in healthcare globally and for certain groups domestically? Where could you engage to make a difference? It may mean writing a letter to your politicians or local healthcare community. Make a plan to work toward liberation in this space.

Voice of Liberation: Dr. Debbie Stevens

BE THE BRIDGE MEMBER AND SUPPORTER DR. DEBBIE STEVENS IS a psychiatric nurse practitioner with a PhD in nursing. She discovered her passion as a young nursing student at East Carolina University, where she had the opportunity to treat an African American patient who'd been sexually assaulted by her brother. The patient had been incarcerated and institutionalized most of her life as a result of the trauma she endured as a child.

Dr. Stevens said, "She was selectively mute and physically aggressive, so many of the young white students were deathly afraid to approach her." But Dr. Stevens felt a connection with the young lady just by reading her medical charts, and she expressed that care from the first encounter. "I went in and gave her a bed bath," Dr. Stevens continued. "I talked to her and prayed in my head for her. It's hard to articulate the deep feeling I had in those moments. Now that I look back, I think it was because I felt this communal connection with her. I understood her pain and that it had landed her in this situation. I had compassion for her."

As she worked with the woman, Dr. Stevens understood that she was created to help those struggling with mental health issues, those who are in the margins and often seen as the least of these in society. So, upon graduation, she made an intentional decision about how and where she'd practice.

For the past eight years, Dr. Stevens has been practicing in a shelter-based clinic in downtown Atlanta, caring for primarily unhoused African American men who suffer from severe, persistent mental health disorders and substance abuse. In a community of marginalized, mostly BIPOC people, Dr. Stevens has an easier time than most people connecting with those of any race and background, given her own Korean and Black ethnic heritage. She sees herself as a safe person who understands the systemic issues her clients face, thus allowing her to approach their care with compassion and deep empathy.

Dr. Stevens has the opportunity to work with some of the most marginalized communities in the mental health field as well as some of the most financially privileged. She says that although her clients have much in common, the separation marked by access and support.

Often, when her patients walk into her office, she notes a visible look of relief on their faces. Some have told her, "I thought you were going to be a white man." Knowing some of her patients have felt dismissed by other doctors, she takes the time to listen and understand their needs and culture. She creates a safe place to talk and ensures they feel seen.

As an educator, Dr. Stevens has worked for Emory University, Florida International University, and Chamberlain University, providing coursework to educate future nurses on racial disparities in the practice and getting them to explore their own biases. She has also started a private practice to help those within all economic brackets achieve an improved mental health level. She tells each client, "I see you, and there is hope for you."

CHAPTER 4

Liberty and Justice for Some?

<hr>

THE JUSTICE SYSTEM

<hr>

"I PLEDGE ALLEGIANCE TO THE FLAG OF THE UNITED STATES OF AMERICA, and to the republic for which it stands, one nation under God, indivisible, with liberty and justice for all." These are the first words I remember hearing on my first day of kindergarten in 1978. The United States had passed civil rights legislation in 1964—just fourteen years prior—though at the time, I didn't know the first thing about legislation or civil rights—or the pledge for that matter. As a kindergartener, I'd never had the thought cross my mind that I lived in a country where liberty and justice for *all* was a myth. I didn't know that the history of my country was stained by racism. I didn't know that some still saw me as inferior because of my skin color. I was just looking forward to coloring, recess, and snack time.

I now know that my liberty, and the liberty of many people of color, was won at a great cost. It was fought for through the Underground Railroad, the Civil War, and the civil rights movement. It was attained through the blood, sweat, and tears of my ancestors. If I had known those truths and been old enough to understand them back in kindergarten, I might have thought a lot harder about the words of the pledge. I might have questioned what it meant to pledge allegiance to a nation that had treated people who looked like me as if they were property, a nation that stole lands from Native Americans, a nation that interred Japanese Americans during World War II. I might have asked hard questions about why the historical treatment of people of color was manifestly unjust.

In the early eighties, as a child, I was a benefactor of the difficult civil rights work done over a decade earlier by African Americans who were unafraid to claim they were "Black and proud," including my dad, who told me he listened to the 1968 James Brown song "Say It Loud— I'm Black and I'm Proud" on cassette while he drove to basic training in 1971. And of course all those people had every reason to be Black and proud. They'd joined in a collective struggle with their forefathers— many of whom were martyrs, including Dr. Martin Luther King, Jr.—to usher in an age of greater equality. Their protests, sit-ins, and marches had paved the way for the passage of the Civil Rights Act of 1964, the law that prohibited discrimination in public places and in federally funded programs, among other things.

Four years after the passage of the act, in the wake of the assassination of Dr. King, their outcry led to even more reforms with the passage of the new Civil Rights Act. The Indian Civil Rights Act of 1968 guaranteed Native Americans full access to the protections of the Bill of Rights and prohibited housing discrimination based on race, religion, national origin, and sex. The Hart-Celler Act, also known as the Immigration and Nationality Act of 1965, phased out the racist "national-origins quota" system that all but prohibited immigration from countries outside of Western or Northern Europe,[1] and by 1968, the national-origins quota was abolished.

The passage of these civil rights laws advanced rights for people of color. But this new age of equality didn't bring justice overnight. The right laws passed, but the systems meant to enforce those laws still had a residue of racism. And we're still dealing with that residue today.

As a young elementary school child, I could never have imagined that a Black boy could be gunned down in the street by police officers for carrying a toy gun—that wouldn't be liberty and justice *for all*. But that's exactly what happened to Tamir Rice, who was killed on November 22, 2014. It would never have crossed my mind that police officers would barge into a Black woman's apartment without justification and shoot her dead, but that's exactly what happened to Breonna Taylor on March 13, 2020. As a child, I would have been shocked to hear that a Black man could be suffocated in the streets for allegedly passing counterfeit money, and yet that's what was done to George Floyd on May 25, 2020.

Many of us among the BIPOC communities have admitted we have not felt safe from unjust policing practices. The past few years haven't alleviated our fears, because we know that police brutality and injustice can happen to any of us, even an elderly Black woman who could have been my grandmother.

KATHRYN JOHNSTON: THE PATTERN OF INJUSTICE

Kathryn Johnston was born in 1914. She had lived through two world wars, the Spanish flu, the Great Depression, the Korean War, the Vietnam War, Jim Crow, the civil rights movement, and 9/11, witnessing many transformations in America along the way. A country that had once made her drink from separate water fountains and use separate bathrooms had changed its laws (if not its ways) and promised her equal protection. But on the night of her death, those promises evaporated.

On November 21, 2006, Ms. Johnston was alone behind the barred windows of her northwest Atlanta home in a neighborhood known for violence. Because of reports that an elderly woman in the area had been raped in her own home weeks before, Ms. Johnston kept a loaded gun by her side.

Around seven o'clock that night, Atlanta undercover police officers Jason R. Smith, Gregg Junnier, and Arthur Tesler raided her home. According to reports, the plainclothes officers carried riot shields when they barged through the front door without identifying themselves.[2] Terrified, Ms. Johnston fired at them from a revolver. The officers returned fire. Of the thirty-nine rounds that left their weapons, five or six struck the ninety-two-year-old woman, who was killed instantly.[3]

I can only imagine the horror of Ms. Johnston's last minutes on this earth. She wasn't surrounded by children, grandchildren, nieces, and nephews. She was alone, scared, and likely confused about the three men breaking into her home. When the shooting stopped, when the smoke cleared, a woman who had witnessed so much change in America was a victim of its police force.

An investigation followed, and the officers claimed that they'd received a tip that a drug dealer had been selling drugs outside Ms. Johnston's house earlier that day. That's why they'd obtained a no-knock warrant—a warrant authorizing officers to enter a residence without announcing themselves—and barged into Ms. Johnston's home. The investigation determined that she was the only one inside and that there was no indication of any drug activity in the home. Instead of owning up to the tragedy, the police officers lied and tampered with evidence to cover up the crime. But thank the good Lord, it all eventually came to light.[4]

Despite the officers' claims that they believed a drug dealer was in the home, further investigation revealed Ms. Johnston had no connection to the drug trade, and had her neighbors been interviewed prior to the raid, the officers would have discovered as much. What's more, the investigation uncovered that when the officers realized their mistake, they planted three bags of marijuana in Ms. Johnston's home, hoping to justify their actions.[5] As horrible as that is, that wasn't all. The evidence suggested that one of the officers—Officer Jason Smith—had called an informant and asked him to lie by reporting that he'd bought crack cocaine at Ms. Johnston's house earlier that day.[6]

The three officers eventually pleaded guilty to a conspiracy to violate the civil rights of Ms. Johnston that resulted in her death. Officers Smith and Junnier also pleaded guilty to committing voluntary manslaughter and making false statements under Georgia law. Officer Tesler was sentenced to five years in federal prison, Officer Junnier six years, and Officer Smith ten years.[7] Then came the civil suit. Almost four years after the tragic shooting, the Johnston family was awarded civil damages of 4.9 million dollars.[8]

Some point to the verdicts in the Johnston matter—including the multimillion-dollar civil judgment—as proof that the justice system ultimately works. But as a Black woman who hopes to live well into her nineties, I think the sentencing was crazy. Six to ten years for taking the life of an innocent Black woman and then intentionally lying to cover it up? That doesn't sound like justice to me, especially when a conviction in Georgia for possessing weed—a crime that Black people in Pickens County, Georgia, are "97.2 times more likely to be arrested for . . . than whites"—can earn up to ten years in prison![9]

No sentence is high enough and no measure of money can bring Ms. Johnston back from the grave. The legacy of her life was worth more than that. This is one of those times when I think the justice system ought to be ashamed of itself.

Ms. Johnston should never have died, nor should George Floyd, Breonna Taylor, Tamir Rice, Amir Locke, Atatiana Jefferson, Michael Brown, Sandra Bland, Freddie Gray, and so many others. (We'll discuss Brown and Gray in a later chapter.) As I read these cases and so many others, it is clear to me that the system isn't simply broken. It was never just in the first place—at least, not for everyone. Is it any surprise that so many in the BIPOC communities—and the Black community in particular—carry so much fear and outrage when it comes to policing in the United States?

Policing—A System Rooted in Racism?

Perhaps you're wondering why I began this discussion about the justice system with abuses in policing. Why not look to the civil rights movement, the discrepancies in white and Brown prison sentencing, or the ways the "war on drugs" has disproportionately affected BIPOC communities? Why not look at the racial disparity among state and federal prosecutors or judges?

While all these areas deserve attention, non-white people know this simple truth: Many of our experiences with American injustice begin with the police. We have come face-to-face with officers at unwarranted traffic stops. We've been confronted while walking down the sidewalk in a predominantly white neighborhood. The police have been called on us while we waited for business partners at the local Starbucks. (More on that in chapter 5.) This is the reality of many BIPOC communities in an America where police procedures seem to differ depending on one's skin color.

A white friend recently told me, "I rarely think about the police, the exception being when I'm intentionally speeding or when I forget to renew my car tags." I wish my Black and Brown brothers and sisters could say the same. A report of the Public Policy Institute of California found that, as of 2019,

> Black Californians are more than twice as likely to be searched as white Californians, at about 20 percent versus 8 percent of all stops.
>
> Searches of Black civilians are somewhat less likely to yield contraband and evidence than searches of white civilians. . . .

Black individuals are almost twice as likely to be booked into jail as white individuals.[10]

There are probably hundreds, maybe even thousands, of cases of racial disparity in policing in other states. Is it any wonder so many within the BIPOC communities are either scared or outraged at what a white person might call a routine traffic stop? As much as it pains me to say it, traffic stops rarely feel routine to people of color. Instead, they often seem like opportunities for people with unlimited authority—the police—to alter the course of a life. And what if they get it wrong? Because police officers enjoy qualified immunity—a doctrine that limits the liability and accountability of officers who violate a person's civil rights—there's very little recourse for those who were unjustly incarcerated. It makes "liberty and justice for all" a fairy tale.

Why does America, a country founded on the idea that "all men are created equal," one whose Pledge of Allegiance promises "liberty and justice for all," continue to have racial disparities in its policing? As we'll see, it grows from our history. Here's a fair warning as we continue: This won't be comfortable for any of us, so let's enter together with open hearts and open minds.

In an article for *Time* magazine about the origins of policing in America, author Olivia Waxman interviewed Gary Potter, a crime historian and an emeritus professor at Eastern Kentucky University.[11] Potter noted that the first city-organized police force was founded in Boston in 1838 as a way to protect property shipped into Boston and to secure its transportation out of the city. Instead of paying for the protection of their goods with private security forces, the merchants argued that the "collective good" of the entire community required public funding of a security force.[12] Protecting the goods shipped into Boston protected the city's economy.

While the police force in Boston began for a seemingly good reason, some police forces in the American South began for different, less honorable reasons. The police in the South were tasked with hunting down, capturing, and returning runaway slaves.

Slavery was abolished through the passing of the Thirteenth Amendment, section 1 of which reads: "Neither slavery nor involuntary servitude, except as a punishment for crime whereof the party shall have been duly convicted, shall exist within the United States."[13] In this wording many state legislatures in the Reconstruction era—particularly those in the South, which were composed of wealthy, white former plantation owners—recognized a loophole: convicted felons could be used as cheap labor. So they passed loitering, vagrancy, and curfew laws, enabling sheriffs to continue targeting Black people. Once convicted and imprisoned, Black people were subject to "convict leasing," which gave privately owned railway companies, mines, and plantations the right to "lease" labor.[14] In his Pulitzer Prize–winning book *Slavery by Another Name*, Douglas Blackmon addressed this sort of neo-slavery system.[15]

While small steps were taken by the federal government to reform and integrate police departments during Reconstruction, most of the progress Black people experienced was short-lived. (This post-Reconstruction Jim Crow era ushered in segregation laws validated by court cases like *Plessy v. Ferguson*, which I discussed in chapter 2.) The result? The police force was tasked with enforcing blatantly racist laws—including the segregation of public transit, segregation of public schools, and prohibition against marriage between white and BIPOC people. Anyone who chose to defy the laws—whether Black or white—would be subject to arrest and the potential imposition of jail time, fines, or even death at the hands of a lynch mob. Though Southern states adopted anti-lynching laws during the Reconstruction era, they were rarely enforced.[16] For instance, Virginia passed an anti-lynching law in 1928, but no white person was ever convicted of lynching a Black person, even though lynching continued in the state until at least 1968.[17] Put another way, the justice system turned a blind eye to true justice.

By the mid-1950s and early 1960s, people of color had had enough. On March 2, 1955, after studying the history of courageous Black leaders like Sojourner Truth and Harriet Tubman, fifteen-year-old Claudette Colvin refused to give up her seat on the bus while traveling from her Montgomery, Alabama, high school to her home.[18] She was cuffed, arrested, and taken to jail. In December of that same year, Rosa Parks boarded a bus in the same city. She made her way to the section designated for non-white riders as required by a Montgomery city ordinance, but when a white rider boarded the bus and didn't have room to sit in the whites-only section, Parks was ordered to give up her seat to accommodate the passenger. You probably know the story, which has been more widely publicized than Colvin's. Parks refused, and as a result, she was arrested, fingerprinted, and had her mug shot taken. But this time, the arrest sparked protests.

On December 5, 1955, the day she was to be tried in municipal court, approximately forty thousand Black bus riders instituted a boycott of the transit system. These boycotters represented the majority of the system's patrons. The boycott continued for just over a year, until the United States Supreme Court upheld a June 5, 1956, lower court ruling (one that the city had appealed) declaring the city ordinance unconstitutional. On December 21, 1956, the Montgomery bus system was integrated.[19]

Other protests against unjust enforcement of Jim Crow laws broke out in the South. In January 1957, sixty Black pastors—including Dr. Martin Luther King, Jr.—met in Atlanta, Georgia, to coordinate nonviolent protests against laws legalizing discrimination and discriminatory policing. In February 1960, four African American students demanded service at the whites-only lunch counter at Woolworth's, and other sit-ins spread across the South. My great-uncle James Ray and his sixteen-year-old daughter, Shirley Ray Harrison, were among those arrested in Greensboro, North Carolina, for participating in a sit-in protest. In 1961, the Freedom Riders (a group of Black and white students who joined forces in protest) took bus trips across the South to protest segregated bus terminals, and many of them were arrested for violating discriminatory laws.[20]

In August 1963, 250,000 people participated in the March on Washington, which culminated in Dr. King's "I Have a Dream" speech. In that speech, Dr. King took on the American policing system.

> Some of you have come fresh from narrow jail cells. Some of you have come from areas where your quest for freedom left you battered by the storms of persecution and staggered by the winds of police brutality. You have been the veterans of creative suffering. Continue to work with the faith that unearned suffering is redemptive.[21]

Still, things didn't change overnight. There were more protests, more sit-ins. But after a bombing at the Sixteenth Street Baptist Church in Birmingham, Alabama, on September 15, 1963, that killed four Black girls, and the protest that followed, President Lyndon B. Johnson and the United States legislature had had enough. They capitulated, passing the Civil Rights Act of 1964. As no small aside, no conviction was made in connection with those bombings until 1977, when Robert E. Chambliss was sentenced to life in prison. Despite the fact that the FBI had solid evidence and good leads relating to the bombing, no further indictments were brought until May 2000.[22]

THE CONTINUATION OF RACE-BASED POLICING

Equal justice under the law requires more than just passing legislation. For justice to be equal, the laws have to be enforced consistently— whether by police or other law enforcement administrations—in regard to all people. Unfortunately, the laws have not been applied with equity. Just law enforcement doesn't treat Brown folks differently than white folks. It doesn't suffocate some for certain conduct—such as allegedly passing a counterfeit bill—while simply letting others go with a warning for engaging in that same conduct.

Mark McCoy, a white, middle-aged archeology professor at Southern Methodist University, tweeted:

> George Floyd and I were both arrested for allegedly spending a counterfeit $20 bill. For George Floyd, a man my age, with two kids, it was a death sentence. For me, it is a story I sometimes tell at parties. That, my friends, is White privilege.[23]

Now, you might argue that this is a cherry-picked example, but what if there's something deeper at work? In 2006, the FBI released a report entitled (U) *White Supremacist Infiltration of Law Enforcement*. The report stated that "white supremacist leaders and groups have historically shown an interest in infiltrating law enforcement communities or recruiting law enforcement personnel."[24] Describing those infiltrators, the report notes,

> Since coming to law enforcement attention in late 2004, the term "ghost skins" has gained currency among white supremacists to describe those who avoid overt displays of their beliefs to blend into society and covertly advance white supremacists causes. One Internet posting described this effort as a form of role-playing . . . [that] has application to ad-hoc and organized law enforcement infiltration. At least one white supremacist group has reportedly encouraged ghost skins to seek positions in law enforcement for the capability of alerting skinhead crews of pending investigative action against them.[25]

The FBI report also indicates that the Ku Klux Klan (KKK) has historically found support in local communities, including within local police departments. As noted in a 2016 article by PBS, ten years after the FBI report,

> The bulletin was released during a period of scandal for many law enforcement agencies throughout the country, including a neo-Nazi gang formed by members of the Los Angeles County Sheriff's Department who harassed black and Latino communities. Similar investigations revealed officers and entire agencies with hate group ties in Illinois, Ohio and Texas.[26]

Perhaps you wonder: "Yes, but Tasha, that report was from 2006. Surely things are different?" It's true that the FBI report is almost twenty years old, but so little has changed. In 2014, the FBI outed two Florida police officers as members of the Ku Klux Klan.[27] In September 2015, a North Carolina officer was fired because he was a little too comfortable giving a Nazi salute.[28] In June 2015, five days after a white-supremacist shooter took the lives of nine Black congregants at Mother Emanuel AME Church in Charleston, South Carolina,[29] the North Charleston police department fired an officer for posing online in Confederate flag underwear.[30] In 2020, three Wilmington, North Carolina, officers were fired after making racist comments in the wake of Black Lives Matter protests, including one officer who said, "Wipe 'em [meaning Black people] off the f———map. That'll put 'em back about four or five generations."[31] In August 2022, the Vincent, Alabama, city council voted to dissolve the police department after one of its three officers sent a racist text message about slavery.[32] In short, although racism within the police ranks has been a known concern for years, no legislation or new policies have been created to deter the infiltration, and the problem persists.

In light of the FBI's findings and the continual surfacing of offenses by officers, we ought to take a closer look at our country's policing, since policing tainted with *any* racial bias undermines liberty and justice for *all*. As Christians who are called to liberation, we should take any race-based injustice seriously because, as Solomon wrote in Proverbs, "Acquitting the guilty and condemning the innocent—the LORD detests them both" (17:15).

If the police system in America is to work for all people, all people can get involved. Let's prepare ourselves and the system for renewal by recognizing and confessing the truth of the system and lamenting it. Let's dedicate ourselves to changing the system, too, whether through legislation (such as removing qualified immunity from officers), reformation (such as initiating community policing efforts), or the redistribution of resources that lends to reimaging the purpose of policing (such as allocating a portion of bloated police budgets to mental health efforts). Through all of this, we can begin to move toward the liberation of modern policing. What could these steps look like?

THE PREPARATION TO RESTORE JUSTICE

In the Old Testament scriptures, Isaiah addressed the people of Israel who conveniently ignored the marginalized and mistreated in their midst. Focused on their own wealth and ease, they'd lost sight of what justice meant. As a result, Isaiah spoke a fiery word from the Lord over the people:

> Stop bringing meaningless offerings!
> > Your incense is detestable to me.
> New Moons, Sabbaths and convocations—
> > I cannot bear your worthless assemblies.
> Your New Moon feasts and your appointed festivals
> > I hate with all my being.
> They have become a burden to me;
> > I am weary of bearing them.

When you spread out your hands in prayer,
    I hide my eyes from you;
even when you offer many prayers,
    I am not listening.

Your hands are full of blood!

Wash and make yourselves clean.
    Take your evil deeds out of my sight;
    stop doing wrong.
Learn to do right; seek justice.
    Defend the oppressed.
Take up the cause of the fatherless;
    plead the case of the widow.

"Come now, let us settle the matter,"
    says the LORD.
"Though your sins are like scarlet,
    they shall be as white as snow;
though they are red as crimson,
    they shall be like wool." (1:13–18)

God was clear: Stop throwing your parties and enjoying your lavish lifestyles while people are suffering in the streets. Wash yourselves and learn to do what's right.

The first act of preparation, according to Isaiah, was for the Israelites to purify themselves. That purification required the wealthy and those in power to acknowledge their sin, namely the ways they'd discriminated against the marginalized. The call to the Israelites is not so different from the Lord's call to us today. Perhaps we can look at our history to see the ways our criminal justice system has segregated and discriminated. Maybe we can examine the ways the system has led to unjust results: to the torturing, killing, and incarceration of many people of color. When we do—when we see our "sins are like scarlet"—we can allow the tears of our lament to pierce our hearts and lead us deeper into the truth that God wants justice for *all*.

But pausing to lament—being purified of our sin—is only the first part of preparation. In the words of the prophet, we must "learn to do right; seek justice." That learning won't be comfortable. We'll have to wrestle with a simple truth: Though legislation and certain high-profile cases remedied some of the racism baked into the system, they have not undone it. Changing the system means educating ourselves and those in our communities about the historical and present disparities in law enforcement, lamenting those disparities, and examining alternatives. We can partner with local communities to imagine new ways of policing, ways that root out inequities in the system and create more just outcomes.

This kind of reimagining can prepare us for change and lead us to repair broken systems. How can we begin that work of repair? Through dedication.

Dedication Is Active

Through Isaiah, God called the people to prepare themselves to do the uncomfortable work they'd neglected for so long. They were to dedicate themselves to justice, which meant defending the oppressed instead of neglecting them. They were to take up the cause of fatherless young men and women instead of treating them as burdens of society (much less objects of incarceration). They were to advocate for the widow instead of allowing her to be exploited by unjust men and unjust systems.

The life of Georgia Ann Robinson, a woman who dedicated herself to police reform, is an inspiration for those who seek justice for all. She was born in Opelousas, Louisiana, in 1879. She grew up to be an activist who found her voice in the women's suffrage movement and the early civil rights movement. She was the first treasurer of Los Angeles's chapter of the NAACP.[33] When the Los Angeles Police Department faced a police officer shortage in 1916 due to World War I enlistment, they recruited Robinson, who had established a reputation as a tireless worker for justice. She accepted the volunteer position.[34]

Three years later, Robinson was officially sworn in on June 10, 1919,[35] and became one of the first two Black policewomen in American history,[36] serving as a jail matron. With that distinction came responsibility. Robinson received an inside look at the system and cared for the needs of the women inmates. She later worked as an investigator, focusing on juvenile cases and homicides. But she wasn't just an officer. Knowing the risks posed to women and children on the streets, she helped to create a safe haven for them—the Sojourner Truth Home for women and girls.[37]

A head injury forced Robinson into early retirement, but she never quit working toward the goal of restorative justice. She became involved in desegregation efforts in California and continued to be a prominent member of the NAACP until her death in 1961, just three years before the passage of the Civil Rights Act.

Robinson didn't simply acknowledge the need for reformation. She entered the work.

I'm proud to highlight Robinson's work. (Talk about a hero!) After all, so many stories of transformation and influence by people of color have yet to be told. We don't often get the credit we have earned.

But it shouldn't be only people of color who put their bodies on the line to reform the police system. If we're going to get any traction in police reformation, we all need to come together to reform policing.

DEDICATION LEADS TO LIBERATION

In 2013, NBC News reported on Camden, New Jersey, a city just across the Delaware River from Philadelphia. Anchor Brian Williams called it the most dangerous and poorest city in America. He reported, "Roughly 77,000 people live here; there were 67 homicides last year and 266 shootings. That's one every 33 hours, and that's the worst in the nation."[38]

People were scared to leave their homes, and not just because of the criminals. As reported by Katherine Landergan in an article for *Politico*, "In 2010, five officers in the department were charged with evidence planting, fabrication and perjury. Later, state and federal courts would go on to overturn the convictions of 88 people who had been arrested and charged by those officers."[39] In the same article, Landergan reported that in 2011, there were thirty-seven complaints against the city police for using excessive force, though none were sustained.

Policing in Camden was clearly not working. The people were afraid of both the criminals and the police. Out of money and credibility, the Camden city council approved the elimination of the city police department and established a county law enforcement department that took a much different approach to policing—a community approach.

Officers of the county effort began by asking residents whether or not they felt safe. They stood on street corners and interacted with people, and they didn't make petty misdemeanor arrests. They were there to build relationships and shut down the most violent crimes.[40]

The Camden County Police Department has adopted a community policing initiative it calls Unity Policing. According to the police department's website, "Unity Policing is CCPD's very own new style of policing built on the principles of de-escalation, wellness, leadership, transparency, and empathy."[41] The initiative calls on the police, government, residents, businesses, and schools of Camden to work together to create a safer community. As part of its program, the department promoted five women to the rank of captain, including Vivian Coley, an African American woman.[42] Together, these women and those they supervise encourage other officers to get out of their cars and engage in positive interactions with the community. They participate in school programs,[43] community events, and city sports.[44] The officers interact with the communities. They don't see themselves as participants in a war; they see themselves as community builders.

The results? In a 2020 article, the City of Camden reported a "70% decrease in homicides and a 46% drop in violent crime over the past 7 years."[45] The Camden County community policing effort, which prioritizes community interaction and programs as a way to build trust, has been a success, and in November 2022, the Department of Justice allocated more than two hundred thousand dollars to the department to fund local community policing initiatives.[46]

The changes in Camden came about because community members, politicians, and the police dedicated themselves to reform. Those reforms have liberated an entire town from fear—both the fear of violent crime and the fear of being unjustly treated by the police. Isn't this the kind of liberation we should want for our own communities? For every community?

As we dedicate ourselves to producing this kind of change nationwide, we must first determine what aspects of our state and local justice system aren't operating justly, and then we must work toward change in those areas. We can help create law enforcement systems that are seen as allies to the community in the pursuit of equal justice. Encouraging increased accountability is another practical step—for instance, lobbying our local police forces to always wear body cameras or sending letters to our politicians asking for the removal of qualified immunity from police officers.

For my white brothers and sisters, things might get pretty uncomfortable if you dedicate yourself to liberation of the law enforcement system. You might have to use your voice to speak out against police brutality and oppression. You might need to join a protest, even if you get labeled liberal or woke. Everyone should want to see a more just system of policing; it benefits everyone, including saving the lives of officers. But using your voice may not be enough. You might also need to use your physical presence. Make your presence known. It'll show support to your BIPOC brothers and sisters, it will hold your local police department accountable, and it might lead to true liberation.

LIBERATING POLICING: MEET UNCLE TROY

While I love the story of Camden, another story of liberation is closer to my heart: the story of my uncle, Police Chief Troy McDuffie, who dedicated his life to liberating a community and embattled police department in Spring Lake, North Carolina. He has led with accountability and integrity, and it made a difference.

Uncle Troy served thirty-five years in law enforcement. When he entered the force, America was only a few decades removed from the dismantling of Jim Crow laws. He knew being a Black police officer would not be easy in the historically white space of policing. But through hard work, integrity, and concern shown for his fellow officers and the people in his community, he set himself apart. He climbed the ranks and, ultimately, became a chief in a time when few people of color were given the opportunity to achieve such a position. He wanted to use that opportunity to leave a legacy.

My uncle valued integrity, accountability, and respect, and he made sure the officers under his command embodied those values in the station and in the community. He was clear with his officers: He would always support them as long as they followed department procedures and led with respect for themselves and those they were called to serve. Part of showing respect meant reforming some of the procedures and personnel of the department, which included dismissing officers with questionable track records.

During his tenure as police chief, from 2009 to 2021, police brutality entered the national spotlight. In an effort to make sure his officers didn't engage in this behavior, Uncle Troy instituted mandatory de-escalation training, teaching his officers to restore calm and order to tense situations. His aim was to build a bridge between the department and the community by hosting community fundraisers, including 5k fun runs, and sponsoring community Secret Santa events. These kinds of events and partnerships allowed the community to see the police officers as servants of the people and helped the police officers see the humanity of each person in the community. This was the thrust of his career. In fact, a militaristic mindset in many police forces across America is what he believes led to so many instances of police brutality.

Uncle Troy didn't stop with community involvement. He implemented yearly psychological checks for officers and advocated for greater accountability through the use of body cameras. He supports a national registry for disciplined police officers, much like a sex offender registry. With a new focus on the mental health of officers, and with the ability to track them through the system, he's hopeful that problematic officers will be weeded out of the system.

The efforts of Uncle Troy, a member of NOBLE—the National Organization of Black Law Enforcement Executives—have created true liberation for the community and for the officers of color serving under him. During his eleven-year tenure as police chief, Uncle Troy's department did not have a single charge of police brutality or excessive force brought against it. "The officers understood," he stated, "what type of culture we were aiming to create—a culture the community could trust."[47] He believes in the reimagination of the policing system to make it equitable and just for all.

Liberation within the American justice system is possible if we all get involved to create better, safer, more sustainable communities. Let's work together to create more equitable systems. Let's remember that we're a family connected to one another under the umbrella of the United States Declaration of Independence, which declares that all of us are created equal. Let's set our sights on creating communities where the words of the Pledge of Allegiance ring true, that there is "liberty and justice for all."

QUESTIONS FOR REFLECTION

1. What is your first thought when you encounter a police car while you are driving? How does your personal experience shape that response?

2. As you reflect on the history of policing as discussed in this chapter, what, if anything, surprised you? What impact do you think it has on today's policing practices?

3. Research policing policies in your state and/or local community. Enlist a friend to research with you. What do you notice about police inequity in your state? In your community?

4. How can your local police department begin to build a bridge of justice, restoration, and reconciliation among the marginalized in your community? How could you be involved in that work?

Voice of Liberation: Shawn Henderson

BE THE BRIDGE MEMBER SHAWN HENDERSON, A FORMER DALLAS police officer, was responsible for one of three sectors in the city. Understanding the racial tensions that accompany policing, Henderson often reinforced the hard truths of policing history with his subordinates. Among those truths, Henderson shared, was the fact that "you don't have to go too far back in our nation's history to see law enforcement used as a tool to enforce systems of racial oppression."[48] Because of that, Henderson said, many people don't trust officers, and it was important that the officers earn back that trust. How would they do it? Through adjustments in attitude, tone, demeanor, and commitment to true justice. His advice to his officers: "Treat people the way you'd want someone to treat your mom in the same situation, and always remember, [police officers'] interactions have the potential to humanize or dehumanize."

Henderson is no longer on the police force. Today he teaches training classes for law enforcement agencies about things like evidence collection and management. "Even though my class is not directly intended to address social justice or racial reconciliation," he said, "there are multiple themes through the course that touch on social justice issues." Why? Henderson said, "It is our obligation as officers to ensure that any interaction with law enforcement leaves our citizens with no legitimate reasons to reinforce past negative personal biases about law enforcement."

He wants to see citizens and officers return home safe at the end of each day, and he wants that for people of *all* colors. That's why he feels it's important to discuss the difficult and hidden conversations that continue to divide us. Through his work, he has taken one small step at a time to bring about change.

CHAPTER 5

The Black Market

THE MARKETPLACE

Y OU'VE PROBABLY HEARD OF BRENÉ BROWN, THE PROFESSOR, RE-
searcher, and *New York Times* bestselling author. But have you
heard of Casandra Brown? Until recently, I hadn't. It turns out
Brené Brown and Casandra Brown are the same person. In her book
Braving the Wilderness, Brown shared how, as a child in Louisiana in the
late sixties and early seventies, she was not often invited to birthday
parties. Why? The class roster listed her as Casandra Brené Brown.
When the parents of her white classmates sent invitations out, they
passed over her, assuming she was Black.[1]

The story didn't surprise me. Most people who see my name or hear
it spoken probably assume I'm Black. (Have you ever known a white
Latasha? There are a few, and they likely have stories to tell.) I'm sure
my first name has caused me to be passed over for party invitations, job
opportunities, or inclusion in certain clubs and civic organizations. But
hearing this kind of story from a white woman felt different. She was in
a position of privilege yet suffered discrimination and isolation because
her name was not deemed "white" enough.

After learning this, I shared the story with a Black co-worker, though I failed to mention that Brown was white because, in my defense, I assumed she'd know who Brené Brown was. She didn't seem bothered. "Who's that again?" she asked.

I stood up straight, raised my brow, and said, "You don't know who Brené Brown is? The white woman who's written on vulnerability and shame and has helped almost every white person I know?"

It was her turn to sit up straight. "Her name is Brené and she's white?"

We stared at each other for an awkward moment. Then we died laughing.

Our funny exchange demonstrates a very human truth: Names carry a lot of meaning. They can signal ethnicity, race, gender, and even religion. In a racialized world, they can indicate other character attributes too. Don't believe me?

Let's play a game. What do you picture when you read the following names?

Luke
Maria
Rasheed
Tam
Mohammed

Do you make certain assumptions about skin color, gender, and religion based solely upon the names, even if you'd rather not? Do any of those names conjure feelings of trust or mistrust? Do you assume one of those people is smarter than others? Do you assume one is Muslim, one is Catholic, or one is Protestant? To be honest, I do.

Name bias is a real thing, and many of us carry these biases with us every day. How do I know? Because many people in this country—both BIPOC and white immigrants—have changed their names to assimilate and to conceal their ethnic origins.

For example, in the mid-nineteenth century, Charles Steinweg was a German immigrant to New York City. He was a phenomenal instrument maker, but English instruments were deemed superior, and his name was anything but English. So the famed piano maker did what so many European immigrants of the age did. He changed his name.[2] The anglicization of his name must have worked, because today the world's best pianists play on Steinway pianos.

Commentators have also noted that many Jewish people in the early twentieth century changed their names to blend into American society and secure better employment. In an article for Michigan State University, Kirsten Fermaglich highlighted Dora Sarietzky, a stenographer and typist who changed her name in the 1930s in order to get more work. Fermaglich commented, "Since most petitioners were native-born Americans, this wasn't about fitting in. It was a direct response to racism."[3]

Steinweg and Sarietzky (I'll use their birth surnames) knew that a name could determine whether they were accepted or rejected by society. It could limit their opportunities to sell pianos or gain employment. That's still true today.

Names can have a deep impact on the way people are treated in the American marketplace. They can determine who gets certain opportunities and who does not. Names can open and close doors.

What's in a Name?

In 2004, economist Marianne Bertrand and former Harvard economics professor Sendhil Mullainathan (who was born in a small village in India and is now a professor at the University of Chicago) published research on the effect of names in the hiring process. Their research found that applicants with white-sounding names received 50 percent more callbacks for interviews than those with Black-sounding names.[4] So women named Latasha were far less likely to receive callbacks for jobs than women named Liv. Men named Tom were more likely to receive callbacks than men named Treyvon, and this was true even if the candidates had similar qualifications.

But that was almost two decades ago. Surely things have changed, particularly considering the heightened awareness around racial reconciliation, right?

Wrong.

In a 2021 study by economists from the University of California, Berkeley and the University of Chicago, 83,000 job applications were sent to over one hundred Fortune 500 companies. Half of the applicants had Black-sounding names and the other half had white-sounding names. The result? Applicants with Black-sounding names had a reduced chance of hearing back from an employer by 2.1 percentage points when compared to applicants with white-sounding names.[5] The study's results come with a caveat, though. According to a Bloomberg report on the study,

> differences in contact rates varied substantially across firms. About 20% of the companies were responsible for roughly half of the discriminatory behavior in the experiment, according to the working paper recently published by the National Bureau of Economic Research.[6]

In other words, the worst offenders were *really* offending.

This is why applicants of African American, Asian, and Latino descent have chosen to "whiten," or delete aspects of, their cultural heritage on their job applications and résumés. In a 2016 study, researchers created résumés for 1,600 entry-level jobs in sixteen metropolitan areas across the United States. Some of those résumés provided racial clues, while others were whitened. Twenty-one percent of Asian candidates with whitened résumés received callbacks, while only 11.5 percent of Asian candidates who kept racial references in their résumés received callbacks. For African Americans, 25 percent of those with whitened résumés received callbacks as opposed to the 10 percent who received callbacks without whitened résumés.[7]

Our ethnicity—including the names we pass down from generation to generation—has a practical impact on our economic opportunity. Hiring discrimination is not a problem of the past. It is a persistent problem today because innately biased people—including you and me—make up our economic systems. This discrimination only deepens economic inequity and creates BIPOC cultural erasure from predominantly white workspaces.

ECONOMIC BELONGING AND *THE SOULS OF BLACK FOLK*

If you're white, ask yourself: *What would it take for me to decide to change my family name?* It's likely not a decision you'd take lightly. But for Brown people, changing our identity to fit into a white world is a frequent—though demoralizing—concession. It's not just our names either. We "whiten" our hair, clothing, and speech patterns to assimilate. The choice to whiten our identity might mean the difference between being followed in a store by a suspicious white manager or being left alone. It can mean the difference between getting a job or getting passed over.

It's exhausting to consciously weigh every little personal identity decision, whether we're applying for a job, making a trip to the corner market, or simply walking down the street at night. This way of thinking and acting is a product of what the African American intellectual and political figure W.E.B. Du Bois called "double consciousness."

In his 1903 book *The Souls of Black Folk*, he wrote:

It is a peculiar sensation, this double-consciousness, this sense of always looking at one's self through the eyes of others, of measuring one's soul by the tape of a world that looks on in amused contempt and pity. One ever feels his two-ness,—an American, a Negro; two souls, two thoughts, two unreconciled strivings; two warring ideals in one dark body, whose dogged strength alone keeps it from being torn asunder.

The history of the American Negro is the history of this strife,—this longing to attain self-conscious manhood, to merge his double self into a better and truer self. In this merging he wishes neither of the older selves to be lost. He would not Africanize America, for America has too much to teach the world and Africa. He would not bleach his Negro soul in a flood of white Americanism, for he knows that Negro blood has a message for the world. He simply wishes to make it possible for a man to be both a Negro and an American, without being cursed and spit upon by his fellows, without having the doors of Opportunity closed roughly in his face.[8]

More than one hundred years after Du Bois wrote these words, African American, Latino, Asian, Indian, Native American, Middle Eastern, Indigenous, Pacific Islander, and multiracial people still wrestle with a double consciousness. We want to remain true to our cultures—our names, styles of dress, and our traditions—but at the same time, we're caught in the paradox of assimilating to belong in white spaces.

Take a simple thing like hair. In 2019, a national alliance called the CROWN (Creating a Respectful and Open World for Natural Hair) Coalition was founded by Dove, the National Urban League, Color of Change (a racial justice organization), and the Western Center on Law & Poverty in an effort to end hair discrimination.[9] According to Dove's 2019 research study, when compared to other women, Black women are 1.5 times "more likely to be sent home from the workplace because of their hair," 3.4 percent more likely to have their hair judged as "unprofessional," 30 percent "more likely to be made aware of a formal workplace appearance policy" than their co-workers, and 80 percent more likely to change their natural hair to meet social norms.[10] Put another way, Black women are singled out and discriminated against because of an immutable characteristic—their God-given hair. In fact, hair discrimination is such an issue that the CROWN Coalition has pushed for the passage of legislation called the CROWN Act to end discrimination against people of color based on their hair.[11] As of September 2023, twenty-three states and counting had enacted the CROWN Act into law![12]

Discrimination based on immutable characteristics begins very early in life—so early in fact that many people of color don't remember the first time they felt discriminated against. The paradox of belonging begins early as well. My best friend is an Asian and African American (biracial) woman formerly married to Black man. She shared a comment with me that their ten-year-old son, Jude, had recently made as he listened to our conversation over the speaker in the car. As a self-identified Black boy, he said, "I understand what it feels like to be white."

She told me that she looked at her son with curiosity, not really taking him seriously.

"Being white feels like freedom," he continued. "Everyone believes you. You get chance after chance." Though not yet in middle school, he understood the disparity between white and Black people and knew how to interpret that disparity. He also understood that to navigate the world, he'd have to change parts of who he was so he could be more believable, more free, more . . . *white.* That's the double consciousness Du Bois wrote about. Jude understood it, though no one taught him.

THE PARADOX OF BELONGING: A BIBLICAL EXAMPLE

Du Bois's double consciousness—where Black people struggle to remain true to themselves and their culture while at the same time having to suppress a part of themselves to fit into white culture, including economic spaces—is not strictly an American phenomenon. This has been a reality for millennia.

In the book of Genesis, we meet Joseph, the favored son of Jacob, the ancestor of the people of Israel. You likely know the story, so I won't recount it in detail. But here are the highlights (and lowlights) of Joseph's life and how he dealt with his double consciousness.

Joseph was sold into slavery by his brothers and then sold to a military officer named Potiphar (see Genesis 37). While Potiphar was away, his wife enticed Joseph sexually then accused him of rape when he refused her advances. Joseph was placed in prison, an innocent man punished for a crime he didn't commit (see Genesis 39). Many people of color can relate to that scenario.

Left to rot in prison, Joseph made a name for himself as a dream interpreter. When Pharaoh had two mysterious dreams, Joseph was called from his prison cell to offer an interpretation. In the first dream, Pharaoh stood by the Nile watching as seven fat cows emerged from the water. Seven skinny cows followed, and they devoured the fat cows. In the second dream, seven heads of healthy grain sprouted from a single stalk. Then seven sickly heads of grain "scorched by the east wind" (Genesis 41:6) sprouted, and they devoured the healthy grain. After hearing the dreams, Joseph gave the interpretation: A famine was coming in seven years, and in the interim years of plenty, Egypt needed to prepare.

Pharaoh believed Joseph's interpretation and promoted Joseph to the highest levels of government, second in charge only to himself. Pharoah commanded him to prepare the nation for the famine. There was only one problem: Joseph wasn't Egyptian, and he didn't have any clout in the Egyptian marketplace. Joseph surely understood this, and he knew that because of his minority status, everyone—from Potiphar's wife to the jailer to the average person on the street—looked at him as an outsider. So what did Pharaoh do? He made Joseph acculturate, which is often a beginning stage of cultural assimilation (requiring a minority group to adopt the language, traditions, customs, religious practices, and even the fashion of the dominant culture).

The Scriptures record that Pharaoh gave Joseph an Egyptian ring and dressed him in Egyptian clothes. He put an Egyptian chain around his neck and ordered him to be carried through the town in an Egyptian chariot while Pharaoh's men shouted, "Make way!" before him (Genesis 41:43). Pharaoh gave Joseph a new, Egyptian name as well—Zaphenath-Paneah—essentially Egyptian-washing (a form of cultural assimilation) his résumé in order to rid him of any ethnic clues. For all practical purposes, Joseph became an Egyptian, and throughout the story, he never objects. Why? I can't be sure, but I wonder whether it's because Joseph knew that his safety and security rested on being on good terms with the ruling class. We know that Joseph ultimately would use his power and space for good.

Years later, at the height of the famine, Joseph's brothers traveled to Egypt to buy grain. When they came before Joseph, they didn't recognize him. He had so assimilated that nothing of his previous identity was left. But Joseph remembered his brothers, and after speaking with them, he turned his back and began to weep (see Genesis 42:24). Why did he weep? The Bible doesn't say, but let me venture my interpretation. Yes, he missed his brothers and his father. But might he also have missed his identity and connection to his family? This is exactly what I felt when I visited Africa for the first time. It was not my fault that my ancestors were sold into slavery, that their cultures were completely stripped from them. But something was missing as I engaged the people with whom I shared common ancestors. I was homesick for my people, even though I didn't know them.

I can imagine Joseph felt the same way, but even more acutely. Maybe the double consciousness welled up in him, as he was aware that he was a child of Jacob, even though he looked Egyptian and had an Egyptian name. Though he'd been completely assimilated, he was still connected to his history and identity. He remembered who he was, and he knew his real name.

Eventually, Joseph revealed himself to his brothers, and he used his assimilated identity as a means for providing for his family economically, ultimately setting aside lands for them in Egypt (see Genesis 45–47). But though those lands would sustain his family for generations, his descendants never fully assimilated like he did. Maybe it was because the Israelites' religion wouldn't allow them to fully participate in Egyptian customs or worship Egyptian gods. Maybe it was because they wouldn't Egyptianize their names. Whatever the case, they didn't receive the full approval of the new pharaoh or his people, even though they grew wealthy in Egypt and could have been powerful allies. Because their prosperity *and* difference threatened the people of Egypt, and because the Israelites did not assimilate, the Egyptians turned and oppressed the people of Israel (see Exodus 1).

Often, those who have gained prosperity through assimilation use their affluence for the good of their BIPOC community. But that kind of assimilation comes with a cost—namely giving up aspects of their identity to fit in with the dominant class. On the other hand, refusing to assimilate comes with its own costs, such as loss of opportunities and freedom due to discrimination.

This begs the question: How can BIPOC remain truly authentic to who we are and still access the marketplace without limitations, punishment, discrimination, or dismissal? Unfortunately, it's a question for which we still don't have great answers. A look at the factory, the boardroom, and the storefront shows us as much.

THE FACTORY: THE MODERN PLANTATION

The plantations of the American South are a thing of the past. There are no longer large ranches where enslaved laborers pick cotton for the privilege of simply staying alive. Still, that doesn't mean that some of the badges of the plantation economy haven't filtered into the modern economy. Those who cannot fully assimilate into white economic spaces—whether because of education, privilege, or principle—seem to feel the effects most.

In recent years, disturbing stories have surfaced from the Tesla factory in Fremont, California. In an article published in the *Los Angeles Times*, three Black employees at the electric car manufacturer described a pattern of racist harassment at the factory. They claimed supervisors used "racist slurs in English and Spanish." They further asserted that Black workers were segregated, given more difficult tasks, and denied promotions. According to the article, one former employee, single mother Monica Chatman, complained that she worked too much overtime. Even though she was paid overtime wages, she was exhausted. Chatman told the *Times,* "There was a time where I worked three months straight—no days off"; she believed she had no choice but to take those overtime shifts to keep her job. Tesla, she said, was "modern-day slavery."[13]

In that same article, Nigel Jones, another former employee, discussed his experience in the factory. Jones claimed he noticed signs of racism early, but it wasn't until he was promoted to fleet manager that overt racism became the norm. He indicated that a supervisor used the word "monkeys" to refer to Jones and two other Black co-workers. That same supervisor once walked away from them saying, "Oh you lazy n—."[14]

Jones could have kept his mouth shut. He could have done his best to assimilate. Instead, he reported the incidents and initially thought he'd see some traction. That was a dream. Ultimately, Jones was fired. But that wasn't all. He claimed he was blacklisted from employment at any other Tesla factory, so when a friend at another location tried to hire him, he was ineligible.[15]

Allegations like these became the subject of a February 2022 lawsuit filed by the California Department of Fair Employment and Housing, claiming rampant racism at the Tesla Fremont factory. An article on the lawsuit published by the *Guardian* noted:

> In the suit, filed on 9 February in an Alameda county court in California, the agency says Black workers reported they were subjected to racist slurs and drawings and were assigned the most physically demanding jobs. "Workers referred to the [Tesla] factory as the 'slaveship' or 'the plantation', where defendants' production leads 'crack the whip'," the agency said in the complaint.[16]

That lawsuit came on the heels of another lawsuit by former Tesla employee Owen Diaz, who alleged fellow employees called him the *N*-word, that he was subjected to racist graffiti, including in his workspace, and that he was told by co-workers to "go back to Africa."[17] The case was submitted to a jury, which found that Diaz was subject to racist treatment and awarded him 137 million dollars in damages. Talk about hitting the bottom line! The award was ultimately substantially reduced in a later order by Judge William Orrick because the award was unconstitutionally high. But in his order, Judge Orrick agreed that Diaz experienced "profound" emotional harm.[18]

No matter the size of the award, I can see why Tesla has earned the nickname "the plantation." It seems that marginalized groups are demeaned and given the more difficult jobs while white people maintain the power. This kind of discrimination doesn't just happen at Tesla, though. It's a phenomenon that affects many companies, and the statistics show as much.

Consider the limitations on the advancement of BIPOC to positions of leadership. Only six Fortune 500 companies had African American CEOs in 2022,[19] while forty S&P 500 and Fortune 500 companies had Asian American CEOs and twenty had Latino CEOs in 2021.[20] In

2019, only 16 percent of corporate board seats were held by people of color.[21] According to management consulting firm McKinsey & Company, which reviewed data from the Bureau of Labor Statistics, the US Census Bureau, and the Equal Employment Opportunity Commission (EEOC),

> Our analysis found that Black workers are underrepresented in the highest-growth geographies and the highest-paying industries. Meanwhile, they are overrepresented in low-growth geographies and in frontline jobs, which tend to pay less.[22]

It's difficult to feel like you belong in the marketplace when people who look, talk, and dress like you are underrepresented there. Underrepresentation leads to much of the discrimination in American economic spaces. The EEOC reported 22,064 charges of workplace discrimination based on race in 2020 alone.[23]

If anything is certain, it's that companies won't make meaningful changes without being pushed. We can use our voices and our purchasing decisions to put pressure on companies that create inequitable market conditions, whether at the factory, in the C-suite, or at the storefront.

HOW THE CUSTOMER CAN INSPIRE LIBERATION

In a marketplace as big as America's, particularly one built on a foundation of racism, issues will persist. American companies may still hire racist employees despite their best screening efforts, but when instances of discrimination happen, employers should return to the foundational principles of creating more equitable systems for all people, including BIPOC employees. It's not just on the employers, though. As consumers, we have to make our voices heard too.

In 2018, employees at a Philadelphia Starbucks called the police on two Black business partners, Donte Robinson and Rashon Nelson. Upon entering the store, Nelson asked to use the restroom but was told the restroom was for customers only. Nelson and Robinson then chose a seat in the back, and when asked by the manager whether they needed any help with drinks, the two men said they were waiting for a business meeting. The manager left the table and immediately called officers. Six minutes after Robinson and Nelson walked into the Starbucks, officers came to arrest them for trespassing.[24] Their only "crime" was sitting while Black.

After the arrest, the truth came out. Robinson and Nelson had indeed been waiting for a third business associate to arrive, which is why they hadn't yet ordered.[25] But that wasn't the only truth that came to light. A video of the arrest surfaced and went viral, sparking nationwide outrage. People protested. Starbucks boycotts followed. People demanded change from the largest retail coffee seller in the world, and the company felt the impact. Sales tanked. Though Starbucks could simply have settled any legal claim with the patrons and weathered the storm, instead they listened to their customers and used the moment to institute change.

The company entered a time of preparation and dedication to fixing their internal problems. They closed more than eight thousand stores for one afternoon so they could train 175,000 employees on racial bias, particularly in places of public accommodation, and they did it by elevating the voices of people of color.[26] The estimated cost in lost sales due to the training closure was 16.7 million dollars,[27] but executive chairman Howard Schultz affirmed the company's "commitment to creating a safe and welcoming environment for every customer."[28]

At the training, associates were shown a film by the Black documentarian Stanley Nelson that examines the experience of Black people in public spaces.[29] The film—comprising historical footage of violence against Black people, footage of modern discrimination, and recent interviews with non-white people—showed that the advancement of civil rights, particularly in the economic spaces of the 1960s, did not come without struggle. Black people were denied tables in restaurants and overnight accommodations in hotels. Black and white students trying to desegregate buses were firebombed. BIPOC patrons were dragged from lunch counters. Civil rights workers were beaten.

The short film demonstrated that though civil rights legislation was passed to mandate equal rights in commercial spaces for BIPOC patrons, that didn't always translate to being *welcomed*. BIPOC consumers shared their experiences of feeling unwelcome in retail stores. How they're often followed around by security or harassed by employees. Then the video asked this question: "What can you do to make our schools, our parks, our stores, our restaurants as welcoming and as inclusive as they can be? What kind of country do we want to live in? Who do we want to be?"[30]

Now, here's the kicker: The documentary was funded by Starbucks. Though the company's executives were aware that diversity training and the production of a short film would not fix the issue overnight, it was a first step in training their employees to create a more equitable environment. Long-term change would require a more long-term strategy. Still, the move by Starbucks, which was undoubtedly triggered by consumer backlash, was taken deliberately, with great preparation and dedication toward creating a liberated environment for its patrons and employees.

COMPANIES LEADING LIBERATION

As you can see, when we raise our voices in the marketplace, when we speak in favor of liberation, American corporations are compelled to engage in their own acts of preparation, dedication, and liberation. Thankfully, some companies are embracing the message of liberation before some incident of racism hits the national news and customers instigate a protest. Consider Microsoft, a corporation that seems to have engaged in its own acts of intentional liberation. In 2020, over 39 percent of its board of directors was composed of ethnic and racial minorities, and its workplace was nearly split between white people and ethnic minorities, with 41.3 percent of its managers being minorities.[31]

Or take a look at Biogen. As of 2020, the Massachusetts biotech company stated that 51 percent of its management team are women and 30 percent are people of color. (Biogen is also one of the top places to work for people with disabilities.)[32]

Gap, the clothing retailer found in nearly every major city in America, stated that about 55 percent of its labor force are people of color and 30 percent of its managers are BIPOC.[33] Apparently, they're committed to liberating us from more than bad style. They're committed to liberating us from the historical badges of racism in the marketplace.

These three companies—Microsoft, Biogen, and Gap—have dedicated themselves to the liberation of their spaces, and many other multinational companies and smaller local companies are leading in liberation as well. By normalizing diversity in every level of the labor force, companies like these send a clear message: All are welcome.

DEDICATING YOUR OWN SPACE TO LIBERATION

Whether you're a Fortune 500 executive, a manager of a moderate-size division, a small business owner, or a barista at a coffee shop, you have a part in creating an equitable workplace or storefront. Note I said equitable, not diverse. What's the difference? Take the example of the Tesla factory. Was it diverse? Sure. Many BIPOC worked at the factory. But was it equitable, putting non-white and white people on an equal playing field? Now consider Microsoft, Biogen, and Gap. They certainly work toward not only creating a diverse workplace environment but also a more equitable workplace through their efforts to promote non-white individuals into managerial positions. See the difference?

If you want to do your part to cultivate a more equitable environment in your workplace and storefront, you can start by examining the issues raised in the short documentary *The Story of Access*, shown by Starbucks.[34] Consider the ways BIPOC customers have been treated in the past and ask yourself what kind of world you want to live in: one in which discrimination is the norm, or one in which everyone has an opportunity to thrive? Then set out to be the change you want to see. Spend your hard-earned dollars at stores and with companies that are creating that kind of world.

If you're in a managerial position, commit to hiring a diverse staff, giving a fair opportunity to people in your community who don't look like you. Many employees of color have been forced to navigate historically white market spaces in this country in order to survive and thrive. On the other hand, in many homogenous communities, white people can attend mostly white colleges and other schools, and can join the marketplace without having meaningful connections with BIPOC individuals. Hiring non-white people puts white people in proximity to their BIPOC brothers and sisters and helps them understand the struggles faced by non-whites. Institute mandatory trainings and continued learning for all employees to improve cultural intelligence. Make sure the value of belonging is part of the hiring process. This leads to getting candidates who reflect your values. It broadens perspective in the workplace, too, exposing people to a wider range of ideas and customs and providing richer perspective regarding the diverse community being served.

Consider hiring and promoting more BIPOC managers and executives. A diverse leadership elevates the voices of non-white people and enables staff members to hear perspectives not otherwise heard. You might also create mentorship programs specifically for BIPOC employees to connect them with upper management. This allows for the creation of a more diverse management pipeline, which paves the way to a more equitable marketplace. It also connects white managers with their colleagues of color and could help them understand the double consciousness Du Bois wrote about.

You might also consider providing a place for BIPOC employees to report any racial grievances anonymously. Many incidents go unreported due to a fear of backlash and firing. If you think discrimination can't happen in your company, you're wrong. (Unless, of course, you have no employees of color, which is an even bigger problem, and you should set some goals for belonging and diversification.)

If you don't have a diverse staff, ask yourself why. Do you have a cultural problem in your organization? Ask your employees of color (even if you have only one) what they think. Hire a consultant to advise you in how to build a more equitable workplace. Invest in organizations like Be the Bridge, which can help you perform diversity audits and provide racial literacy training. Host racial literacy book clubs with incentives to promote racial bridge building. While it should go without saying, let me be clear: Don't do these things just to check a box; be sure to actually incorporate what you learn.

If you operate in a place of public accommodation—a restaurant, hotel, or retail shopping space—make sure you're treating BIPOC patrons as well as you treat white patrons. If you wouldn't follow a white customer around in your store, don't follow a BIPOC customer. If you wouldn't call the police on a white customer who hadn't ordered a drink yet, don't call the police on someone with a different skin color; it's absurd.

If we're going to create more equitable economic spaces, we need to create spaces of welcome. Black and Brown people shouldn't have to whiten their names and résumés to gain employment opportunities. We can celebrate diversity, knowing that true liberation looks like creating economic stability for people of all ethnicities.

QUESTIONS FOR REFLECTION

1. What would you do if the company you worked for discriminated against people of color? Have you ever seen instances of this at a company? How did that make you feel?

2. Why is promoting workplace equity more important than promoting diversity?

3. Take stock of the brands and companies you like. Do you know whether they have or support initiatives to advance equity in the marketplace? If you don't know, do some research and determine whether they deserve your hard-earned dollars.

Voice of Liberation: Craig Williams

CRAIG WILLIAMS, A FRIEND AND MENTOR OF MINE, IS A GRADUATE of Benedict College—one of the top HBCUs. He spent eleven years climbing the American corporate ladder. After receiving his MBA at Northwestern University's Kellogg School of Management and having worked at some of the largest companies in the world—Kraft Foods and Coca-Cola—he became president of Nike's Jordan Brand.

As a committed family man and HBCU supporter, Williams aims to be for others what he didn't have in his early start in corporate America: a mentor and role model to BIPOC businesspeople. In most rooms, his co-workers don't look like him, which causes him to feel out of place at times. So he tries to change the room by doing the highest quality work. He knows performing in his job allows him to make changes from the top down, including creating more diverse and equitable workplaces and compensation structures.

Williams believes corporations and their leadership must be

accountable for the outcomes related to diversity and equity and sees value in tying these results to compensation. He's convinced this connection between equity initiatives and salary can produce more urgency in corporate America. More specifically, he knows that when leaders receive more compensation for making cultural shifts related to diversity and equity, it will move the needle.

Williams may be only one man managing one brand, but he's making a difference by shifting the policies within the company he manages. These changes are bringing opportunity and liberation for the BIPOC and white communities under his care.

CHAPTER 6

The Code of Silence

THE MILITARY

WAS AN ADULT WITH A COLLEGE DEGREE AND CAR PAYMENTS BEFORE I learned the full context of my maternal grandfather's military service, though I knew Troy E. McDuffie, a Black man from rural North Carolina (and the father of Police Chief Troy McDuffie from chapter 4), had served his country in two wars. As an inquisitive child with no filter, I'd asked my great-grandmother if she was old enough to have been a slave. (She was not, much to my surprise.) I'd also asked my grandfather why he always went to the VA hospital, why he had those "big ole" army-issued hearing aids, and why I always had to shout at him during any conversation. It was because of his time in Korea and Vietnam, he said.

It wasn't until my adult years that I became truly curious about his time in the military. In part, my interest was spurred by my love for my grandfather and our family's history. It was also prompted by what I'd learned about the treatment of people of color in the military, historically and presently. It made me wonder what my grandfather's experience had been like. Why did he, a Southern Black man living in the era of segregation and legalized discrimination, join the military?

My grandfather had been reared in Robeson County, North Carolina, which, as you might remember from chapter 4, was one of the poorest counties in the country when he was a child. Growing up, he didn't have much, and his father ran out on the family when my grandfather was only ten years old. This meant my grandfather was left to carry his father's weight. But with limited career opportunities outside sharecropping or day labor at the nearest factory, he knew he needed a better way to support his family, and young though he was, he made a bold move. He forged a birth certificate and enlisted in the army in 1952, well before his eighteenth birthday. He would later earn his GED in the military.

The early 1950s were a time of racial segregation, including state-sponsored Jim Crow laws that legalized it. Just a few years before my grandfather joined the United States Army, President Truman had issued Executive Order 9981 on July 26, 1948. In part, the order stated:

> It is hereby declared to be the policy of the President that there shall be equality of treatment and opportunity for all persons in the armed services without regard to race, color, religion or national origin. This policy shall be put into effect as rapidly as possible, having due regard to the time required to effectuate any necessary changes without impairing efficiency or morale.[1]

It was a dramatic order, one meant to lead the United States Armed Forces into a period of racial equality. With the promise of equality, more than a few Black men enlisted, particularly those who needed a way out of systems of economic injustice in the South. My grandfather was among them.

Of course, all those men—including my grandfather—probably knew an executive order wouldn't change things overnight. They were joining a military full of white senior officers, and they'd lived enough life to know there's no switch you can flip to turn off racism. My grandfather probably knew he'd likely receive more difficult assignments than his white counterparts, that he'd be subject to wage discrimination, and that he wasn't as likely to be promoted as those with lighter skin. Still, he measured his opportunity and took the risk, believing that participation in an inherently racist system could help him break his family's cycle of poverty.

As he expected, military desegregation was slow, despite the executive order. Soldiers of color, whether skilled or unskilled, were mostly segregated and placed in unskilled labor units within the military ranks. My grandfather was placed in a primarily Black mechanics unit, where he served during the Korean War. Though this skill was one he would later use after retirement from the military, his opportunities for advancement while in the ranks were limited in his early army days. When Vietnam rolled around, he found himself surrounded by other Black men who'd been drafted or who enlisted to avoid the draft.

According to Erica Thompson, "Despite making up only 11% of the civilian population, [Black men] accounted for 16.3% of the draft and 23% of combat troops in 1967," and while in the war, many of those soldiers saw the worst of it.[2] In fact, a 1988 study indicated that 20.6 percent of Black veterans suffered PTSD compared to 13.7 percent of white soldiers.[3] My grandfather knew many of those men. My grandfather *was* one of those men. For the rest of his life, he suffered from Agent Orange effects, hearing loss, nightmares, night sweats, and a psychological disconnection from his family.

Returning from the war, my grandfather continued his military career. He discovered that although the official policy of the United States Armed Forces was to integrate Black and white soldiers and strive for racial equality, the reality on the ground was much different. Years after the shift in formal policy, African American soldiers were still treated inequitably. Opportunities for advancement were limited. Pay was inequitable. Black communities were not accommodating to those who'd fought in a "white man's war,"[4] and according to a 1972 study, Black veterans were over twice as likely to have difficulty finding full-time employment as white men.[5]

My grandfather survived two wars and remained in the military long enough to break the cycle of poverty in which he'd been raised. This is not to say he rose to a high military rank or that he achieved fame, glory, and wealth. He didn't. But his willingness to defend his country in a racially unjust time makes him a true hero. If you could sit down with him and have a shouting conversation like the ones I've grown to love, you'd come to understand that truth.

So how did the military, a structure meant to defend every citizen of the United States, regardless of skin color, come to be racially unjust? The truth is, it was baked into its DNA, just as it was in the other systems and structures of our country.

The Whitewashed History of the United States Military

Many of us love war heroes: General George Washington, General Ulysses S. Grant, Sergeant Alvin York from World War I, and General George S. Patton. But though historians have noted that African Americans and Native Americans have fought in every major American war, including the American War of Independence,[6] how many Americans can name those heroes? Let's meet some of them to learn from their stories.

In the early days of the Revolutionary War, Black soldiers were initially passed over for service. George Washington—our first president and one of our greatest national heroes—was opposed to training and arming enslaved people, who might use that training and those arms to instigate a slave revolt.[7] But as the war gained steam, and the British offer of freedom to Black men who joined their ranks began having an impact on the war effort, Washington reassessed the situation. He needed more men—there was a troop shortage—and the young union couldn't suffer the loss of a primary means of labor. So Washington made a pragmatic decision. He would open the rank and file to Black soldiers.

After Washington sent word to legislators that he needed additional men, Congress required each state to institute a draft and provide a quota of men based on their population. Since Rhode Island, the smallest state of the young union, didn't have enough white men to fill its two battalions, it proposed supplementing its militias by drafting both free and enslaved Black men. Though hesitant, Congress and Washington agreed; thus, the First Rhode Island Regiment became America's "first Black miliary regiment."[8]

The First Rhode Island Regiment was one of a handful of Black regiments that served throughout the American Revolution, and it was distinguished on the battlefield. In the Battle of Rhode Island, the regiment was tasked with protecting a defensive position. History shows that the regiment not only defended the position, but they also pushed back three German regiments fighting for the British army. According to an article by Farrell Evans, "Major General John Sullivan spoke for Washington's satisfaction at the regiment's performance when he said, 'By the best information the commander-in-chief thinks that the regiment will be entitled to a proper share of the honors of the day.'"[9] In the final days of the war, this regiment joined with the Second Rhode Island Regiment, and together, as the Rhode Island Regiment, they fought in the Battle of Yorktown, Virginia, in 1781. It was this battle that led to the British surrender.[10]

In 1778, Rhode Island passed the Slave Enlistment Act, which stated that any enslaved person who fought in the Rhode Island regiments would be "immediately discharged from the Service of his Master or Mistress, and be absolutely FREE, as though he had never been encumbered with any Kind of Servitude or Slavery."[11] But despite the success of the regiment and the legislation that freed the Black men in it who survived the war, the Black heroes who served did not receive the recognition they deserved. In fact, according to scholar Cameron Boutin, regardless of the contributions of Black effort to independence, many leaders across the upstart country opposed legislation allowing the enslaved to enlist.[12]

During the Civil War, freed slaves did their part to advance the cause of the North, and not just men either. Harriet Tubman, the great abolitionist who'd been born into slavery, served as a scout, a spy, a nurse, and a military leader. Continuously placing herself in harm's way, she led formerly enslaved African Americans northward during the Combahee River raid (June 2, 1863),[13] which prompted many of those freed men to fight for the Union army.[14] Tubman was a formidable secret weapon, yet despite the Union army's dependence on her skills, her name was kept out of military documents. As a result, Tubman initially was granted only a widow's pension of eight dollars per month in 1888. Her response: "You wouldn't think that after I served the flag so faithfully, I should come to want under its folds." Tubman remained uncompensated for her service until Congress passed a bill that was signed into law by President William McKinley in 1899—thirty years after her work for the Union. The law recognized Tubman's contributions and awarded her an increased pension for her wartime service in the amount of twenty dollars per month, five dollars less than other veterans.[15]

The abolition of slavery in 1865 didn't eliminate discrimination in the ranks of the military. Though men and women of color served in World War I and World War II, they were segregated from white soldiers, endured some of the worst conditions, and often didn't receive recognition for their contributions.

In World War I, the 369th Infantry Regiment, known as the Harlem Hellfighters, was assigned to the French army and fought on the front lines. Among the Hellfighters was Private Henry Johnson, the son of North Carolina tobacco farmers.[16] While on sentry duty 115 miles outside of Paris, no fewer than twelve German soldiers surprised Johnson and another soldier, Needham Roberts.[17] Early in the fighting, Roberts was wounded, and after running out of grenades, Johnson held off the enemy with little more than a knife, avoiding capture. When the dust cleared and the Germans retreated, Johnson discovered he'd suffered twenty-one wounds. But he'd killed at least four Germans and kept the advancing party from busting the French front line. Johnson—who earned the nickname "Black Death"—and Roberts received France's highest military award, the *Croix de Guerre.* They were the first American privates to receive the decoration.[18]

Likewise, the 370th Infantry Regiment fought valiantly in World War I. After being ambushed on a supply run, the regiment was met with fierce resistance. Over the following days, one member of the regiment—Emmett Thompson—ran supplies from the regiment's supply wagon to the frontline trenches while the 370th pushed back the German front. The defeated Germans gave the regiment a nickname—"the Fighting Black Devils"—and it stuck. Two members of the Black regiment received high honors for their roles in the battle. Lieutenant Frank Robinson received the *Croix de Guerre,* and Sergeant Emmett Thompson received the Distinguished Service Cross "for extraordinary heroism in action."[19]

In World War II, many Native Americans were conscripted as Code Talkers, who used their tribal language to communicate top-secret messages on the battlefield. Receiving orders in English, they transmitted those orders in their native languages—either as a direct translation or coded message, depending on the nature of the orders—to other Code Talkers via handheld radios. According to the Smithsonian Institute's National Museum of the American Indian, the United States Army "recruited Comanche, Meskwaki, Chippewa, Oneida, and later,

Hopi, people to transmit messages in code during World War II," whereas the Marines enlisted the help of the Navajo.[20] Among them was a Comanche man named Charles Chibitty.[21]

Chibitty—whose last name means "holding on good" in the Comanche language—was born in 1921 in Comanche territory in Oklahoma.[22] He was sent to the Fort Sill Indian School, an institution founded to force assimilation of Native children into white culture. According to the United States Army's website, "The schools used humiliation, punishment and coercion to separate the children from their native religion, language and traditions."[23] He and his classmates were prohibited from speaking their tribal language and were punished if they disobeyed. But in 1940, the government decided to use Native American languages—languages unknown to the Germans and Japanese—to pass encoded messages. In 1941, Chibitty enlisted.

Chibitty and his fellow Comanche Code Talkers created a code that was never deciphered by the Germans. According to the Smithsonian's National Museum of the American Indian, Chibitty didn't just develop the code; he "participated in some of the fiercest fighting in the war, including the D-Day landing in Normandy."[24] His distinguished service earned him five campaign battle stars and "a cavalry officer's saber from his tribe, an honor comparable to the Medal of Honor among the Comanche."[25] After decades without official recognition for their work, the Comanche Code Talkers were celebrated by the French government in 1989 with the presentation of the Chevalier of the National Order of Merit. (A chevalier had the rank of a knight.) A decade later, the Pentagon presented Chibitty with an award as the last surviving member of the Comanche Code Talkers.[26]

Women of color also served this country's military honorably. Consider the 6888th Central Postal Directory Battalion of World War II, 855 women of color led by Major Charity Adams,[27] who held the highest rank of any African American woman.[28] While stationed in Britain, Adams and her battalion were tasked with ensuring the delivery of a backlog of mail to and from the front lines, and though she believed her battalion was expected to fail, she set out to make her unit "the best WAC [Women's Army Corps] unit ever sent into a foreign theater."[29] Adams more than succeeded. Her unit processed sixty-five thousand pieces of mail per shift and, according to some sources, cleared a six-month backlog in three months.[30] However, despite their significant contributions, they didn't receive formal recognition in the United States for their service until the 1990s,[31] when the army finally awarded the battalion the Meritorious Unit Commendation in 2019. Sadly, few lived to see the honor; Adams herself died in 2002.[32] As of February 23, 2022, there were only six living members of the battalion.[33]

Lack of recognition on the battlefield was bad enough. When they returned home, many Brown soldiers not only failed to receive commendation, but they were also deprived of the opportunities given to white soldiers. In fact, though Congress had passed the GI Bill to help veterans get back on their feet after they returned from World War II, many Brown veterans were denied its privileges. Because of segregated schools, they didn't receive the same educational opportunities under the bill. Some were denied mortgages because they could not purchase homes in white neighborhoods. According to journalist Erin Blakemore:

> While the GI Bill's language did not specifically exclude African-American veterans from its benefits, it was structured in a way that ultimately shut doors for the 1.2 million Black veterans who had bravely served their country during World War II, in segregated ranks.[34]

Walt Napier, a 514th Air Mobility Wing historian, credits President Truman's 1948 executive order declaring that there "shall be equality of treatment and opportunity for all persons in the armed [forces] without regard to race, color, religion or national origin" for instigating change in the military. Still, it didn't change fast enough. For instance, the United States Air Force—by their own admission—didn't come into compliance with Truman's executive order until 1952.[35] The other branches did their best to follow suit, but the army—the branch of the military my grandfather joined—wasn't fully integrated until 1954.[36] Still, full integration did not alleviate the inherent injustices in the system, which continued to treat BIPOC soldiers differently than their white counterparts.

CONTINUING EFFECTS OF RACIAL INJUSTICE IN THE MILITARY

Many brave BIPOC soldiers—men and women alike—fought for freedom, despite the fact that the military did not grant them the same liberties as white soldiers. While the system has changed for the good, some aspects of it still seem to be "stacked against" non-white people serving in the military.[37] Major Daniel Walker knows that firsthand.

Major Walker was a fighter pilot in the US Air Force. In an interview with David Martin for CBS's *60 Minutes,* Walker shared his experience as one of only fifty African American fighter pilots in the US Air Force.[38] Specifically, Walker said that he continued to experience the effects of racism even in 2020, more than eight decades after his great-uncle Norman Scales served as one of the first Black fighter pilots in a group called the Tuskegee Airmen, whose job was to fly perilous missions during World War II. Walker said that, like other African Americans, he'd had to moderate his behavior and speech so white people wouldn't feel threatened. He was told he was too confident and needed to dial it back, then told that he was too quiet. Realizing that he was treated differently than white pilots, which limited his professional opportunities, he left the military after eleven years.[39]

Walker's experience is not unique. In a 2017 Department of Defense workplace survey of active-duty members, over 30 percent of Black military members reported that they had experienced racial or ethnic discrimination or harassment in the previous year.[40] The report also indicated that white service members participated less in diversity efforts and tended to believe their units were inclusive.[41] The conclusion? The report indicated "certain active duty members inhabit different worlds within the military."[42]

What's more, according to an Associated Press article on military discrimination, the United States military indicated that it fielded more than "750 complaints of discrimination by race or ethnicity" in 2020. Civilians working in military-support roles also filed 900 complaints of racial discrimination and more than 350 complaints of discrimination based on skin color.[43] It has been further reported that, despite integration, African Americans in the military are more likely than white soldiers to be disciplined and less likely to be promoted. Reflecting on this reality in an interview with *60 Minutes*, Secretary of Defense Lloyd J. Austin stated,

> There's probably not a job that I had since I was a lieutenant colonel where some people didn't question whether or not I was qualified to . . . to take that job. It's a world I live in. And I'm sure that the other officers that you talked to would probably say the same thing. There's not a day in my life . . . when I didn't wake up and think about the fact that I was a Black man.[44]

PREPARATION FOR MILITARY CHANGE

The military has historically downplayed the contributions of its Black heroes while offering white soldiers higher pay, more leniency in disciplinary measures, better advancement opportunities, and better post-service education and career opportunities. If that were not enough, a handful of military bases are named after Confederate soldiers: for example, Fort Gordon, which is named after John Brown Gordon, a Confederate soldier alleged to be the head of his state's Ku Klux Klan, and Fort Benning, named for Henry Benning, another Confederate general. Both are in my home state of Georgia.

One may ask: Why name military bases after people who committed treason against the United States rather than those who fought for the ideals of freedom and liberty? When I first put pen to this chapter, there were *zero* military bases named after Black or Indigenous soldiers who were also heroes and contributors to our country's independence and continued freedom. That changed in 2022, when it was announced that nine military bases named after Confederate leaders would *finally* be renamed, and some would now honor BIPOC military leaders.[45] (Fort Benning and Fort Gordon will get new names by 2024.)

The evidence is overwhelming. The military, one of this country's first and oldest white spaces, has a history of, and continues, privileging white people over people of color. If we're going to completely rid the military of racism, we must prepare it as a space for liberation. How?

Preparation requires that we identify the issues, lament them, and repent from them. Weeding out racial bias might entail stripping military bases of names, flags, or symbols that carry vestiges of racism. It might also mean repenting of any disciplinary injustice based on race and creating systems that level the playing field for soldiers of color.

As we prepare, we must imagine new ways forward, and we can't do this alone. In larger governmental systems like the military, this kind of preparation will require citizens to demand change, politicians to push for legislative reforms, and white soldiers in power to stand up for racial equity. Put another way, when dealing with large community systems of racism, change requires every citizen touched by that system to prepare themselves and the system itself for liberation.

ACTIVE DEDICATION

Liberation in any space—military included—requires collective and intentional action as a people. What might that action look like? First, we could demand policies that bring equity in representation, pay, and promotion across all levels of the military, including at its highest ranks. Increasing representation at the highest ranks of the military would certainly affect the way soldiers of color are treated throughout the ranks.

Another suggestion is to examine the historical records and honor soldiers of color who served our country so valiantly. We could then formally recognize the accomplishments of those previously overlooked, just as President George W. Bush did in 2007 when he awarded the Congressional Gold Medal to the Tuskegee Airmen. In his speech at the ceremony attended by the surviving airmen, he said, "I would like to offer a gesture to help atone for all the unreturned salutes and unforgivable indignities. And so, on behalf of the office I hold, and a country that honors you, I salute you for the service to the United States of America."[46] Note his use of the word *atone*. When we atone, we make amends for the past. Though this gesture to the Tuskegee Airmen was only the beginning of true atonement, it sent a message to the BIPOC military members: *You belong in this space.*

How else could we engage in the dedication of white spaces? As I mentioned, there were very few military bases named after Black or Brown soldiers as of December 2022. This, despite the fact that thousands of BIPOC soldiers have served their country with honor and distinction. Don't more of those soldiers deserve to have military bases named after them? Couldn't we dedicate more military bases to Black and Brown war heroes like the Tuskegee Airmen, Harriet Tubman, or Code Talker Charles Chibitty?

The practice of dedicating certain historically white spaces to Brown people isn't just ceremonial, and neither should we imagine it will cure all the ills of the system. We'll still have to commit ourselves and the system to the equitable treatment of Brown people. Even so, this kind of initial dedication sends a clear signal: The military is a space for *all* American citizens to serve and protect *all* American citizens. Dedication of historically white spaces to *all* people builds bridges of true, holistic racial reconciliation. It atones for the sins of the past.

THE LIBERATION OF THE MILITARY

If we're going to create systems of liberation, we must do the hard work of understanding the need for liberation, and then we must replace inequitable systems with systems that strategically lift those who have been disenfranchised. For those of us who are Christians, who believe that God created all men and women to be equal, this kind of liberation is not optional. We are to "speak up for those who cannot speak for themselves, for the rights of all who are destitute," and to "defend the rights of the poor and needy" (Proverbs 31:8-9).

Following in Christ's footsteps means doing what he did. Quoting the prophet Isaiah, Jesus said,

The Spirit of the Lord is on me,
    because he has anointed me
    to proclaim good news to the poor.
He has sent me to proclaim freedom for the prisoners
    and recovery of sight for the blind,
    to set the oppressed free. (Luke 4:18)

Liberation—from sin and systems of oppression—is a foundational message to the Christian faith. What could this look like today? It might mean providing compensation to the soldiers who were denied the GI

Bill. And if those soldiers are no longer with us? Maybe the government could provide their families with educational opportunities to set right the wrong. Or perhaps it could compensate the descendants of those soldiers for the generational wealth stolen from them.

We can also ensure that Black veterans are not denied benefits at a higher rate than their white counterparts. The Black Veterans Project has investigated inequities and disparities in services suffered by veterans. Their research has helped advance equity for those who've served in the military. If we did those things, if we demanded liberation, what would we see? We'd begin to see our Brown brothers and sisters walking in new freedom as they serve their country.

We must not simply acknowledge the wrongs to our veterans. Repair is required. That repair involves honoring those BIPOC soldiers who served with distinction. It requires promoting Brown soldiers who've been passed over because of their skin color. It means providing them access to programs that advance their health and economic security. If we do this, we'll see our BIPOC soldiers holding their heads high, knowing that they play an integral role in protecting the rights and freedoms of *all* people. They will walk in a new freedom as they serve their country. That's the kind of dignity that marks liberation.

Creating the conditions for liberation isn't about removing opportunities or taking away rank or pay from those in power. Instead, we set out to lift those who have historically experienced disparity to their rightful place by encouraging conditions for advancement and discipline that are not based on skin color. In making things right, we can begin to repair the wrongs that have been done and ensure that BIPOC soldiers of the future have meaningful, honorable, and equitable careers in the military.

QUESTIONS FOR REFLECTION

1. If you've been in the military or around those with military backgrounds, in what ways have you noticed the disparate treatment of people of color in any branch of service? What changes do you think need to be made?

2. What expectations, if any, have you had about military service? How do you think those expectations were formed? (For example, through books or movie depictions of war.)

3. If you have suffered racial disparities in the military, read about the GI Bill Restoration Act. If you're a white person who knows a former soldier of color, consider sharing the information with him or her.

Voice of Liberation:
Megan Brown

WHILE ATTENDING A CONFERENCE WHERE THE WORK OF BE THE Bridge was represented, Megan Brown discovered our curriculum and woke to her identity as a biracial woman after having identified primarily as a white woman for much of her life, despite her Asian heritage. The experience propelled her to commit to the work of racial reconciliation, particularly in her community as a military spouse.

Trying to understand her biracial identity within a diverse but divided military community, Megan decided to bring together women interested in learning more about racial reconciliation from a biblical perspective. They didn't have to be Christian, just a military spouse who was willing to meet once a week in Megan's home in Warner Robins, Georgia, where the Robins Air Force Base is located.

It wasn't easy at first. Many who attended were not used to having conversations about race with a diverse group of people from different cultures and with different histories and biases.

One attendee even used a racial slur in the midst of the Bible study. Some didn't see the connection between racial issues and biblical discussions. Megan herself was still on a learning curve as she attempted to lead these discussions, trying to unlearn unhealthy racial patterns she had grown up with and process her own racial identity. Still, she continued, and over time, the Bible study became a place where people of color and white people could come together to discuss the hard work of racial reconciliation.

As she continued deeper into the work, she began to speak out and write more about the racial issues faced by military members. Megan, a military missionary dedicated to racial equity as an expression of the gospel, used the Be the Bridge discussion curriculum to expand the conversation beyond her group to other sectors of military life. She's even written an article on the *Military Spouse* website about becoming an agent for racial healing.[47]

Megan does more than write, though. She has nominated women of color as Military Spouse of the Year to break the homogeneous hold in those circles. Women who previously felt isolated have been able to connect and discuss issues in a newfound community. She has also created pathways for other women of color to lead within the military space. In fact, she was invited to the Pentagon to meet with the US Air Force's chief of chaplains's office to discuss how to use the gospel to push forward the work of racial healing.

Megan is not afraid to have hard conversations about racial issues in the military. As she pushes into this space, she's becoming an agent of liberation for military members and their spouses.

CHAPTER 7

Land of Broken Promises

PROPERTY OWNERSHIP

Land acknowledgment: I would be remiss if I didn't acknowledge those who first cultivated and inhabited the land on which I live as we prepare our minds to discuss systemic injustice as it relates to land ownership. I honor the Muscogee (Mvskoke) tribe, which dwelt on these lands in the Atlanta metropolitan area.

I N 2012, I RECEIVED AN UNEXPECTED CALL FROM A PASTOR IN AUSTIN, Texas, who asked whether I'd consider taking a job on the staff of his church. At the time, I was working for a non-profit organization that was fighting modern slavery, but I had been contemplating going to seminary. Though I enjoyed my work, I wasn't sure it was my career path, and I was doing my best to discern where God might be leading me. I thought this unexpected phone call might be a sign.

The pastor explained that he'd been given my name and thought I might be the right fit for their children's ministry program. Even though

I was a committed Christian who'd been involved in the church, I hadn't considered joining a church staff, much less becoming a children's minister. But as I thought and prayed about the opportunity and then made my way through the interview process, it seemed like the right step. So I accepted the job, and a few months later, I packed my bags and moved deep into the heart of Texas.

Now, I understand how state pride works. I am a native North Carolinian who now lives in Georgia, and both states are close to my heart. I love dogwood season in North Carolina and the summer cookouts where the South's best vinegar-based barbecue is served up. I love peaches, the Atlanta fashion scene, Black entrepreneurs, and Monica as much as any native Georgian. But when I moved to Texas, I realized many Texans take state pride to another level. Everything there is bigger, bolder, maybe even Texas-sized—houses, trucks, cowboy hats, and drinks. The state flag seems almost a symbol of worship. I saw it flying outside homes, painted on the sides of buildings, and waving above bridges. And if I heard it once, I heard it a thousand times: "Don't mess with Texas."[1] (What does that even mean?)

Many Texans are kind and self-determined people. Some are big, loud, and proud. If they want something, they'll go get it. Nothing stops them. This larger-than-life Texas personality grew through the resilient individualism embodied in many of the people involved in the state's history. Unfortunately, much of that history is colored by white supremacy.

THE FIRST TEXANS

Texas was once home to scores of Indigenous tribes, including the Apache, Comanche, Wichita, and Caddo. But as is the way of so much of Western history, the land claims of these Native tribes were thwarted by the arrival of the first European settlers.

In the late 1680s, the Spanish, who'd already laid claim to much of what is present-day Texas, began to colonize the territory. They established a foothold near El Paso.[2] By 1718 a group of Spanish-speaking settlers founded a mission and fort along the San Antonio River, and the Spaniards continued to push across the territory.[3] Spain continued to occupy the territory known as Spanish Texas until 1821, when they were defeated in the Mexican War of Independence.[4]

Just before Mexico gained its independence, Moses Austin, a Connecticut-born colonizer, negotiated the right to form a new colony in Texas.[5] Moses died in Missouri before he could realize his dream, but his son, Stephen F. Austin, traveled to San Antonio, where he secured his father's right to settle from the Spanish government.[6] Austin found adventurers willing to take a chance on the territory, and soon colonization was underway.[7] Nearly three hundred American men—the Old Three Hundred, as they were called—many of whom brought enslaved people with them to work their land, were granted titles. According to the Texas State Historical Association, "by the fall of 1825, sixty-nine of the families in Austin's colony owned slaves, and the 443 slaves in the colony accounted for nearly a quarter of the total population of 1,790."[8]

In 1829, eight years after the Spanish had lost control of the region, the Mexican government abolished slavery,[9] which, as you might imagine, angered the settlers. The government further restricted immigration and imposed tariffs, and by 1832 the Texas colonists had had enough. The settlers held conventions in 1832, 1833, and 1835—the final convention being that which led to the Texas Declaration of Independence.[10] Though some scholars argue whether the abolition of slavery played a role in the Texas Revolution, there's no debating this: After its independence, Texas adopted a constitution that protected the practice of enslavement.[11]

Things weren't easy in the new republic. Native tribes like the Comanche and Cherokee raided the white settlements.[12] The people of Texas fought back to defend the territory they'd claimed. It was a tumultuous time in the republic, and in March 1842, things grew more tumultuous. Mexico, which refused to recognize Texas's independence, invaded the republic. Battles continued throughout the 1840s, and tensions increased between the native Mexicans—the Tejanos—and the Anglo-Texan settlers.

White settlers began to push the Tejanos to the margins, requiring them to sign loyalty pledges. They enacted and enforced strict voting laws and taxes as well.[13] If the Tejanos didn't own property or couldn't pay the tax, they couldn't vote. As a result, the white settlers amassed land and power.

By December 1845, all claims to Texas were settled when the United States made a deal with Texas and formally added it as the newest state of the union. As part of that deal, Texas was annexed as a slave state.[14] What's more, the discriminatory practices against the Tejanos continued, though the perceived threat of Mexican government dissipated. Throughout the late nineteenth and early twentieth centuries, many Tejanos were victimized by the Texas Rangers, a law enforcement arm of the state of Texas.[15]

Raúl Ramos, a professor of history at the University of Houston, indicated that many of the Tejanos "essentially went broke trying to defend themselves against frivolous lawsuits contesting their claims to land ownership."[16] So in a historical pattern as old as the United States itself, the positions of power in the Lone Star State became primarily occupied by white men.[17]

Attitudes toward Indigenous people haven't changed much over the years. Many have been marginalized since the time of Stephen Austin, a fact Latin Americans know all too well.

While I served the church in Austin, I connected with many in the Latino community who often observed, "We didn't cross the border; the border crossed us." They could trace their roots back generations, long before white people settled in the area, and many of their ancestors had lived in the territory that became Texas long before it was an independent republic or annexed by the United States. Though their ancestors may have believed their cooperation with white settlers to form the great state of Texas meant that they would have a fair shake at property ownership, they were crossed—as in double-crossed—by those who drew the borders. Their lands were taken. Their voices were silenced. They were pushed to the margins, and that marginalization had generational effects.

Black people in Texas can say much the same thing, except that instead of the border crossing them, they were taken across the border as enslaved persons. Even after the abolition of slavery, Texas adopted Jim Crow laws that mandated racially segregated high schools, prohibited marriages between people of different races, instituted the charging of poll taxes, and required segregation in all public carriers.

Housing discrimination also occurred. Austin, for instance, was intentionally designed to be racially segregated. In its first city plan in 1928, the city of Austin passed race-based zoning laws, designating a "Negro district,"[18] and a recommendation to move Black residents out of the city center to East Austin. The city government recognized that "the Texas legislature had previously enabled racial zoning at the local level," granting municipalities the "'power and authority' to 'segregate and separate . . . the white and Negro race.'"[19] What's more, the city restricted services to African American residents who lived outside of East Austin, including closing integrated city schools and moving students to segregated schools in East Austin.[20] It was a historical song and dance—move the borders, traffic the people, retain the power.

In an interview with *Vice*, Andrew Busch, then a visiting professor at Miami University, provided additional context:

> The first city plan that Austin leaders came up with was designed to be segregated, but they couldn't legally write that into effect. . . . The city was built to be separate but equal under Jim Crow. Parks were built for African Americans, and parks for

whites and Latino schools were placed in very specific parts of the city. In 1930 you'd see African Americans scattered all over the city, but ten years later they were all on the east side. Then, in the early '60s, the city built I-35 right through the divided area.[21]

That same highway still stands as a dividing line in the city, and many people of color still feel this division. Is it any surprise that many in Austin's Black community are leaving,[22] even as the city remains one of the fastest-growing major cities in the nation?[23]

Texas serves as a microcosm for the rest of the country. Historically, across the United States, Native people were displaced and treaties were broken. White power brokers pushed Black people to the margins so they could retain their dominance. As wise King Solomon wrote, "What has been will be again, what has been done will be done again; there is nothing new under the sun" (Ecclesiastes 1:9). This reality applies to every kind of injustice, but we see it play out time after time in the ways governments—local, state, and national—allocate property rights.

What Good Is a Treaty?

Over the years, the United States has negotiated numerous treaties with Indigenous people, many of which dealt with tribal lands. Unfortunately, many of these treaties were broken. According to Hansi Lo Wang of National Public Radio (NPR), "more than 370 ratified treaties have helped the U.S. expand its territory and led to many broken promises made to American Indians."[24] Reporting on an exhibit of those treaties in 2015, Wang highlighted the Treaty of Canandaigua, which was signed in 1794. This agreement between the United States and the Haudenosaunee Confederacy (Six Nations tribes) of New York secured a partnership between the fledgling government and the Haudenosaunee after the Revolutionary War, when the newly formed American government needed peace to get its footing. The treaty promised the return of more than a million acres to the Six Nations and committed to the tribes 4,500 dollars in goods, "which shall be expended yearly forever."[25]

The government did not live up to its end of the bargain. According to Wang, much of the territory of the Six Nations has been taken back over the years. In 1960, the US Army Corp of Engineers began construction on the Kinzua Dam in Pennsylvania, which flooded ten thousand acres of land subject to the treaty.[26] This created a hardship for the Seneca Nation. Likewise, industrial pollution of the Saint Lawrence River, which flows through the lands, has led the Environmental Protection Agency to mark a portion of Mohawk Nation an "Area of Concern," thus making even more of the land assigned by the government to the Six Nations unusable or undesirable.[27] According to Wang, the United States has broken all but one promise—the promise to provide 4,500 dollars' worth of goods annually.[28] Maybe this goes without saying, but 4,500 dollars in goods isn't nearly what it was in 1794.

Though it's been twisted beyond recognition, the Treaty of Canandaigua still stands, at least in part. But so many other treaties were broken. In an article for *Smithsonian Voices,* the blog of *Smithsonian* magazine, Dennis Zotigh reported that in 1778, the United States Continental Congress sent a delegation to negotiate a treaty with the Lenape people. These members of the Delaware tribe had been forced westward as far as present-day Pittsburgh and Detroit. But at the start of the Revolutionary War, the Continental Congress needed to secure allies just as badly as the Delaware needed to secure their own territory. So the two nations signed a peace treaty.[29]

This is that moment where I read history and want to shout back through time, "No! Don't do it, Lenape leaders!"

The terms of the treaty provided that each nation forgive the other for past disputes. They pledged "perpetual peace and friendship" to each other and promised to assist each other in any "just and necessary war with any other nation or nations."[30] Of course, what constituted a just war was subject to a white man's definition. The treaty also ensured Americans safe passage across Delaware lands to attack the British and guaranteed the Lenape would provide supplies to Americans. In addition, it guaranteed the Lenape would provide the United States Army with experienced warriors.

Zotigh wrote,

In the last article of the treaty, the United States recognizes Delaware sovereignty. The new nation promises "to guarantee to the aforesaid nation of Delawares, and their heirs, all their territorial rights in the fullest and most ample manner, as it hath been bounded by former treaties, as long as they the said Delaware nation shall abide by, and hold fast the chain of friendship now entered into."[31]

The treaty went on to suggest that the Delaware might invite friendly tribes to join their nation, and that the confederation should become a new state with representation in Congress. As I'm sure you're aware, no such state was formed for the Delaware Nation.

The treaty with the Lenape didn't last. Not only was the United States unable to defend the Ohio territory from the British, but it also couldn't defend it from American settlers. Fewer than four years after the treaty was signed, Pennsylvania militiamen killed ninety-six Delaware people in what's known as the Gnadenhutten Massacre in an Ohio town by the same name. The militiamen claimed they were avenging raids on white settlements, but history has shown that the slaughtered Native Americans had nothing to do with any alleged raids.[32]

As a result of the massacre and broken promises, some of the Delaware fled to Ontario. Others made their way to Spanish territory west of the Mississippi River.[33] Ultimately, the vast majority of lands subject to the treaty were taken by white settlers.

Of course, treaties that benefited white settlers were strictly enforced. On May 28, 1830, President Andrew Jackson signed the Indian Removal Act. Five years later, United States representatives met with a group of Cherokee leaders in New Echota, Georgia. There, the parties signed the Treaty of New Echota, in which the Cherokee Nation traded seven million acres of land for five million dollars and land in territory west of the Mississippi. Most Native Americans opposed the treaty, but Congress still ratified the agreement.[34] In 1838, the government sent soldiers to carry out the treaty, forcing approximately sixteen thousand Cherokee people on a journey to Oklahoma that stretched some five thousand miles.[35] By the time the journey was over—a journey known as the Trail of Tears—almost four thousand had died.[36] And by 1839, approximately one hundred thousand Native Americans had been forced to relocate under similar conditions,[37] earning President Jackson the nickname "Indian Killer."[38]

White settlers continued moving west, claiming lands throughout the territory. This expansion west and the continual taking of Native American land was fueled by the belief that God had ordained the white man to populate the entire continent. The belief became known as *manifest destiny*.

The newly formed and supposedly Christian nation could claim God all they wanted. But God didn't ordain the taking of Native American land, and because there's been no formal government recognition of, repentance from, and reparation for the sins of our past, the injustice done to our Native American brothers and sisters continues to have implications today.

In the pamphlet *Lifting as We Climb: Women of Color, Wealth, and America's Future,* Dr. Mariko Chang (with the help of Meizhu Lui and others) discussed her findings on Native American wealth—that it is a fraction of the wealth owned by the average white person. Based on a longitudinal study in 2000, Dr. Chang wrote, "Median wealth for Native Americans . . . was $5,700 whereas the median wealth for the sample overall was $65,000, a ratio of only 8.7%."[39]

FORTY ACRES AND A MULE

In addition to the Native Americans and the Latino community, Black people also have lost land as a result of the government's broken promises. On January 16, 1865, a few months before the end of the Civil War, General William T. Sherman issued Special Field Order No. 15, which commandeered coastal land from Charleston, South Carolina, to the Saint Johns River in Florida. The seized land—all four hundred thousand acres of it—was to be distributed to newly freed Black families in forty-acre plots. The order also encouraged freed slaves to fight for the Union. In an effort to dole out the land, the United States government formed the Bureau of Refugees, Freedmen, and Abandoned Lands (also known as the Freedmen's Bureau), which was authorized to take away land from the traitors—Confederate supporters—and give it to those formerly enslaved and Union supporters. (And yes, since the beginning of time governments have stripped traitors of their lands and reallocated them to loyalists.) Sherman also proposed lending each Black family a mule, which led to the common phrase for reparations, "Forty acres and a mule."[40]

Sherman's order was a valiant attempt to make reparations to newly freed slaves. But I recently discovered that Sherman didn't come up with the idea on his own. In fact, on PBS's *The African Americans: Many Rivers to Cross* website, Henry Louis Gates, Jr., explains that the idea came from a meeting Sherman and the presiding secretary of war, Edwin M. Stanton, had with a group of Black ministers. Those ministers, it was reported, were asked what they wanted, and their spokesperson, Garrison Frazier, who'd been a slave until 1857, told Sherman and Stanton, "The way we can best take care of ourselves . . . is to have land, and turn it and till it by our own labor." Days later, Sherman signed the famous order.[41]

This order was radical for its time, but it embodied justice that was more than two hundred years overdue. It held the potential to change the trajectory for generations. Of course, you know how this story played out since there's no block of land on the East Coast owned by Black people. How was the promised land taken away? After the assassination of Abraham Lincoln, vice president and Southern sympathizer Andrew Johnson became the new president. President Johnson overturned Sherman's order in the fall of 1865 and returned most of the land to the previous white owners, the very people who'd fought for the Confederacy and who—for the most part—had previously enslaved the now-freed African Americans.[42] Those former Confederates would go on to subjugate the African Americans Sherman tried to help.

If Sherman's order had been enforced, imagine what might have been. Black people could have had their own territory, a territory governed by African Americans and not subject to discriminatory Jim Crow laws. They could have generated wealth to hand down to future generations. Imagine the benefit to all Americans. Our liberation is tied together. Instead, the only generational inheritance given to Southern African Americans was discrimination, segregation, poverty, and pain.

President Johnson's decision made clear that too many Americans were not ready to see African Americans as equals. This kind of mentality was reinforced by discriminatory propaganda like *The Birth of a Nation*, discussed in chapter 8.

BROKEN PROMISES LEAD TO BROKEN PROMISES

One broken promise paves the way for the next. If you exclude a class of people from land ownership once, the second, third, fourth, or one-thousandth time becomes much easier. During the Reconstruction era, for instance, lawmakers instituted policies that physically separated people by race so that white people could maintain the highest valued land, solidifying their wealth. In the Jim Crow era, racially restrictive covenants required white people to sell their houses to white people to keep the neighborhoods free of people of color. In some communities, like Detroit in the 1940s, physical walls were built to separate white homes from Black homes.[43]

During the Great Depression, President Franklin D. Roosevelt signed the National Housing Act of 1934, which aimed to make home-ownership for the middle class a reality. The act paved the way for the thirty-year mortgage, allowing people to finance their homes over long periods of time. But this system left Black and Brown people behind for many years.

Lenders engaged in redlining—the practice of drawing red lines on a map to indicate geographic areas of lending risk. Some lenders re-fused to offer loans to homeowners in supposedly riskier redlined areas, while some insurers refused to cover the properties or charged astronomical fees to issue a policy. And wouldn't you know, those red lines were drawn around predominantly urban neighborhoods with a high percentage of BIPOC residents. When white people fled from these urban areas and moved out to the suburbs in what's commonly called white flight, non-whites were left in the distressed areas. Due to their inability to get financing to purchase their homes, they were often subject to paying rents to slumlords. Redlining and white flight locked people of color into less desirable, less valuable properties, which didn't allow them to build wealth at the same rate as white homeown-ers. Policies like this further entrenched the inequity in many of the spaces discussed in this book.

Today, not much has changed. According to the Pew Research Cen-ter, 27.4 percent of Black mortgage applications and 19.2 percent of Latino mortgage applications were denied in 2015, compared to only 10.9 percent of white mortgage applications.[44] Granted, these denial rates may be predicated on BIPOC savings and credit scores, but those wealth disparities were born from the ways people of color have been locked out of property ownership over the years.

If being denied for a mortgage isn't bad enough, imagine finally obtaining a home, only to have it ripped out from under you. That's what happened to many Black homeowners in Detroit. According to reports, the city of Detroit illegally assessed property taxes against predominantly Black and non-white residents between 2010 and 2016, forcing many of them into foreclosure. Reporting in 2022 indicates that approximately one hundred thousand Detroit citizens lost their homes, and the city owed them around six hundred million dollars. Most of those affected were Black.[45] As of the writing of this book, those who've lost their homes haven't been compensated.[46]

TAKING PROPERTY IN THE NAME OF GOD

Whenever I write about these things, I can't help but think about the calls for justice from the prophet Isaiah. Remember his words I quoted in chapter 4?

> Take your evil deeds out of my sight;
>   stop doing wrong.
> Learn to do right; seek justice.
>   Defend the oppressed.
> Take up the cause of the fatherless;
>   plead the case of the widow. (Isaiah 1:16–17)

I'm also reminded of the words of Christ. In the gospel of Matthew, Jesus rebuked the Pharisees, those with religious power and authority:

> Woe to you, teachers of the law and Pharisees, you hypocrites!
> You give a tenth of your spices—mint, dill and cumin. But you

have neglected the more important matters of the law—justice, mercy and faithfulness. You should have practiced the latter, without neglecting the former." (23:23)

Isaiah and Jesus could not have been clearer. God's people were demonstrating acts of religious righteousness while neglecting the poor, ignoring injustice, and taking by force what wasn't theirs to take. These people were practicing what theologians call *syncretism*, which, simply put, is the combining of two different philosophical or religious systems. They were attempting to worship both God and wealth, which led them to ignore the very things God cared about most—justice, mercy, and faithfulness to him.

Americans aren't much different. Over the centuries, we've adopted a kind of syncretized Christianity, a combining of the faith with capitalism, which relies upon land ownership. With such a mindset, treaties could be broken, and agreements undone, to benefit the people in power. And doctrines like manifest destiny could take hold.

LIBERATING AMERICA'S PROPERTY STRUCTURE

We live in a time where we can fly, send a person to the moon, and float cities on the ocean, yet we can't figure out how to make property ownership an affordable reality for more people of color. That leads to a fundamental question: Are we really unable to fix systems of racism in property ownership, or do we just not want to? That question points to a host of additional questions.

Will we, collectively as Americans, continue to ignore our country's history of broken treaties, promises, and the ways we've taken property for the benefit of white people?

Will we continue to send politicians to our city halls, our state capitals, and Washington who continue to ignore the systemic racism embedded in our country's property ownership policies?

Will our religious systems and leaders ignore the destruction of wealth in BIPOC communities while continuing to raise their hands in worship to God?

Will we allow greed and indifference to keep us from undoing the systemic injustice in property ownership?

Or . . .

Will we prepare ourselves to bring liberation by learning the history of American property rights, particularly in relation to BIPOC communities?

Will we repent of the ways we've taken land from Native Americans, the Latin American community, African Americans, and others?

Will we dedicate ourselves to liberation, demanding reforms that allow people of color better access to capital markets and homeownership at fair rates?

Put simply: Will we be agents of liberation in historically white property spaces?

As with any other system we've discussed in this book, creating space for Brown faces in the white space of property ownership is going to take preparation, and preparation begins with education. We've looked at the ways property was unjustly taken or kept from Tejanos, Native Americans, and the African American community. But there are other stories too. During World War II, many Japanese Americans were moved to internment camps, and while they were incarcerated, their homes were vandalized and even destroyed.[47]

There are so many stories like these, and telling them would require multiple books. I encourage you to do the work to understand how discrimination has affected property ownership rights in your state by searching the internet for "minority discrimination property [insert your state]." I guarantee you'll find at least one article showing how a person of color has been the victim of property discrimination.

Once you understand the landscape, dedicate yourself to righting the wrongs. You might not be a lender or a legislator. Maybe you're not in a position to change policies or practices. But you can dedicate your most precious resource—your time—to bringing about justice. You can write letters to your local, state, and federal policymakers, demanding programs that level the playing field for BIPOC property ownership.

In addition, consider supporting banks that invest in BIPOC communities. According to a *Shelterforce* article by Shelby R. King, in June 2020, Bank of America and PNC (both in the top ten largest lenders) each committed one billion dollars to racial equity initiatives. In September of that year, Citigroup committed one billion dollars to an "Action for Racial Equity" initiative, and Truist committed forty million dollars to help "racially and ethnically diverse small-business owners, women, and individuals in low- and moderate-income communities."[48] According to the same article, Wells Fargo committed four hundred million dollars to Black- and minority-owned businesses. JPMorgan Chase, the largest bank in the United States, committed thirty billion dollars over five years to increase minority "entrepreneurship and homeownership."[49] It's true that some of these organizations may have been part of the problem of discriminatory lending in the past, and they don't get a pass for that. But if they now do the measurable work of promoting and supporting Black property and business ownership, they're at least taking steps in the right direction.

You might also support BIPOC-owned banks and credit unions. Many of these institutions provide services to lower-income communities. OneUnited Bank, for instance, is the "first Black digital bank and the largest Black owned bank in the country," and they've won ten Bank Enterprise Awards for lending to low-to-moderate-income communities.[50] They support various justice movements like #TakeAKnee, the movement started by Colin Kaepernick (see chapter 9).[51] OneUnited Bank is using capital to make a difference, and the more capital they have, the more significant the difference they can make! So consider banking with institutions like OneUnited or other BIPOC-owned financial institutions and tell them *why* you've made them your bank of choice.

You can also take direct action like Bob Fletcher, who paid the mortgages and taxes on three farms owned by Japanese Americans so they would not lose their property during the internment of World War II. This act of resistance and justice came at great personal cost. Still, he did the work.[52] We could learn a lot from outliers like Fletcher. Prayerfully consider what you might do, such as speaking out against inequities in housing in your hometown.

You can also encourage your church to get involved. Don't overlook the run-down parts of your community. Don't overlook look Black farmers. Form relationships with those doing the hard work of renovating properties in traditionally BIPOC communities, and ask how you can support them. (Note: Don't simply move in and assume you can be the savior, because that's just manifest destiny under a different name.) Maybe you and your church can support minority-owned businesses in a predominately Black area, which can increase wealth and help advance the goal of homeownership for owners and employees of color. Maybe members of your faith community can purchase or restore an apartment complex and provide affordable housing for families.

Whatever you do, dedicate yourself and your community to the liberation of property ownership. We can be better. Let's heed the words of the prophet Micah:

He has shown you, O mortal, what is good.
    And what does the LORD require of you?
To act justly and to love mercy
    and to walk humbly with your God. (6:8)

QUESTIONS FOR REFLECTION

1. What are your thoughts on our country's broken treaties? Spend some time reflecting and journaling on it.

2. How do you feel knowing that some mortgage lenders have race-based policies? What do you think needs to happen to change this system?

3. How can the people of God be a beacon of justice and righteousness when it comes to property ownership or property funding? What are some things you think can change this system?

4. Research the Native American nations that may have lived in your area or state. Where are they now? In what ways can you be of support to them?

Voices of Liberation:
Derrick and Paige Jackson

AFTER MORE THAN A DECADE IN THE SPECIAL FORCES, DERRICK Jackson, along with his wife, Paige, decided to move their large Black family to the country, to reclaim and reconnect with the land through farming. Why? Was it because they were multi-generational farmers? Nope. In fact, they're first-generation farm owners. They moved because they believe there is a lack of transparency in food production and that the proper food brings healing to the body.

The Jacksons initially raised chickens, then expanded, purchasing a farm on the outskirts of Durham, North Carolina. Farming—something that might seem foreign to so many people of color nowadays—was once the job of many African Americans, Indigenous people, and members of the Latino/a community. BIPOC farmers were originally the main cultivators of the land, but collectively, they now own less than 10 percent of that land. The Jacksons are reclaiming the narrative of the American farm, particularly as it relates to BIPOC farm ownership.

Although they face issues of systemic racism in their rural community, the Jacksons are finding liberation by educating and giving others power. They use their space to invite others to the table to learn cultivation practices and bridge building. As former Be the Bridge group leaders, they have used their passion for restoration of relationships to address systemic issues. They are true bridge builders. They teach regenerative farming, a holistic approach to farming and animal care, at Grass Grazed Farm and have an online farming shop. The Jacksons host a growing community of Black farmers who are implementing best farming practices on their own homesteads. They're inspiring a new generation of Black landowners and making an incredible impact in the farming industry.

CHAPTER 8

Appreciation Versus Appropriation

U NLESS YOU'RE A MUSIC HISTORIAN OR A FAN OF OLD-TIME BLACK music artists, the odds are slim that you've heard the name Willie Mae "Big Mama" Thornton. The truth is, though I'm a fan of music and Black history, I was only vaguely aware of her role in music history. But all that changed when I visited the National Museum of African American Music (NMAAM) in Nashville, Tennessee.

The museum, a fifty-six-thousand-square-foot facility located in the heart of Music City, tells the story of African American music and shares the impact African Americans played on shaping our country's musical vibes.[1] Walking through the doors, I was met with the sights and sounds of my people—Prince, Aretha Franklin, Chuck Berry, and so many others. As I made my way through the Rivers of Rhythm corridor, I was immersed in a high-tech, multimedia experience of Black music. It reminded me that the Black story and the story of American music are inextricably intertwined.

In the Wade in the Water gallery, I heard the spirituals sung by the enslaved on plantations and witnessed how these songs gave birth to gospel music.

In the Crossroads gallery, I learned how gospel laments became the source of Reconstruction-era blues.

In the Love Supreme gallery, I discovered that the African American desire for freedom and self-expression inspired jazz during the Jim Crow era.

I learned about the story of rhythm and blues (R&B) in the One Nation Under a Groove gallery and how it led to today's rock 'n' roll and pop music.

In the Message gallery, I saw how societal disparities and hope for a better future birthed the hip-hop movement.

Each of these forms of music has been influential over the years and has led to the appropriation of these styles by white artists. Consequently, many of the early Black artists were exploited by the white music industry. This is Big Mama Thornton's story.

Thornton was born in Alabama in 1926. As the daughter of a Baptist minister, she was surrounded by church music from her infancy, and she began singing in church at an early age.[2] Her talent was apparent, and by the age of fourteen, she decided to pursue a bigger dream—a professional career in music.

In her early twenties, Thornton moved to Houston, Texas, and it didn't take long for her to make a mark on the club scene of the day.[3] Record executives came calling, and in 1951, she signed a recording contract with Peacock Records. Her star was rising, and in 1952, she performed at the Apollo Theater, the famed venue for Black performers in Harlem, New York.[4] That year, she recorded "Hound Dog"—yes, *that* "Hound Dog," written by Jerry Leiber and Mike Stoller—which rocketed up to number one on the R&B charts. Her performance led to the song's commercial success, reportedly selling a half-million albums. Though the song made Thornton a star and set the stage for a new genre of music (rock 'n' roll), she didn't see much of the profits.[5]

Four years after Thornton's "Hound Dog" hit, a young white man from Tupelo, Mississippi, recorded his own version of the song, channeling Thornton's bluesy sound.[6] This time, the song rocketed into the stratosphere, selling ten million copies and cementing the singer as "the King of Rock 'n' Roll." The artist? Elvis Presley.

This wouldn't be the last time the white music industry appropriated Thornton's sound. In the early 1960s, she wrote and recorded "Ball and Chain" with the record company Bay-Tone Records. Bay-Tone did not initially release the song, but they retained the copyrights. So when Janis Joplin recorded the song later in the 1960s, Big Mama Thornton was once again cut out of the profits, at least officially.[7] Joplin didn't use the song without Thornton's permission, and in fact, the raspy-voiced rocker later gave Thornton songwriter credit and a portion of her royalties.[8] But Joplin's goodwill doesn't change the fact that the music industry, which was run by white men, set the conditions for the exploitation of Black artists like Thornton.

Before visiting the museum, I didn't know Thornton's full story, but I can't say I was surprised. For years, I'd learned that many songs recorded by white artists were appropriated from Black artists; in that museum, I saw the facts. Black artists had written and performed songs, and created the sounds and genres, that were later appropriated by white record labels and artists who capitalized on them. Some of Presley's earliest hits included "All Shook Up," "Don't Be Cruel," and "Return to Sender," each of which was written by a Black musician—Otis Blackwell. Elvis sang those songs for white audiences in a style quite similar to Blackwell's earliest recordings, but very few people know Blackwell's name today.[9] What's more, there's no doubt Elvis's sound was reminiscent of other Black musicians of the day, including Chuck Berry, who was quickly overshadowed by Presley's fame. Why? Because Presley looked like the record executives and audiences.

Thornton and Blackwell weren't the only Black music performers whose songs were taken and popularized by white artists. Little Richard and Dorothy LaBostrie wrote the song "Tutti Frutti," which Little Richard recorded in 1955. But the song was made famous by white artist Pat Boone in 1956.[10] As Lisa Tomlinson, a professor at the University of the West Indies, indicated,

> [The record company] couldn't have a Black man shaking his booty, the sexuality of it, or any other stereotypes associated with Blackness. Boone's image was much more tame and family-like, much more softened, compared to Richard's gyrations.
>
> The record company circulated those types of images in the form of whiteness to appease white people, and they have that power because of the institutional system. . . . To a great extent, the media is controlled by white men, and they're the ones who use their monetary influence, and dictate who is going to be seen.[11]

Record companies offered African American music in a palatable, white package to appease white people. The result? A generation of Black artists who might have been forgotten had it not been for music historians and organizations like the National Museum of African American Music.

As I left the museum, I thought about the ways Black artists have historically been pushed to the side in the humanities, particularly in entertainment spaces. Black music is just a microcosm of the exploitations many Black and Brown people have experienced in the entertainment industry, whether in music, film, or even literature. It led me to wonder: What are the origins of Black exploitation in the humanities?

The Celebration of Whiteness in the Enlightenment

Elevating whiteness and denigrating or objectifying Blackness in artistic spaces is nothing new. Though some version of such discrimination is as old as history itself, it took a firm hold on Western thinking during the Enlightenment period of the seventeenth and eighteenth centuries. In that era, Western intellectuals began substituting reason for more spiritual explanations of the world. They applied that reason to all areas of the human experience and began categorizing the world according to rigid classifications, arguing that natural laws governed the world. That reasoned approach led to scientific, philosophical, religious, and even artistic advancements and reforms, but it also led to the solidification of racial hierarchies.

During this time period the false notion that white people were inherently smarter, more capable, and more human than non-white people became accepted worldwide. In fact, it was Enlightenment philosophy that led to Thomas Jefferson's personal justification of slavery. According to the website dedicated to Monticello, Jefferson's home estate,

> Enlightenment philosophy strongly influenced Jefferson's ideas about two seemingly opposing issues: American freedom and American slavery. Enlightenment thinkers argued that liberty was a natural human right and that reason and scientific knowledge—not the state or the church—were responsible for human progress. But Enlightenment reason also provided a rationale for slavery, based on the hierarchy of races.[12]

Oh, goodness.

This twisted philosophical position found its way into every facet of Western thinking. Consider, for example, Shakespeare's famous play *A Midsummer Night's Dream*. In act 2, scene 2, Lysander, enchanted by a love potion, spurns the dark-skinned woman he previously loved (Hermia) for a white-skinned woman (Helena), saying, "Not Hermia but Helena I love: Who will not change a raven for a dove?"[13]

How do we know that Hermia was darker skinned and Helena

lighter skinned? In act 3, scene 2, Lysander asks Hermia to leave him, saying, "Away, you Ethiope [meaning Ethiopian]! Out tawny Tarter, out!"[14] (A friend who studied Shakespeare said some scholars believe Hermia was actually white, but after Lysander is enchanted, he begins to associate her with dark skin simply *because* she is unattractive. In other words, no dark-skinned woman could be attractive, which is an even more offensive interpretation of the text.)

The play itself deals with themes of light and dark, day and night, showing how lightness is preferable to darkness. In Hermia's unattractiveness, Lysander associates her with darkness. She was classified as lower in the hierarchy of desirability.

These creative choices by Shakespeare are not coincidental. His view of race was a built-in feature of the era. In her article titled "Anti-Racist Shakespeare," Farah Karim-Cooper, professor of Shakespeare studies at King's College London and the co-director of education and research at Shakespeare's Globe, wrote, "In Renaissance texts related to beauty, behaviour and courtesy, whiteness is figured as an ideal in the interior as well as exterior terms." Whiteness, she said, was linked to virtue. Appearance, even the physical complexion of a person's skin, was viewed as a reflection of that person's inner self, and by extension, his or her worth.[15]

Words matter. How beauty is described and written about matters. If pure, holy, chaste, and desirable women are portrayed artistically as white, what does that say about Black and Brown women and their worth?

The white supremacy of the Enlightenment took a firm hold in America. Racial hierarchies were solidified through slavery, and those hierarchies infected American thinking. Black and Brown people were viewed as inherently inferior to white people in all things, including the arts, which is likely why many people probably didn't think twice about white artists appropriating music from African Americans. This philosophy set the stage for overt exploitation of Black people in the earliest forms of American entertainment.

THE RISE OF AMERICAN ENTERTAINMENT:
A LESSON IN BLACKFACE

In the 1830s, Thomas Dartmouth Rice performed in minstrel shows that featured a white male performer in blackface, caricaturing the songs and dances of the enslaved. For historical reference, the most well-known song and dance performed by Rice was "Jump Jim Crow," the title of which would later inspire the name of the discriminatory and segregationist laws following the emancipation of the enslaved.[16]

Rice's minstrel shows began in Louisville, Kentucky, and as they gained in popularity with white audiences, others began popping up across the country.[17] In fact, one of the earliest minstrel companies—the Christy Minstrels—had an act on Broadway for nearly ten years.[18] Stephen Foster, the songwriter who wrote classic American songs like "Oh! Susanna" and "Camptown Races," wrote for the Christy Minstrels, a theatrical company developed by Edwin Christy.[19]

The tropes and stereotypes that came from the traveling minstrel shows made their way into other media, including the first Hollywood blockbuster, a 1915 silent film called *The Birth of a Nation,* which was directed and produced by D. W. Griffith.[20] The film was based on a novel and play, *The Clansman,* written by Thomas Dixon, Jr., a segregationist minister, and was set during the Civil War and Reconstruction.[21] It portrayed African Americans—particularly Black men—as evil, lazy, animalistic, violent, and, ultimately, unworthy of freedom.

The plot of *The Birth of a Nation* is simple, fictional, and racist. The film claims that during Reconstruction, Black forces took over much of the South and abused both power and white women. Quoting President Woodrow Wilson, the film notes, "The white men were roused by a mere instinct of self-preservation . . . until at last there had sprung into existence a great Ku Klux Klan, a veritable empire of the South, to protect the Southern country."[22]

It's worth noting that President Wilson once wrote a textbook praising the Ku Klux Klan, describing it as "an 'Invisible Empire of the South,' bound together in loose organization to protect the southern country from some of the ugliest hazards of a time of revolution."[23]

The primary villain of the film is a "mulatto," Silas Lynch, one of the film's many characters in blackface, who rises to become the lieutenant governor of South Carolina. After setting up operations in Piedmont, he induces the Black townspeople to quit working, live off the government dole, and eventually, through acts of voter fraud, take over the state legislature.

In the film, actors portraying Black state representatives are shown shoeless, drinking, and eating fried chicken while working at the legislature. The movie climaxes when Lynch, who has solidified his power through Black legislators and militiamen, attempts to coerce a white woman to marry him. Just before the wedding, a band of gun-wielding heroes rides into town—the KKK. The Klan liberates the woman and the rest of the people from the ruling mob of crazed African Americans and returns power to where it rightfully belongs—the white man.

The movie was controversial from the beginning, and it's been called "the most reprehensibly racist film in Hollywood history."[24] Still, it was popular among white audiences across the nation and became the highest grossing motion picture of its day. It galvanized segregation efforts and inspired the reorganization of the Klan. In fact, a few months after the release of the movie, Colonel William J. Simmons, a preacher, led a cross burning on Stone Mountain, Georgia, which many recognize today as the rebirth of the Klan.[25]

The Birth of a Nation was met with mass protests from African Americans and the NAACP. It galvanized an early civil rights movement as Black people, the mostly white leadership of the NAACP, and novelists like Upton Sinclair joined together to campaign against the film.[26] These early activists understood that the film wasn't simply an artistic expression—it was a statement about the worth, identity, and place of Black people. The film's not-at-all-subtle underlying message was that the darker-skinned community wasn't meant to rule; instead it was meant to be subjugated, even if violence was required to make that happen.

FAMILY-FRIENDLY ENTERTAINMENT OR MINSTREL LEGACY?

The racial stereotypes and caricatures of the minstrel shows were incorporated into other, seemingly more innocent forms of entertainment. Take, for instance, the early animation of Walt Disney. His breakout character, Mickey Mouse, was based on blackface minstrels. During an episode of NPR's *Code Switch* podcast, Nicholas Sammond, a professor of film at the University of Toronto, explained that the 1928 film *Steamboat Willie* features the mouse as a steamboat captain who played a song originally known as "Old Zip Coon," which was created for the minstrel shows. According to Sammond, Mickey Mouse's "facial characteristics, the gloves he sometimes wears, the way that he acts, his bodily plasticity, his ability to take punishment, all are kind of markers of the minstrel that . . . [were] established by the time he came on the scene in the late 1920s."[27] His conclusion? In his 2015 book, *Birth of an Industry: Blackface Minstrelsy and the Rise of American Animation*, Sammond wrote,

> Commercial animation in the United States didn't borrow from blackface minstrelsy, nor was it simply influenced by it. Rather, American animation is actually in many of its most enduring incarnations an integral part of the ongoing iconographic and performative traditions of blackface. Mickey Mouse isn't *like* a minstrel; he *is* a minstrel.[28]

The caricaturing of Black people continued as Disney's animation catalog developed. In *Dumbo,* released in 1941, a group of crows mimicking the inflections of Black voices tries to teach Dumbo how to fly. One of the crows is called Jim Crow. A controversial 1946 release, *Song of the South,* depicts a Black Uncle Remus, who seems perfectly content to remain in subjugation on the plantation. (The song "Zip-a-Dee-Doo-Dah" comes from this film.) In 1953, the company released *Peter Pan,* which perpetuates stereotypes about Native Americans, referring to Indigenous people as "redskins" and featuring a song titled "What Made the Red Man Red?" The 1955 film *Lady and the Tramp* uses anti-Asian stereotypes in the depiction of two Siamese cats. *The Jungle Book,* released in 1967, uses multiple tropes to denigrate Brown people, and Disney's 1970 film *The Aristocats* depicts a Siamese alley cat named "Shun Gon" in a caricatured way.[29]

The Rise of the Mammy

Black women may not have been portrayed as being violent or animalistic like the men in *The Birth of a Nation,* but American entertainment stereotyped them in other ways, often in radio and television shows that were considered more family friendly. Where white women were portrayed as virtuous and beautiful—a carryover from the Enlightenment days—their Black and Brown counterparts were depicted as less beautiful, less intelligent, and perfectly content in their subjugation.

From the 1800s through the Jim Crow era of the mid-1900s, the Black "mammy" caricature arose in literature, radio, film, and even advertising. The mammy was a larger-than-life, good-natured, and always-smiling woman who was happy to serve at the plantation. She was proof to white audiences that slavery was a social good, and it allowed them to conveniently ignore the sexual exploitation of slave women that was all too common on Southern plantations. Mammy characters appeared frequently—even on the sides of syrup bottles.

(In 2020, Quaker Oats announced the rebranding of the Aunt Jemima brand due to its racist origins.[30])

The first African American to win an Academy Award was Hattie McDaniel, who won Best Supporting Actress in 1940 for her portrayal of Mammy in *Gone with the Wind* (the 1939 film directed by Victor Fleming). McDaniel played a mammy character in numerous films over the course of her career.[31]

Mammy stereotypes gave way to new racial stereotypes of Black women. Starting in 1928, the *Amos 'n' Andy* radio show featured white men portraying—and mocking—Black characters, much like in the earlier minstrel shows. In the show, George "Kingfish" Stevens was a ne'er-do-well con artist who was always broke and unable to provide for the needs of his wife, Sapphire, who was loud, sassy, and overbearing. For instance, in the episode "Sapphire's Easter Outfit," Sapphire confronted Kingfish about being a bum because he couldn't afford to buy her a new dress and manipulated him until he finally broke down and bought her a new Easter outfit.[32]

Sapphire was an emasculating caricature, and the stereotype became even more mainstream when *Amos 'n' Andy* was adapted for television in 1951 and ran until 1953. As described on the Jim Crow Museum website maintained by Ferris State University,

> The Sapphire Caricature portrays black women as rude, loud, malicious, stubborn, and overbearing. This is the Angry Black Woman (ABW) popularized in the cinema and on television. She is tart-tongued and emasculating, one hand on a hip and the other pointing and jabbing (or arms akimbo), violently and rhythmically rocking her head, mocking African American men for offenses ranging from being unemployed to sexually pursuing white women. . . . The Sapphire Caricature is a harsh portrayal of African American women, but it is more than that; it is a social control mechanism that is employed to punish black

women who violate the societal norms that encourage them to be passive, servile, non-threatening, and unseen.[33]

If you keep your eyes open, you'll see the residue of Mammy and Sapphire in more contemporary shows and movies. In the 1970s and 1980s, Aunt Esther on *Sanford and Son* (played by LaWanda Page) and Florence Johnston, the housekeeper on *The Jeffersons* (played by Marla Gibbs) were Sapphire characters.[34]

Even today, some celebrities and public figures have been unjustly saddled with these labels based on perceptions of either being non-threatening and matronly (Oprah Winfrey) or being angry Black women (Serena Williams and Michelle Obama).

BRUCE LEE: ELEVATING BLACK AND BROWN FACES IN WHITE ENTERTAINMENT SPACES

Narratives that began in the Enlightenment and carried over into the modern era of radio, film, and television have reinforced the negative stereotypes held by white audiences. They've brought shame on the Black and Brown people who are stereotyped. When I've seen a Mammy or a Sapphire on film, I often wonder, *Is this how white people really see me?* In this way, I, and many of my brothers and sisters of color who've been caricatured by the media, have been misrepresented by white stereotypes.

Thankfully, some have done their part to bring liberation to Black and Brown people in entertainment.

Bruce Lee was a powerful, lightning-fast, and precise martial artist who cared deeply for his culture and the film industry. Lee, the son of an opera singer in Hong Kong and a student of martial arts, was not a stranger to performing. He appeared in films as a child and was often cast as a street kid or delinquent, but his delinquency carried over into his real life.[35] He joined a gang. He got in trouble with the law.[36] So when he turned eighteen, his family sent him to Seattle, Washington, to complete his education.

In Washington, Lee opened his first martial arts school. Then, in 1964, he made his way to Oakland, California, to found a second school. There he developed his own technique,[37] Jeet Kune Do (which means "Way of the Intercepting Fist").[38] This technique combines various styles of martial arts, boxing methods, and even fencing techniques. He garnered quite the reputation in the region, and after a kung fu demonstration in Los Angeles, he caught the attention of a television producer, who offered him a role in the television adaptation of the superhero radio show *The Green Hornet*. Lee, however, wouldn't be cast as the hero. Instead, he would play the role of Kato, the Asian chauffeur and sidekick to the masked Green Hornet.[39]

Lee was well received in his role, and his action sequences in the show were spellbinding.[40] But Lee was typecast—the Asian servant of the white hero. The show only lasted a season, running from 1966 to 1967. After the cancellation of *The Green Hornet*, Lee found himself without another leading role.

According to Lee's widow, Linda Lee Cadwell, in 1971, Lee pitched an idea for a television show to Warner Bros., which would have created a breakout role for the Chinese actor.[41] The show was promising, but it was reworked and renamed, ultimately becoming the television series *Kung Fu*. Lee should have been a natural fit for the role, but he didn't get the gig. Instead, David Carradine, a white actor who was not a martial artist, was cast as Kwai Chang Caine, a biracial Shaolin monk who traveled through the American West looking for his half-brother, Danny Caine. Why? The directors felt viewers didn't want to watch an Asian-led show.[42] So his material was appropriated and sanitized, and Lee received none of the credit.

Sound familiar? Big Mama Thornton would probably have thought so.

Lee strove to portray the best version of himself, his culture, and his community, which meant avoiding stereotypes. Because he was choosy about his roles in an era when it was difficult for Chinese people to get a break in Hollywood, he returned to Hong Kong in hopes of creating his own opportunities. There he landed a leading role in the film *The Big Boss,* which made him an international star and led to a series of successful films released between 1971 and 1973.[43] Weeks before the last and most successful of those films, *Enter the Dragon,* was released, Lee died.

Lee broke through the racist barriers of the day to win fame and fortune. Along the way he became allies with BIPOC actors, entertainers, and everyday people in their fight against injustice. He elevated their voices even as he became an international superstar.

One of Lee's first students was a Black man, Jesse Glover, who'd taken up martial arts because he needed a way to protect himself after being victimized in an altercation with the police. Lee ultimately promoted Glover to the position of assistant instructor. He also struck up a friendship with his student and basketball superstar Kareem Abdul-Jabbar, who taught Lee about racism in American society.

Lee incorporated much of what he learned from people like Glover and Abdul-Jabbar into his films. In *Enter the Dragon,* Lee featured Black actor Jim Kelly and portrayed the police harassment experienced by many in the Black community while highlighting the Black martial arts movement. His other films addressed issues of diversity and racial equity. According to Daryl Maeda, former assistant professor of ethnic studies at the University of Colorado Boulder (now dean and vice provost of undergraduate education),

[Lee] preached constantly that in martial arts, distinctions of race and nation must be discarded. . . . In "Way of the Dragon" he admonishes a student who says he prefers Chinese boxing—

Kung Fu—over Japanese karate because the latter is "foreign." His character, Tang Lung, replies that nothing is foreign, everything must be evaluated on how effective it can be in particular circumstances.[44]

Bruce Lee was a trailblazer. He proved movies could advance equity by including a diverse cast of characters and touching on complex issues of race and inclusion—and that it could be done without sacrificing profitability. His biggest films have grossed well over two billion dollars when adjusted for inflation, as of the writing of this book.[45] Not bad for an actor who couldn't get a leading role in Hollywood because of his race.

Preparation: Cultivating a Holy Imagination

As followers of Christ, we're called to use our artistic talents—singing, songwriting, writing, directing, and acting—to the glory of God. Sometimes we use these talents in direct support of a worship service, and sometimes we use them in the secular world. No matter where we use these gifts, though, we shouldn't mimic the culture. We should be mimicking the Scriptures.

When I think of biblical scenes that would make for a compelling movie, I can't help but think of the book of Revelation. In the book, a great struggle of good versus evil takes place. There's a dragon and a bunch of angels and a warrior Jesus. There's an apocalyptic war involving the saints. There's a victorious ending too. Perfect content for a film, right?

If we were to bring that book to life, what would we see? We would see a whole host of folks of all ethnicities playing key roles, and by that, I don't just mean a Brown-skinned Jesus. In John's vision, he wrote,

After this, I looked, and there before me was a great multitude that no one could count, from every nation, tribe, people and language, standing before the throne and before the Lamb. They were wearing white robes and were holding palm branches in their hands. And they cried out in a loud voice:

"Salvation belongs to our God,
      who sits on the throne,
      and to the Lamb." (Revelation 7:9–10)

John saw all different kinds of people in his vision—Middle Eastern, African, white, Asian, Latino. Even though he heard them declaring God's salvation, the text implies that he heard that praise in various languages—Hebrew, Greek, Amharic, Native American languages. No one ethnicity was elevated in John's vision. There was no appropriation or assimilation in the vision. Instead, each person was fully themselves and fully represented in the most sacred of spaces.

It is important to remember John's vision, particularly because we live in a society that carefully curates its artistic spaces to elevate certain cultures and exclude others. If we're going to change things in the entertainment industry, we must prepare ourselves and our spaces for change. That preparation should start with cultivating a biblical, holy imagination.

Imagine what it might look like for your music, your local theater, or the television shows you watch to have a cast resembling those from the book of Revelation. That's what it looks like to cultivate a holy imagination.

CELEBRATE THOSE WHO DEDICATE THEMSELVES TO LIBERATION

Once you've cultivated a more holy imagination, one that sees color as beautiful and necessary in the world, how can you dedicate yourself to the liberation of BIPOC in artistic spaces, including the entertainment industry?

First, notice how Hollywood and other forms of entertainment treat white and Black people. Consider the 2009 feel-good film *The Blind Side,* about a poor Black football player being "saved" by a middle-class white woman. Sandra Bullock won an Academy Award for portraying the role of white savior. That same year, Mo'Nique—a Black actress—won the Academy Award for her portrayal of the unemployed, profane, abusive mother of the protagonist in the film *Precious.* Tropes aside, it's worth noting that Bullock was paid five million dollars for her role in *The Blind Side,*[46] while Mo'Nique indicated that she was paid only fifty thousand dollars.[47]

Think about the shows you stream into your living room. Are heroes white and villains Black? Are there any non-stereotyped BIPOC people in leading roles at all? Take an inventory and be honest.

Also, scan your bookshelves. Are the written forms of entertainment you consume predominately white? According to one study, as of 2020, 79.6 percent of working writers and authors are white. Black authors—the next highest demographic—make up only 6.11 percent, and Asian authors make up 3.87 percent.[48] So chances are, unless you're intentional about the books you buy, your bookcase is primarily filled with the work of white authors.

Once you've taken stock of the entertainment landscape, consider how you can dedicate yourself to its liberation and to the elevation of BIPOC voices, even in the smallest ways. First, share what you've learned about the entertainment industry. Teach others about the history of the American entertainment system and ask them to consider how they might have supported films with white-supremacist themes, even if they didn't realize it.

Don't stop there, though. Support artists of color in music, literature, art, and film who are sharing amazing, complex, and intensely human stories.

Shonda Rhimes, for example, is a genius! Rhimes has her own production company, Shondaland. She produces and writes some of the best shows on television today and has contributed to popular shows like *Grey's Anatomy, Station 19, Scandal, How to Get Away with Murder, Bridgerton,* and *Inventing Anna,* among others. Each of these shows features a diverse cast of complex characters that defy racial stereotypes. (Warning: Her shows can be racy and are not intended for all audiences.)

Rhimes entered the industry hoping to disrupt the notion that African American creators must create and write solely for their own communities. She wanted to write for broader audiences and create beautiful and complex characters of all ethnicities. In 2012, she broke the mold by introducing Kerry Washington in *Scandal,* who became only the second Black woman to star in a leading role in a prime-time television series. (The first was Diahann Carroll, star of the show *Julia,* which ran from 1968 to 1971.)[49] In 2014, *How to Get Away with Murder* featured yet another Black leading lady in a television drama, Viola Davis. Washington and Davis portrayed powerful, beautiful, strong Black women who challenged the more traditional . . . ahem . . . *white* notions of beauty.

Rhimes celebrates Black and Brown people in her work, and she does it in a way that makes us examine our own prejudices and shatters our stereotypes—and not just the stereotypes of white people. I remember the first time I saw the trailer for *How to Get Away with Murder,* I was surprised. Why? Because I knew seeing a middle-aged Black woman—someone I could identify with more than a young blond leading lady—wasn't normal. Seeing that trailer, I was set free in a peculiar type of way, one in which I can't quite explain.

Also look at Chance the Rapper, who has produced some of the best music over the past decade. In 2017, he won three Grammys for Best Rap Album, Best New Artist, and Best Rap Performance. He's also received and/or been nominated for numerous awards from BET, the NAACP, Soul Train, iHeartRadio, Billboard, and BMI, among others. Though not all his music is appropriate for all audiences, his art is unashamedly Black, positive, and fun. But he's doing more than breaking stereotypes. He's using his platform to liberate other Brown people. In the spring of 2017, he donated one million dollars to public schools in his hometown of Chicago, and later that year, his nonprofit increased the donation amount to 2.2 million dollars, with the additional funds set aside specifically for art and education programs in twenty schools.[50] Because of his art and philanthropy, he appeared in *Time* magazine's list of 100 Most Influential People in 2017 and became the youngest entertainer to win the BET Awards' Humanitarian Award that same year.[51]

Anita Baker, the Black singer-songwriter who rose to prominence in the 1980s, publicly thanked Chance the Rapper at a Las Vegas show in 2022. There, with Chance in the crowd, she shared that the young rapper helped her regain control of her original master recordings, which had been claimed by her former record label. He liberated her art![52]

I share my love of Rhimes and Chance the Rapper because their lives are a testimony to liberation in the entertainment industry, and in that, they've liberated me. There are so many artists of color who deserve credit and support, including literary talents like Toni Morrison (Black), Amy Tan (Chinese American), Mindy Kaling (Indian American), and Tommy Orange (Native American). Seek them out. Watch their films, television shows, and performances. Listen to their music. Read their books. Celebrate their art, and as you do, understand that you are liberating yourself and others from the shackles of white supremacy. You're liberating BIPOC artists from appropriation and objectification and exploitation.

You're making space for Brown faces in traditionally white artistic spaces.

QUESTIONS FOR REFLECTION

1. How have movies, TV shows, and other forms of entertainment shaped or reinforced stereotypes about different ethnic groups or countries? List some specific examples.

2. Why is it important to tell stories that avoid representing characters of color as monolithic? Can you name some movies or books that provide a more nuanced view of people of color?

3. Who are your favorite artists and entertainers of color? What will you do to promote their art?

Voice of Liberation: Dawn Bynoe

WHEN DAWN BYNOE—THE DAUGHTER OF BLACK IMMIGRANTS from Antigua—was only five months old, she was hospitalized for a serious illness. The doctors told her parents that Dawn wouldn't survive, so they went into her room to say goodbye. There, her dad heard her cry for the first time—a long but beautiful cry. In that moment her dad knew that she would live and that her voice would be a gift.

Dawn did, in fact, survive. She grew up to be a musical prodigy, eventually attending LaGuardia High School in New York City, the school of music, art, and performing arts that served as the basis for the movie *Fame*. There, she attended school with actresses Tichina Arnold and Melissa De Sousa, just to name a few. She was in the presence of greatness, but could she do great things in the entertainment industry?

Dawn was signed by a music talent agency at the young age of sixteen, and she sang for the mayor of New York as a young adult. She became a successful singer and voice-over actress.

She even earned a role on Broadway, which she later had to give up when she became pregnant. But despite all that promise, she realized that to achieve as a Black woman in the entertainment industry, she'd have to learn to assimilate. And she did. In fact, a white male agent once said her greatest asset was that she could sound white.

Dawn finally signed with an African American agent, which is a rarity in publishing and acting. She now worries less about her hair or her speech patterns. She's taken back her power, turning her talents to coaching, training, and writing. She has found liberation in the entertainment industry by sharing her story and experiences with her Be the Bridge group. Through it, she's helped white women understand the pressures faced by Black and Brown women in entertainment, and she's encouraged more of her sisters of color to stop waiting for others to open the doors and instead create their own doors.

CHAPTER 9

Shut Up and Dribble

SPORTS

I N 2020, MY FRIEND JAMIE CALLED AND TOLD ME OF AN INCIDENT THAT happened to her sons, both of whom are adopted—one is biracial and the other a proud Haitian American. She shared that as her kids were preparing to participate in a Little League game, someone came up to them and warned them not to kneel during the national anthem.

This was not shocking, seeing as how it was a time when sports protests were in the national spotlight, and I'd received numerous calls, emails, and texts from friends—and even strangers—trying to navigate similar situations with their own children.

That day, I suggested that if Jamie's sons continued to play sports, and if they decided to protest the national anthem, she could first help them learn to articulate the *why* behind the protest. As athletes, they had a platform they could use to talk about injustices experienced by people of color in America. In doing so, they would follow in the footsteps of some of their sports heroes—heroes like LeBron James.

In January 2018, there was no bigger sports star than professional basketball icon LeBron James. He was a perennial All-Star and four-time MVP of the league. Even more impressive, in the seven previous seasons, he'd led his teams—the Miami Heat and the Cleveland Cavaliers—to the NBA finals, winning three of those finals and claiming the title of MVP two times.[1] He was poised to make another run in the 2018 playoffs, though his Cavaliers would eventually lose to the Golden State Warriors, led by Kevin Durant and Stephen Curry.

James didn't just shine on the court. He was a philanthropist and a fierce advocate for social justice and particularly for young people in the BIPOC community. He'd donated millions to the Boys & Girls Clubs of America and to after-school projects. In 2016, he donated 2.5 million dollars to the Smithsonian's National Museum of African American History and Culture to help fund an exhibit honoring the life of boxer Muhammad Ali.[2] He also founded a school in his hometown of Akron, Ohio, called the I Promise School, which is "dedicated to helping kids who are falling behind and at risk of falling through the cracks."[3]

James was a loving husband as well—one who'd been with his wife since high school—and the father of three. He was a friend and mentor to younger players.

In 2018, when ESPN reporter Cari Champion invited James and Kevin Durant for a car-ride interview while exploring James's childhood stomping grounds in Akron, their conversation covered subjects other than basketball. In the interview, which can be seen on YouTube, James spoke honestly about race. Violence against people of color was a regular topic in the news, and the Black Lives Matter movement had taken hold. President Donald Trump was in the White House, and his incendiary comments offended many BIPOC communities. So in that moment, James didn't hold back. He shared his own inflammatory opinion: President Trump didn't care about folks who looked like James and Durant. When Champion acknowledged that many people assume James's success made him numb to the experience of being a Black man in America, James responded:

I'm a Black man with a bunch of money, and having a crib in Brentwood and having the "[N-word]" spray painted over my gate, that lets you know I ain't too far removed. . . . No matter how [much] money or access, or how you become in life as an African American man, female, they will always try to figure out a way to let you know that you still beneath them.[4]

Right-wing pundits and sports commentators criticized his statement on social media. Days after the interview aired, Fox News host Laura Ingraham responded, calling James's comments "barely intelligible" and "ungrammatical," which is crazy if you spend the time to *actually* listen to the interview. She went on, "It's always unwise to seek political advice from someone who gets paid $100 million a year to bounce a ball. . . . Keep the political commentary to yourself. . . . Shut up and dribble."[5]

SHUT UP AND DRIBBLE?

Ingraham fell into a classic white supremacist trap. She looked at a Black man, discounted his intelligence and wisdom, and reduced him to his physical attributes and abilities. But James is more than a great basketball player. He's an overcomer, the son of a single mother who wasn't raised in economic privilege. His early years were shaped by the inner-city experience of Akron, Ohio.

James responded to Ingraham through his athlete-empowerment brand, Uninterrupted. In a short video from the Uninterrupted Twitter account, simple text messages appeared across the screen.

Shut up and dribble. Shut up and tackle. Shut up and stand. Shut up and get paid. Shut up and just do your job. Shut up and take off that hood. Shut up and stop running. Shut up and put your fist down. Shut up and do you live around here? Shut up and you fit the description. Shut up and put your hands up. Shut up and get out of the car. Shut up and don't move. Shut up and get on the ground. Shut up and lay still.

This is why we can't just stick to sports. Do you understand now?[6]

James's point was simply made. There's too much at stake for Black people in America. Athletes cannot keep silent. They shouldn't shut up and dribble.

Ingraham's comments are not a surprise to many people of color. For decades, many white coaches, pundits, and other commentators have offered their opinions on how Black athletes should behave or speak in and out of the sports arena. Over the years, this arena has been one of the places where systemic racism has played out, and it continues to be a problem today.

Consider the fact that most American sports leagues were segregated well into the mid-1940s. Consider, too, how many team owners are white even though many of the athletes composing the teams they own—particularly in the NFL and NBA—are players of color. In a 2023 article for the *Guardian*, Merlisa Lawrence Corbett wrote, "Despite Black athletes dominating the team rosters in the NFL and NBA, there is only one Black majority owner of a major sports franchise: Michael Jordan, who has controlling interest of the Charlotte Hornets."[7] Now think about how often these athletes are told to stick to athletics and keep their mouths shut. "After all," the owners and pundits imply, "you're getting millions of dollars a year for your physical talents, not your political opinions."

Thankfully, many BIPOC athletes have resisted these calls to "sit down and shut up" over the years.

RUNNING AGAINST THE NAZIS

Throughout the 1930s, Adolf Hitler used sports to promote the myth of white superiority. In 1933, the year Hitler became chancellor of Germany, the country whitewashed its athletic organizations, excluding all non-Aryans (non-whites) from participation. Jewish athletes were excluded from participation in all national sporting facilities and associations.[8] The German Boxing Association removed the Jewish middleweight and light heavyweight champion Erich Seelig from boxing in April 1933.[9] Tennis champion Daniel Prenn was excluded from Germany's Davis Cup team.[10] Jewish track-and-field athletes were kept off the national Olympic team.[11]

In 1936, two years before Germany invaded Austria, the world watched as Hitler hosted the Olympic Games in Berlin. Through those games, Hitler hoped to prove once and for all that the Aryan race was physically superior to all others. Some, including Black American athletes, begged to differ.

In the months leading up to the Olympics, many argued that the United States should boycott, claiming Americans should not participate in Germany's anti-Semitic games. Jesse Owens, the Black son of a sharecropper and the grandson of slaves,[12] was among those persuaded to boycott by the NAACP.[13] But after the president of the American Olympic Committee called those pushing for the boycott "un-American agitators" (saying, in essence, "shut up and dribble"),[14] Owens and seventeen other African Americans agreed to participate.[15]

Under the watchful eye of Hitler, who attended the games with the expectation that his white athletes would dominate, Owens turned the tables. He was the man of the hour at the games, earning gold medals in four events—the 100 meters, the long jump, the 200 meters, and the 4 x 100 meters relay.[16] His victories made him an instant international celebrity. Of Owens's success, Albert Speer, the minister of armaments and munitions in the Nazi regime,[17] wrote,

[Hitler] was highly annoyed by the series of triumphs by the marvelous colored American runner, Jesse Owens. People whose antecedents came from the jungle were primitive, Hitler said with a shrug; their physiques were stronger than those of civilized whites. They represented unfair competition and hence must be excluded from future games.[18]

Owens's participation in the games was nothing short of a political act. He went to Germany, confronted Hitler's racism—*Shut up and don't play*—head-on, and his performance spoke for itself. When he returned to the United States, many treated him as a national hero. In New York City, he was greeted by the mayor, and during a parade in his honor, someone handed Owens a bag of ten thousand dollars—an enormous sum of money at the time, particularly for a Black man.[19]

Still, many treated him as less than equal to his white fellow athletes. After the parade, Owens was invited to a reception at the Waldorf Astoria hotel, but he was not allowed through the front entrance. Instead, he was taken up to the reception in a freight elevator because Black men had a certain place in society, even if they were athletic heroes.[20] And despite Owens's display of heroism in discrediting the racist Nazi regime, President Franklin D. Roosevelt never invited him to the White House nor contacted the Olympic star. Owens would later say, "Hitler didn't snub me—it was our president who snubbed me. . . . The president didn't even send me a telegram."[21]

Still, Owens's victory opened the doors for other Black athletes, who later used their voices as activists for racial equality.

THE PODIUM AS A PLATFORM

In the 1968 Summer Olympics, months after the passage of the Civil Rights Act of 1968, African American sprinters Tommie Smith and John Carlos won the gold and bronze medals in the 200 meters. Roughly thirty minutes before they took the podium, they agreed to use the largest sporting stage in the world to send a message of Black empowerment.[22] When they finished in podium positions, that's exactly what they did.

They made their way to the medal podium, and both received their medals shoeless to represent Black poverty. Smith, the gold medalist, wore a black scarf, representing Black pride. Carlos, the bronze medalist, wore a beaded necklace, the beads representing "those individuals that were lynched, or killed that no one said a prayer for, that were hung and tarred. It was for those thrown off the side of the boats in the middle passage." Both men unzipped their tracksuits to show solidarity with the American blue-collar worker.[23] Under his jacket, Carlos wore a black T-shirt to cover up USA on his uniform to "reflect the shame I felt that my country was traveling at a snail's pace toward something that should be obvious to all people of good will."[24] When they took the podium for the national anthem, they didn't put their hands over their hearts. Instead, they raised black-gloved fists in a Black Power salute. Peter Norman, the white Australian silver medalist, did not raise his hand with the Black athletes, but he wore an Olympic Project for Human Rights badge to show his solidarity.

Though many in the crowd stood with the athletes in silent solidarity, some booed their salute while others shouted the national anthem. Carlos would later write, "They screamed it to the point where it seemed less a national anthem than a barbaric call to arms."[25] There were other repercussions too. The pair was suspended from the US Olympic team and removed from the Olympic Village. They received death threats when they returned to the States. Many Americans saw them as traitors, and Carlos had difficulty finding employment.[26] But their cause was more important to them than the praise of the crowd or even the prospect of future employment.

Smith would later be very explicit about their cause, saying, "We were concerned about the lack of black assistant coaches. About how

Muhammad Ali got stripped of his title. About the lack of access to good housing and our kids not being able to attend top colleges."[27] Put another way, they wanted true and full liberation for African Americans, and they were willing to sacrifice everything to achieve it.

Owens, Smith, Carlos, and so many other BIPOC athletes have used their platforms to stand up for liberation. It's a tradition that's carried on over the years. It's a tradition that's alive and well today.

THE WNBA: A VOICE OF LIBERATION

In July 2016, one week after the killings of Philando Castile and Alton Sterling by police officers, four members of the Women's National Basketball Association (WNBA) team the Minnesota Lynx took to the podium in a pre-game press conference in T-shirts they would wear during their warm-ups. The front of the T-shirts read "Change Starts with Us: Justice & Accountability." On the back were the names of Philando Castile and Alton Sterling and the words *Black Lives Matter*.

In that press conference, Maya Moore, an African American forward, said, "It is time that we take a deep look at our ability to be compassionate and empathetic to those suffering from the problems that are deep within our society. Again, this is a human issue, and we need to speak out for change together."[28]

According to a CNN article, four Minneapolis off-duty police officers who were providing security for the game walked off the job. Lieutenant Bob Kroll, the president of the Police Officers Federation of Minneapolis, later shared criticism of the team's players, intimating that the players didn't know the facts of the shooting and were speaking out too soon. Kroll told the *Star Tribune* newspaper that "rushing to judgment before the facts are in is unwarranted and reckless."[29] And when the *Tribune* asked whether more than four officers walked off the job, Kroll said, "They only have four officers working the event because the Lynx have such a pathetic draw."[30] In other words, he thought the players for the Minnesota Lynx—most of whom were Black—should shut up and dribble.

Not many years before Minnesota officers would murder George Floyd, the women athletes of the Minnesota Lynx exposed the racist underbelly among some Minneapolis police officers. Kroll's remarks would not go unaddressed by city officials. Minneapolis mayor Betsy Hodges came out swinging, with a post on Facebook that said, in part: "Let me be clear: labor leadership inherently does not speak on behalf of management. Bob Kroll sure as hell doesn't speak for me about the Lynx or about anything else."[31]

Moore and others across the WNBA wouldn't let Kroll—who would later defend the officers who murdered Floyd—or anyone else shut them up. During that same month, players from the New York Liberty, Indiana Fever, and Phoenix Mercury wore their own Black Lives Matters shirts.[32] The WNBA responded by fining each team five thousand dollars, and further fining each player who wore the shirts five hundred dollars because the shirts were not league sanctioned. Did that deter these women of courage? No way. On July 14, Liberty player Tina Charles turned her warm-up shirt (which was WNBA sanctioned) inside out in protest. On Instagram, she later wrote, "My teammates and I will continue to use our platform and raise awareness for the #BlackLivesMatter movement until the (WNBA) gives its support as it does for Breast Cancer Awareness, Pride and other subject matters."[33]

Many women in the WNBA continued to fight for racial justice, vocally supporting Black Lives Matter, kneeling in protests, and even taking time off to advocate for racial justice. In fact, Maya Moore took two years off basketball to fight for the freedom of Jonathan Irons, a Black man wrongfully convicted of burglary and assault. Her activism worked—in 2020, Irons was released from prison. Moore met him outside the prison wearing a T-shirt that read, "Do Justice, Love Mercy,

Walk Humbly," a reference to the words of the Old Testament prophet Micah: "What does the LORD require of you? To act justly and to love mercy and to walk humbly with your God" (6:8).[34] Talk about using your sports platform to bring liberation!

These courageous women wouldn't shut up and dribble. The result? Their commitment to using their platform to bring justice and liberation is changing the world.

A PARTICULAR PEOPLE FOR A PARTICULAR TIME

It's never a good idea to discount the work of BIPOC faces in white spaces. People of color were made in the image of God, placed in a particular context for a particular reason, and given tasks and callings.

I've always loved Psalm 139. In it, the psalmist wrote,

Before a word is on my tongue
    you, LORD, know it completely.
You hem me in behind and before,
    and you lay your hand upon me.
Such knowledge is too wonderful for me,
    too lofty for me to attain.

Where can I go from your Spirit?
    Where can I flee from your presence?
If I go up to the heavens, you are there;
    if I make my bed in the depths, you are there.
If I rise on the wings of the dawn,
    if I settle on the far side of the sea,
even there your hand will guide me,
    your right hand will hold me fast.
If I say, "Surely the darkness will hide me
    and the light become night around me,"

even the darkness will not be dark to you;
    the night will shine like the day,
    for darkness is as light to you.

For you created my inmost being;
    you knit me together in my mother's womb.
I praise you because I am fearfully and wonderfully made;
    your works are wonderful,
    I know that full well.
My frame was not hidden from you
    when I was made in the secret place,
    when I was woven together in the depths of the earth.
Your eyes saw my unformed body;
    all the days ordained for me were written in your book
    before one of them came to be. (verses 4–16)

All of us—white and people of color alike, humans—were made by God, in the image of God, for the purposes of God. He knew us when we were being formed and knew the kinds of future work he had for us.

This sentiment isn't just found in the Old Testament. In his letter to the Ephesians, Paul explained, "We are God's handiwork, created in Christ Jesus to do good works, which God prepared in advance for us to do" (2:10). Among the works we've been given is the assignment to advance the core truth that "there is neither Jew nor Gentile, neither slave nor free, nor is there male and female, for you are all one in Christ Jesus" (Galatians 3:28).

I believe these scriptures demonstrate a powerful truth. All followers of Christ—including BIPOC athletes—have been placed in this world at this time to do the good work of exposing inequity and to speak out against any sort of implicit or explicit prejudice or racism. We're here to point out the places where society has fallen short, where whiteness has squeezed out people of color. We're here to shine a light on inequity and to call for justice. We're to use whatever platform we have to advance that work.

But here's the unfortunate thing: As long as there is sin in the world, others will seek to shut down the voices of liberation. They will ask people of color to sit down and do what they're told—to "Shut up and dribble." They will tell white allies of BIPOC athletes not to rock the boat. So we have to resist. We have to stand up for liberation. We have to use our platforms to bring the equity Christ wants for all, even if that lands us in hot water. As the late United States representative John Lewis said, we have to be willing to "get in good trouble, necessary trouble."[35]

TROUBLEMAKER OR LIBERATOR?

Eventually, history will recognize the value of that "necessary trouble" in creating vital change, and I hope they see Christians leading the way. In the meantime, though, it can be costly. Just look at the story of Colin Kaepernick.

In 2016, Colin Kaepernick, then a quarterback for the San Francisco 49ers, began kneeling during the national anthem to protest racial injustice in America. His protest grabbed headlines across the country—and not just on the sports pages. It sparked debate among television pundits, editorial writers, and everyday Americans who weren't particularly interested in sports. As a wave of other athletes began to join in the protest, the National Football League had a full-fledged controversy on their hands. Before Colin Kaepernick's protest—one of the most controversial in all of sports history—he prepared by studying the issues of systemic racism in America and the part he might play in addressing them.

According to an article published in *The New York Times*, in 2010, years before his protest, Kaepernick was a standout quarterback at the University of Nevada. As a biracial man who had been adopted by white parents, Kaepernick began looking for "a deeper connection to his own roots and broader understanding of the lives of others."[36] One way of connecting was to pledge Kappa Alpha Psi, a Black fraternity on campus. His teammate John Bender had this to say about him:

> Finding an identity was big for him, because in some aspects in life, he would get the racist treatment from white people because he was a black quarterback. And some people gave him the racist treatment because he was raised by a white family. So where does he fit in in all this?[37]

Kaepernick wanted to deepen his understanding of what it meant to be a Black man in America. After a successful college career, he took the NFL by storm, leading the 49ers to the Super Bowl. He could have ignored his own issues of identity and rested on his multi-million-dollar contract. Instead, he continued to pursue identity education, even auditing a summer class on Black representation in pop culture taught by Ameer Hasan Loggins at the University of California, Berkeley. According to his professor,

> His intelligence surpasses that in which people give him credit for. . . . Seriously, for many of the students, he disproves the well-worn stigmas and stereotypes that are placed on black athletes.[38]

Which brings us to 2016. With a fuller understanding of the struggle of people of color in America, and recognizing his place in the fight for racial justice as a high-profile Black athlete and Christian, Kaepernick began his protest. (Some writers seem to indicate Kaepernick's faith played a role in his protest.[39]) Instead of remaining seated during the national anthem, Kaepernick chose to kneel upon the advice of retired Green Beret and former NFL player Nate Boyer. It was a protest, but a respectful one. According to NFL reporter Steve Wyche, Kaepernick stated:

> I am not going to stand up to show pride in a flag for a country that oppresses Black people and people of color. To me, this is bigger than football and it would be selfish on my part to look the other way. There are bodies in the street and people getting paid leave and getting away with murder.[40]

Even if you didn't follow the story, you can imagine the response. The 49ers released a statement saying that every American had a right to protest or support the anthem. The NFL commissioner even weighed in on the controversy, saying he didn't "necessarily agree" with what Kaepernick was doing.[41] Plenty of fans told Kaepernick he was being anti-American or unpatriotic. Some said the 49ers should require him to stand during the anthem. Still others—both white and fans of color—supported his decision and defended it as an act of free speech. What about the players? Many joined the protest.

Polls by Reuters indicated that 72 percent of Americans believed Kaepernick's protest was unpatriotic. Sixty-one percent indicated they didn't "support the stance Colin Kaepernick [was] taking and his decision not to stand during the anthem."[42] Kaepernick was not deterred. Despite the controversy, his protest continued throughout the season. After the conclusion of the 2016–17 season, Kaepernick entered free agency, and no team—the 49ers included—signed him to a contract.

Even without Kaepernick in the league, the protests continued. In 2017, players continued to kneel during the national anthem. Their actions led to calls for boycotts of the league.[43] On September 22, 2017, President Trump offered his two cents on the protest, indicating that players who continued to kneel should be fired.[44]

By September 2018, Kaepernick was still sidelined and many—

Kaepernick included—believed he'd been blackballed from the league. Against that backdrop, Nike made him the focal point of a commercial, which stated, "Believe in something, even if it means sacrificing everything." Nike took heat for the ad campaign, with some calling for a boycott of the brand. (The ad would go on to win a Creative Arts Emmy for Outstanding Commercial.)[45]

Despite the growing protests and the new Nike commercial, the NFL released no statement addressing systemic racism and police brutality in America. The NFL, it appeared, was more concerned about alienating its white fan base than about responding to the systemic racism that so affected its players. It was unwilling to take a stand.

The seeds of Kaepernick's protest continued to take root, however. Almost four years after Kaepernick first refused to stand, and after the murders of George Floyd, Breonna Taylor, Ahmaud Arbery, and others, Roger Goodell, the NFL commissioner, finally released a statement on June 5, 2020. Without equivocation, Goodell stated:

We, the National Football League, believe Black Lives Matter. I personally protest with you and want to be part of the much-needed change in this country. Without Black players, there would be no National Football League. And the protests around the country are emblematic of the centuries of silence, inequality, and oppression of Black players, coaches, fans, and staff.[46]

Goodell vowed to listen and seek ways to create a more unified league.

In the wake of these statements, and in light of the Black Lives Matter protests that swept across the country during the summer of 2020, a new poll showed a shift in sentiment as it related to Kaepernick's protest: 52 percent of Americans agreed that kneeling during the national anthem was appropriate.[47]

Meaningful changes came after that statement by the commissioner. Less than a week later, the NFL committed 250 million dollars to a fund with the purpose of combatting systemic racism.[48] In July of 2020, the corporate sponsors of Washington, D.C.'s NFL team began pressuring them to change their name because it was offensive and demeaning to Native Americans. FedEx called for a name change on July 2, and on the same day, Nike removed Washington team apparel from its website. The following day, the league and the team announced that a thorough review of the team's name was underway. That review eventually led to the team's new name, the Commanders.

During the 2020–21 season, the NFL introduced additional social justice messaging. "End Racism" and "It Takes All of Us" were painted in team end zones.[49] The league committed to playing "Lift Every Voice and Sing"—often called the Black national anthem—at major league events[50] and even normalized protests, saying that neither the NFL nor any of the teams would take disciplinary action against players taking a knee during the national anthem.[51] It also continued the practice of allowing players and teams to add decals to their helmets bearing messages like "Black Lives Matter" or the names of victims of police brutality, a practice that was strictly prohibited prior to Goodell's 2020 statement.[52]

These outward changes were only a start, and they came with little discomfort to the NFL. The changes have been performative. Racial disparity remains an issue in professional football, and to be clear, printing messages in an end zone or playing the Black national anthem aren't enduring policy changes that will end systemic racism in the NFL. Substantive policy changes need to be made, especially considering the fact that, as of the 2022 season, more than 75 percent of players identify as non-white[53] but there are only three Black head coaches (out of thirty-two head coaching positions).[54] The NFL has taken some performative first steps, but it has a long way to go.

Following in Kaepernick's Cleats

Kaepernick's preparation and dedication did more than draw awareness. He brought about a change in action and opinion, and inspired other athletes to speak out. Even so, as of the writing of this book, Kaepernick doesn't have a contract. His refusal to *shut up and dribble* cost him so much, though it left a mark on one of the largest sporting institutions in the world. For now, he still hasn't achieved the full liberation he's entitled to.

This begs the question: How can you prepare and dedicate yourself to the cause of liberation of athletes of color? First, you can study the history of activism in sports. Read about Jesse Owens, Tommie Smith, John Carlos, Jackie Robinson (the first Black MLB baseball player), Muhammad Ali (the heavyweight champion who was suspended from boxing because of his own protest), the Black 14, Colin Kaepernick, LeBron James, Maya Moore, Chloe Kim, and others. You might discuss with others the reasons for their speaking out. Imagine yourself in their shoes.

Then, resist the temptation to tell athletes of any color to "Shut up and dribble," and refuse to support those who do. Elevate BIPOC athletes' voices and be a voice for true Christian liberation in your own right. Harness the power of Christian protest, as Kaepernick did. Boycott teams and owners who do not allow BIPOC athletes to speak out about racism and social institutions. If you want to take it a step further, consider supporting brands that support athletes of color and that elevate their voices even when those voices are calling out the establishment. (Both Nike and LeBron James's Uninterrupted brand come to mind.) Supporting those athletes and brands advances the messages of liberation, a message we all need to hear.

QUESTIONS FOR REFLECTION

1. Why do you think activism and sports have shared a connection for many years?

2. How would the prophets of the Old Testament compare to some of today's prophetic voices in sports? Were the messages of the prophets welcome by the hearers of that time?

3. Consider your favorite sports teams and their treatment of people of color. How can you use your platform, money, or influence to support teams who encourage and allow their players to work toward the liberation of others?

Voice of Liberation:
Justin Holiday

JUSTIN HOLIDAY IS AN AMERICAN BASKETBALL PLAYER WHO CUR-rently plays for the Dallas Mavericks. His two brothers, Jrue and Aaron, also play in the NBA. But their mother and father passed down more than serious athleticism to this trio. They also passed down a love for the God of righteousness and justice, the God who called them to action and activism.

I had the opportunity to interview Justin for the *Be the Bridge* podcast in 2020. He shared that amid the racial unrest that erupted in the wake of George Floyd's murder, he considered sitting out the season but ultimately decided to play in the hope of inspiring a generation of future NBA players. Having been influenced by those who had lost their lives to police violence, Holiday chose to make a difference. In order to build bridges of understanding and support, he created a T-shirt that included the names of those who had lost their lives to violence and systemic injustice. His goal was to bring awareness to the present and past racial injustices involving policing and to bring about a change.[55]

Like other players, Holiday spoke out during interviews and wore apparel that sparked conversation. He also became a member of our Be the Bridge community, where he invites others into the work of true racial reconciliation. He and his wife, Shekinah, have lent their voices and leadership skills to help the organization grow and spread its message. Holiday's platform and commitment have made it possible for the work of Be the Bridge to continue as we empower people toward racial healing, racial equity, and racial reconciliation. He is an example of how athletes and other individuals can leverage their power and influence to advance the message of Christ-centered racial reconciliation.

CHAPTER 10

One Body, One Spirit, One Hope

THE CHURCH

I N 2015, I JOINED A GROUP TEXT THREAD WITH NINETEEN OTHER PEO- ple. We had all met around 2000 at a predominately African American church in Atlanta. Fifteen years later, I'd moved to Texas and many of the others on that text thread were spread out across the country. Most of us attended predominately white churches. Because of the state of the world, particularly in regard to race relations in America, we needed a Black support group. And because of our lack of proximity to one another, a mass text thread would have to do.

We had all watched with horror the events that unfolded in Ferguson, Missouri, on August 9, 2014, after an unarmed Black teenager, Michael Brown, was shot and killed by police officers for allegedly stealing cigars. You might remember the aftermath. Ferguson erupted in protests, and police arrived in military gear and tear-gassed the crowds who were protesting police brutality. The event helped galvanize the Black Lives Matter movement, which had begun the year before, and opened a new chapter in America's long book on race relations. Watching this unfold on television was traumatizing for my friends and me. We needed one another because in many of our new circles, we didn't feel safe to bring up the issues our Black community was facing.

Tensions ran high in our country through the end of the year, and just when it seemed things might be settling down, Freddie Gray died after being transported in the back of a police van, with no seatbelt, and allegedly being given a "wild ride."[1] That ride led to Gray's severe spinal cord injury and ultimately to his death.[2] Again, riots broke out, this time in Baltimore, with nightly nationwide news coverage. Pundits provided theories on how our country might fight racism, particularly in the police force. Black folks suffered more trauma.

Eventually, the news coverage of the Freddie Gray case waned. But the BIPOC communities I spoke with still grieved, and there was no place to share that grief. The grief was compounded by the June 2015 shooting at Mother Emanuel AME Church in Charleston, South Carolina (see chapter 4).

It was not merely a hard time for people of color; it was unfathomable. For many of us who worshipped in predominately white spaces—including those on the text thread—it was particularly difficult. Before this year of violence, we hadn't felt particularly seen or heard. But in the aftermath of these deaths in 2014 and 2015, we were flooded with questions about white supremacy by text, email, and while simply walking to our car after church. White people in our churches told us how shocked they were, how they couldn't believe events like these could happen in 2015. We heard too many white people make excuses for the police officers in Ferguson and Baltimore. We heard them defend gun laws even as they condemned the Charleston attacks, and in most of our churches, if anything at all was said about racism, it was rarely said by a pastor or leader of color. Some churches chose to remain silent because they wanted to avoid conversations about gun violence.

Text messages flew among us after the Charleston shooting. My

Black friends and I vented about our rising levels of exhaustion. At the time, I was on staff at a large church in Austin, Texas, and I was frustrated by the lack of communication around the issues of white supremacy and racism. Prayers were offered by the staff. Sympathies were graciously extended. But few were willing to address the fact that racism was baked into the very systems of society, and even fewer were inclined to act in ways that might bring reconciliation.

My friends described having much the same experience, hearing many white people declare that these acts of violence against Black people were isolated events and not a larger systemic issue. It was difficult to understand the complete disconnect between our pain and the business-as-usual attitude of other believers. We witnessed a mix of willful ignorance, deflection, denial, and for some, confusion. All of it left us feeling invisible, unseen, even as we were fully alive and present to witness both the horror of the violence and the silence of our faith community.

The text thread became a sort of lifeline. But during one exchange, it struck me. If someone didn't open a real dialogue in the church about issues of white denial, white silence, and BIPOC exhaustion and police brutality and systemic racism—dialogues like I was having with my Black friends—nothing would change. I wanted better for the church, my friends, my community, the staff. So armed with a bit of knowledge and a lot of naïveté, I went off-script.

I began hosting conversations at the African American Cultural and Heritage Facility in Austin with a group of Christian friends of different ethnicities—white, Black, Latina, and Asian—about racial reconciliation. The parameters of the conversation were simple: We wouldn't hold back, we would speak the truth about systems of racism with love and respect, and we wouldn't interrupt one another. In fact, no one would speak unless they held the talking stick—which was a literal stick we held to signal whose turn it was to speak without interruption. We all agreed the women of color in the group would lead the conversation because we had things to say about what true racial reconciliation might look like. The white women agreed to listen graciously.

In that first meeting, we shared candidly. We were friends, committed to learning from one another. There were tears of sorrow and anger. There were moments of deep empathy and understanding. There was good food, too, which kept us from leaving when the conversations got uncomfortable. When we were finished, we agreed the dialogue was only just beginning and that we had to keep pressing in together. So we scheduled another meeting, and then another, and another. As we persisted, each of us confessed a sad truth: We'd never had these kinds of conversations in our church congregations before.

These meetings became our brave space. We had courageous conversations about hard things. We showed up with our busy lives. We committed ourselves to listening and learning. And over time, our little dinner group grew and multiplied into other groups. After several months and hearing about the impact of the conversations, my friend Jennie asked me to help lead a similar conversation at an event she was hosting. She also asked if I could write a guide to help others. With hesitation, I said yes. (I hesitated because I understood how these conversations typically went around white people.)

Jennie encouraged me to create an organization that facilitated conversations about racial reconciliation. That organization became what's now Be the Bridge. (For more information on Bridge groups, see the QR code on the Additional Resources page at the back of this book.)

By 2016, Be the Bridge was growing, as was the need for tough conversations, particularly in the church. That year, more instances of police violence against Brown bodies broke out, and there was Black retaliation too. Alton Sterling and Philando Castile were killed by police officers on July 5 and 6 respectively. Then, on July 7, Micah Xavier Johnson, a Black man, ambushed a group of police officers in Dallas, Texas, in an act of retaliation. After two years of violence between the police and people of color on the streets of America, I realized that I had heard very little from the church. Friends—Bridge friends, friends on the text thread, and friends in my everyday life—told me that many of their pastors had avoided the elephant in the room on the Sunday following that violent week in July. It was too political, these ministers said, too divisive. The issues were too complex to do them justice in a one-hour service. Some simply didn't know how to navigate the varying views in their congregations regarding issues of race.

Though I was beginning to expand Be the Bridge, I was on staff at a different church in Austin when Sterling and Castile were killed. I did what many of my BIPOC friends did: I hid my grief and kept moving forward. My ancestors had done it for generations, and I figured I could follow in their footsteps.

That week, I had a previously scheduled meeting with one of the campus pastors, Eric Bryant, at a local coffee shop. I decided I wouldn't let myself be disappointed if he treated the meeting as business as usual. I washed my face, put on my makeup, got in my car, and drove to meet him. I took a deep breath before exiting the car and walking into the shop.

But the meeting turned out to be anything but business as usual. Eric led with a startling question: "How are you doing?"

I wasn't prepared and didn't exactly know how to answer. Did he really want to know the truth, that I grieved the deaths of more Black men, that I was frustrated by the fact that so many churches weren't addressing issues of violence against Black people, and that part of my frustration was directed at *our* church? Was I willing to tell him all of this, and then risk hearing a response from him that I might not like?

My emotions must have shown even though I was at a loss for words—a rare occurrence for me. Before I could come up with a meaningful response, he looked at me and said, "I have no words for what is happening. I'm so angry."

His statement broke something loose in me. I felt seen. Understood. I found the words I needed to express my anger and frustration. As I spoke, both our eyes filled with tears. It occurred to me later that this powerful moment only occurred because Eric—a white man—made space for my pain.

Eric Bryant was my hero that day. He was empathetic, and he really saw me. He didn't ask me five hundred questions. He didn't try to make excuses for the police officers. He didn't blame the victims. Instead, he sat in that pain with me and listened. Then he reassured me that the work I had started with Be the Bridge was important.

"It's for such a time as this," he said.

The conversation turned to more practical things. Eric suggested that we lead the church through a lament, and that's exactly what we did. During that week in July 2016, a multiethnic body showed up. We were one body, one church, worshipping, praying, and lamenting the loss of Black lives to police brutality. People of color were allowed to take their masks off and share their pain. White people listened with empathy. I will forever be grateful for Kenny Green and Eric Bryant and others who stood up for me with compassion in that very white space. Their words and actions carry me today. When it was over, many people of color told me how healing the service had been because our local church—typically a white space—decentered the system of whiteness for a day. That decentering had been good for the souls of that congregation.

THE SYSTEM OF WHITENESS: A HISTORICAL PRIMER

The centering of whiteness—a phrase that describes the process of tying white culture to church culture, especially evangelical culture—is not a new thing. In fact, it goes back to the earliest days of our country.

When the Puritans set sail for America, they intended to claim territory in a new land, a land where they could establish themselves as God's chosen people. According to Phil Gorski, a Yale sociologist and the co-author of *The Flag and the Cross: White Christian Nationalism and the Threat to American Democracy*, the Puritans believed that America was the promised land and that they stood in the place of the Israelites. In an interview on his book, Gorski expounded:

> God bestows a Promised Land on the Israelites. They go to that land and find the Amalekites inhabiting it. They conquered the land. This is how a lot of the early settlers of New England, many of them Puritan, understood their situation. Quite literally, they saw themselves, like the Israelites, as a chosen people. North America was the new Promised Land. The Native Americans were the new Amalekites and the Puritans felt entitled to take their land.[3]

It wasn't just the early Puritans who used a misinterpretation of Christian theology to justify subjugating people. The early slave traders from Britain, Spain, Portugal, Denmark, France, Sweden, and the Netherlands centered their whiteness and rationalized their racist atrocities with religion. Taking the Bible out of context, they claimed that slavery was validated by what they called the curse of Ham.

You've probably heard the story from the book of Genesis, how Noah and his family were saved from the Flood by way of the ark (Genesis 6–9). After they made landfall, Noah got drunk. While he was inebriated, his son Ham saw him naked. Biblical scholars disagree on what exactly happened, but it's clear that the event dishonored Noah. When Noah regained his faculties, he cursed Ham's son Canaan, saying, "Cursed be Canaan! The lowest of slaves will he be to his brothers" (Genesis 9:25).

Though Noah didn't curse Ham himself, this "curse of Ham" was used for generations to justify slavery. Plantation owners argued that Black people—like Canaan—were to be servants forever because the owners believed that God had ordained it as part of the curse. Why were Ham and his children assumed to be Black, despite the fact that Scripture never speaks of Noah's family in racialized terms?

David M. Goldenberg, a historian who wrote *The Curse of Ham*, claims that a misreading of Hebrew and other Semitic languages led to the mistaken belief that Ham meant "'dark, black' or 'hot.'"[4]

Slaveholders also twisted other scriptures to justify owning image-bearers of God. Scriptures like these:

Slaves, obey your earthly masters with respect and fear, and with sincerity of heart, just as you would obey Christ. Obey them not only to win their favor when their eye is on you, but as slaves of Christ, doing the will of God from your heart. Serve wholeheartedly, as if you were serving the Lord, not people, because you know that the Lord will reward each one for whatever good they do, whether they are slave or free. (Ephesians 6:5–8)

Slaves, obey your earthly masters in everything; and do it, not only when their eye is on you and to curry their favor, but with sincerity of heart and reverence for the Lord. Whatever you do, work at it with all your heart, as working for the Lord, not for human masters, since you know that you will receive an inheritance from the Lord as a reward. It is the Lord Christ you are serving. (Colossians 3:22–24)

All who are under the yoke of slavery should consider their masters worthy of full respect, so that God's name and our teaching may not be slandered. Those who have believing masters should not show them disrespect just because they are fellow believers. Instead, they should serve them even better because their masters are dear to them as fellow believers and are devoted to the welfare of their slaves. (1 Timothy 6:1–2)

Teach slaves to be subject to their masters in everything, to try to please them, not to talk back to them, and not to steal from them, but to show that they can be fully trusted, so that in every way they will make the teaching about God our Savior attractive. (Titus 2:9–10)

Those slave owners ripped verses out of context to promote the insanity of buying, selling, and owning other humans. They also cut verses out of the Bible. A Bible that became known as "the Slave Bible" (published in 1807) omitted portions of Scripture that might have inspired slave rebellions, including the entire book of Exodus and the letter to the Galatians, with its exhortation that there is "neither slave nor free" (3:28). What about the book of Jeremiah, which pronounced woe to those who make "people work for nothing, not paying them for labor" (22:13)? That also was removed.[5] In fact, more than 90 percent of the Old Testament was removed along with half of the New Testament.[6] What remained was a propaganda tool, one used to teach plantation slaves that God ordained their enslavement, and resistance to their enslavers was resistance to God.

THE MODERN CHURCH AS A WHITE SPACE

Of course, the version of Christianity that centered white bodies, led crusades, and enslaved Brown bodies continued to hold sway well past slavery. It was used to justify Jim Crow laws. Perhaps you recall reading in chapter 2 how Jerry Falwell believed segregation in education was justifiable because God drew "a line of distinction" between the races and "we should not attempt to cross that line."[7] Falwell amassed great political clout in the Conservative movement as the founder of the power-wielding Moral Majority, which helped Ronald Reagan win the presidency in 1980.

White supremacy, twisted theology, and hunger for power have gone hand in hand for millennia. Even today, there is a resurgence of white Christian nationalism in American evangelicalism. How does one identify and define Christian nationalism? Gorski described it this way:

> White Christian nationalists believe that the country is divinely favored and has been given the mission to spread religion, freedom, and civilization. They see this mission and the values they cherish as under threat from the growing presence of non-whites, non-Christians, and immigrants in the United States. . . . It's the view that somebody has corrupted the country or is trying to take it away. White Christian nationalists want to take it back.[8]

The cycle continues. The new white Christian nationalists are on a new crusade, and they're using their brand of religion to justify it.

The rise of white Christian nationalism is bad news for anyone who doesn't fit into their narrative. But when churches avoid discussing the *full gospel*—the liberating gospel that Christ came for all, regardless of political affiliation and ethnic distinction—they create spaces where white supremacist ideas can silently spread like a virus. When those views are finally confronted, the ideas quickly become vocalized and weaponized.

I've heard stories from across the country. Pastors who have tried to preach against the sin of racism have been accused of espousing critical race theory and wokeism (a word co-opted and weaponized by political pundits). These accusations demonstrate a denial of the very real, ongoing issues of inequity we've been discussing throughout this book, and if you're in denial, that ultimately means you support the racial injustices. The result: Pastors have been fired, elders have been removed, and congregants have been asked to leave over challenging their congregations on racist ideologies. Sadly, this is all too common in the church today.

CONVERSATIONS IN THE CHURCH: WHAT ARE WE SO AFRAID OF?

It's important that we have the hard conversations in the church as a way of discipleship, but so often those conversations are shut down, as are the people who instigate them.

A friend in Atlanta struggled to understand why, in a church whose membership is about half white and half BIPOC, none of the executive leadership or elders were people of color. During the social unrest of 2020, her teenage son, Cole, was asked to participate in a video interview with the pastor about his experience of being a student of color in the church. After the interview, which evidently didn't go quite as the pastor envisioned it, the pastor went on a rant. He said everyone should just be colorblind, which would solve all the problems. (This despite the fact that being colorblind is both impossible *and* minimizes the experiences and culture of people who want to celebrate their ethnic heritage.) He went on to downplay everything Cole had shared in the video, making Cole feel unseen and unheard. Cole recounted being angry and wanting to say something, but the youth minister who was in the room stopped him.

Aria Evans, one of our student leaders in Be the Bridge Youth and College, also recalls being asked to be in a video at her church, but she was afraid to speak the truth because she knew it wouldn't be received. So she turned down the request and decided not to share her experience. She went right along pretending everything was fine. Her parents eventually left that church, which allowed her to become more authentically herself, and after attending our Be the Bridge Student Leadership Summit, she found her voice. Aria admitted that she hadn't fully embraced her Blackness but now she sees it as a strength.

My friend and assistant Lauren Brown told me about a white pastor at her former church who said he was tired of having to be so careful about the things he said from the pulpit and that he was bothered by constant correction when it came to how he spoke about race. She responded that if he was tired of being corrected, imagine how tired she must be of hearing his racially biased comments and having to correct him! The pastor didn't appreciate her response and lived experience. So after ten years of toiling to create healthy conversations around race, she and her family, along with several other families, decided to move on from the church. This scene has played out in many churches across the country as BIPOC congregants have engaged the work of racial reconciliation.

For every story like this, I can tell you hundreds more—from churches that hang partisan political signs in the building, to those that ask Brown people not to wear BIPOC positivity apparel, to faith communities that only call on Brown people to share their experiences when it benefits the church. Stories like these have left a trail of trauma experienced by those who tried to speak out, only to be dismissed. When I hear these stories from friends and Be the Bridge members, when I ask why they didn't leave sooner, they tell me they stayed to make a difference. But if the church leadership doesn't make space for their voices—as Eric did for me and so many others—all that effort is wasted.

Christ came to unite us into one church, one citizenship out of many people. He invites us into a single conversation, a conversation about being united in him. The apostle Paul—a "Jew of Jews" *and* a Roman citizen—knew this well. To the church in Ephesus, he wrote,

> Remember that at that time you were separate from Christ, excluded from citizenship in Israel and foreigners to the covenants of the promise, without hope and without God in the world. But now in Christ Jesus you who once were far away have been

brought near by the blood of Christ. For he himself is our peace, who has made the two groups one and has destroyed the barrier, the dividing wall of hostility, by setting aside in his flesh the law with its commands and regulations. His purpose was to create in himself one new humanity out of the two, thus making peace, and in one body to reconcile both of them to God through the cross, by which he put to death their hostility. (Ephesians 2:12–16)

Through the cross, all are made equal.

Avoiding hard conversations doesn't lead to equality or unity in Christ. That's why I believe those who shut down conversations that decenter whiteness in the church will be surprised when Christ calls them to account one day. I also believe that very good pastors like Eric faithfully live out the gospel when they decenter themselves and make space for voices and faces of people of color in white spaces.

Church, Prepare Yourself

As we've seen in this book, preparation for liberation requires us to do the work. We have to be educated about the spaces dominated by white voices. We need to know our history and the ways that history bleeds into today. We have to recognize the ways our thinking—whether our philosophies, ideologies, or theologies—might be tainted by white supremacy. Then, just as Eric did, we must make space for hard conversations—conversations that hopefully lead to liberating action.

I know it can be difficult to have these kinds of conversations in churches these days. I know plenty of pastors who've been accused of being "woke" or "Marxist" or of "pushing the BLM agenda" simply for challenging their congregations to examine their hearts for the sin of racism. (The story of Kevin Thompson, a pastor from Arkansas who left his home church after being called names like these, comes to mind.)[9] Still, we must try.

We must initiate conversations about racism, particularly in the church, because we are brothers and sisters of the same heavenly kingdom. We belong to the family in which God recognizes no distinction between "Jew nor Gentile, neither slave nor free, nor is there male and female, for you are all one in Christ Jesus" (Galatians 3:28). We should "hate what is evil [which includes racism]; cling to what is good [which includes equity and racial reconciliation]" (Romans 12:9). We should strive for reconciliation that allows us to not just worship together as every tribe, tongue, and nation but also allows us to celebrate and elevate one another. Can you imagine the beauty of this kind of church?

Dedication to Liberation: Some Suggestions for the Church

How can we make space in the church for hard conversations about racial healing? When pastors and church leaders ask me what they can do, I suggest they open roundtable discussions with members of color who have experience in the work of racial reconciliation and healing. I suggest they allow those members of color to lead the conversations, sharing about their experiences in the church without interruption. They can also bring in experts to lead conversations and propose action plans for improving their church culture. (As a bonus, the church can actually implement the plan.)

I also suggest that pastors and congregants stop saying "Just focus on the gospel" as a way of saying "Stop talking about race." Isn't the entire point of the gospel that Jesus came to liberate us from sin? And isn't racism sin? So yes, let's talk about racism and how Jesus came to liberate us from it. Let's also talk about how to apply that gospel to create a more equitable church and world.

If you're not a minister and you want to know how you can begin creating a more equitable church environment, consider reading at least five books written by authors of color who are committed to the work of racial reconciliation and biblically based justice before engaging in conversation. Be open to correction and feedback from members of BIPOC communities without retaliation and defensiveness. Consider also submitting yourself to leaders who are different from you, if you're not already doing so. Elevating the voices of people of color provides a check on intolerance, nepotism, and promoting the same kinds of ignorance that landed the church here in the first place. Invest in training, mentoring, and coaching from BIPOC leaders who have committed to the work of racial reconciliation. If you live in an area that lacks diversity, you can find BIPOC-led coaching cohorts and training opportunities online. You can also join an online Be the Bridge group.

Don't just seek diversity; seek to be a racial reconciler. Don't expect people of color to come into your space, especially if you haven't done the work to make it courageous and safe for BIPOC congregants. De-center yourself by visiting churches, communities, and organizations that have BIPOC leadership. Submit to that leadership.

Also, know that people of color may show up in your church looking for enriched children's and youth programs and opportunities to be bridge builders across racial lines. So often, those of us in the BIPOC faith community go in thinking that others want the church to be more multicultural. Don't prove us wrong. Take time to listen to our stories and pain, and be ready to respond. Don't make excuses, blow off feedback, or accuse people of color who share their points of view of acting out of some woke leftist agenda. It's more than just dismissive—it is abusive.

Liberating the church from the empire mentality that centers white power and white supremacy is the work of racial righteousness, and it's going to take a lot of work. Undoing so much history isn't going to happen overnight. But this is the work we've been called to—the work of unity. Let's join together under Christ and put our hands to the plow.

QUESTIONS FOR REFLECTION

1. Does your faith community make a practice of discussing issues of racial righteousness? When was the last time you remember hearing any reference to racial reconciliation from the pulpit?

2. Does your congregation elevate the voices of people of color in a meaningful way? If not, how can you advocate for change?

3. What books are you committed to reading to help you become more educated and equipped to speak out for change in the church? Write them down. Make a promise to do the work.

Voices of Liberation:
Dion and Michele Evans

THE PANDEMIC USHERED IN A MAJOR CHURCH TRANSITION FOR MY
friends Michele and Dion Evans, as they were attending a predominately white church, a place that didn't seem to value our
culture, art, or worship style. They had grown discouraged
about the lack of diversity within the church and were tired of
being reprimanded when they pushed for conversations on the
racism that affected their lives every day.

Michele's daughter had admitted that she didn't feel safe at
church and that she didn't feel like she could fully be who God
created her to be. She was constantly holding back, afraid to
discuss subjects that mattered to her. Michele's son felt he was
forced to assimilate to the white culture of their church. He
confessed that he felt a piece of himself dying on the inside. The
environment was ripping the family apart.

So after years of trying to build bridges within this white-
centered church, when their worship experience moved to more
virtual spaces, the family took the opportunity to reset, heal,

and look for alternative church communities. The Evanses began a Bible study with a few like-minded people of color, determined to create a brave and safe space after learning of the sentiments and the negative impact white church spaces were having on their children's self-esteem.

The Bible study grew, and the families decided not to return to the former church due to the rejection they'd experienced over the years with conversations on racial injustice and ways of restoration. They have now turned their process of healing into a church that honors the *imago Dei*—the image of God—in everyone.

Dion and Michele Evans—the leaders of this church—have set a goal to ensure their process of discipleship is inclusive to everyone. Both are active leaders within our Be the Bridge community and the surrounding community in which they live. They have not given up on the local church and believe it can be the vehicle for bringing racial reconciliation to the world.

Through their church, they are a part of a growing community of believers who are restructuring their faith around the full, inclusive gospel of Jesus Christ. They are creating the places they desire to worship in. Through those spaces, they're finding liberation and bringing it to others. Through their pain and despair, God has given them hope through new communities and commitments to honor the full gospel.

Prayer of Lament

GOD OF COMPASSION AND JUSTICE, HEAR THIS LAMENTATION FOR the persistent scourge of systemic racism that plagues our world. We bow before you with heavy hearts, burdened by the weight of prejudice and discrimination that stains our societies.

We lament for the countless souls who have suffered, their dignity trampled upon by the chains of hatred and bigotry. We lament the divisions that tear at the very fabric of humanity, perpetuating injustice and denying equal and equitable opportunities for all.

Father, we beseech you to grant us the strength and wisdom to confront the roots of systemic racism. Help us dismantle the systems that perpetuate inequality and marginalize our brothers and sisters based on the color of their skin. Illuminate our path with empathy, understanding, and compassion so that we may foster racial healing, racial equity, and racial reconciliation.

May our hearts be filled with a burning desire for righteousness and justice, driving us to challenge the status quo and advocate for meaningful change. Grant us the courage to confront our own biases and prejudices, acknowledging the ways we have unknowingly contributed to this brokenness.

Guide our leaders, institutions, and communities to embrace racial righteousness, racial diversity, and equity as sacred values. May they work tirelessly to dismantle oppressive systems and foster environments where every individual is cherished and respected, irrespective of their race or ethnicity.

Let this lamentation serve as a call to action, a rallying cry for righteousness, justice, and solidarity against systemic racism. May we stand together, hand in hand, as we strive to create a world where justice flows like a mighty river and where the legacy of systemic racism is but a painful memory.

Father, we seek your guidance and strength, knowing that only through collective efforts rooted in love, empathy, and understanding can we overcome the deep wounds inflicted by racial injustice. Amen.

Prayer of Reimagination

FATHER GOD, HEAR OUR PRAYER AS WE GATHER IN HOPE AND ENVISION a world free from the chains of systemic racism. We come before you with hearts brimming with a vision of healing, equity, and reconciliation for all.

We dare to reimagine a society where the color of one's skin holds no power over their opportunities, their worth, or their safety. We envision a world where racial diversity is celebrated as a source of strength and where every individual is recognized for their inherent value, their reflection of the *imago Dei,* and their unique contributions.

Grant us the courage to challenge the racist structures that perpetuate racial inequality and racial discrimination. Inspire us to dismantle the systems that have divided us for far too long. Fill our hearts with unwavering determination to confront our own biases and prejudices, transforming them into seeds of understanding and empathy.

Guide us to create communities founded on respect, compassion, justice, righteousness, and restoration. Help us build bridges across racial divides, fostering dialogue and forging connections that transcend the boundaries of race, ethnicity, and culture. May our interactions be characterized by mutual respect, genuine curiosity, and a deep appreciation for the richness that racial diversity brings.

Empower and convict our leaders and institutions to enact policies that address systemic racism head-on. Give them wisdom and discernment to enact transformative changes that ensure equitable access to education, healthcare, employment, and justice. May they be guided by equity, compassion, and a commitment to repairing the structures that perpetuate racism and keep us from truly upholding liberty and justice for all.

We envision a future where systemic racism is but a distant memory. A future where equity, justice, and opportunity are the birthright of every individual, regardless of their background. May this vision inspire us to work tirelessly toward its realization, fueled by love, empathy, and a shared understanding of our interconnectedness.

Father, as we lift our voices in this prayer, we commit ourselves to the pursuit of a world that embraces the inherent worth and dignity of all people. May our actions align with our aspirations and may the reimagining of a society free from systemic racism become a reality. Amen.

Epilogue

We wear the pain.
Beaten
Bruised
Torn and worn
We were treated like savages and not human form.

We wear the pain.
The pain of our ancestors and their ancestors before them.

We wear the pain.
Our Blackness was once considered a deformity, we wear the pain.
They chose greed and indifference over our image, we wear the
    pain.

Enduring brutality, emptiness, and scorn,
for some since the day they were born,
we wear the pain.

In anguish birthed from chains that left a generational stain on
    Brown bodies across this nation,
we wear the pain.
The scars of dehumanization encapsulate our bodies and
    emotional being,
we wear the pain.

Death has not defined us; we are not demarcated by our pain. We
    are not merely bereft. We are because they were.
We remain because their breath survives through us.
Each breath of pain
The pain
The pain
The pain
The pain we wear has emboldened us, stripped us, and
    strengthened us. It has created paths of faith and restoration.
    We are not our pain alone.

Our hope, strength, and pain exist intertwined in a rhapsody of a
    complex moral arc that always bends toward justice.
We wear the pain.

—Latasha Morrison

First, to all the Brown faces in white spaces: Systemic racism is a painful reality that should never define your worth or limit your aspirations. You are more than the stereotypes and prejudices projected onto
you. Your culture, heritage, and identity are sources of beauty and
strength that should be celebrated. In the face of adversity, remember
to always believe in your own power and potential. Your achievements
and successes are a testament to your resilience and determination. Do
not let the ignorance and hatred of others dim your light. Instead, let it

fuel your motivation to rise above and shatter the limitations imposed upon you.

As we navigate the path toward a more inclusive and just society, your voice is essential. Speak up against injustice, share your stories, and if you choose to do so, educate others with patience and compassion. Your perspective is powerful and can inspire change, even if it's only one person at a time. Even when progress is slow, remember the countless trailblazers who came before you, who fought tirelessly for equality and justice. Their legacy lives on, and you are a part of that legacy. Your contributions matter, and they are shaping a better future for generations to come.

Now, to every reader, BIPOC and white alike, consider this question: What's next?

As we journey from the pages of this book out into the real world, remember the stories. Consider how history plays out every day in the world around you. As a BIPOC person, you may have been insulated from many of these hard truths your entire life. As a white person, you may have benefitted from these historical truths, and it might be easy to forget that, for BIPOC individuals navigating predominantly white spaces, the journey was and still is fraught with challenges, many of which were outlined in this book.

So as we move forward together, let's remember that the fight against racism is ongoing, and it is up to all of us to create a more just and equitable world. We must listen to the voices of those who have been marginalized and work together to build a society that is truly inclusive and welcoming to all. Racism has never been the period on our collective stories. We can write a new ending, finding ways to thrive and fight against adversity for as long as we have breath in our bodies. We must push forward amid silence, apathy, and false narratives. Regardless of where we find ourselves on the journey, I pray that we remain empowered and don't let the obstacles stack against us so that we can rectify the wrongs that have stained our country, communities, businesses, and churches.

As I close this book, I am reminded of Jesus's call in the Sermon on the Mount for his followers to care for humanity. Jesus gave us a road map for creating places of belonging and restoration. He calls us to live with compassion, mercy, justice, and righteousness. Where does he begin this message? As Jesus sat on the mountain with his disciples, he opened with, "Blessed are the poor in spirit, for theirs is the kingdom of heaven" (Matthew 5:3). In our work for racial justice, let's begin with the realization that we are powerless to make change without God. We are his children and we rely on him to bring about his kingdom on earth as it is in heaven. What if we began there, remembering we are poor, and asked Jesus to fill us with his kingdom vision? Would it make a very different, better world? Wouldn't it remove any arrogance, ego, or pride from the conversation?

Now, remembering the poverty of our spirit, how should we move forward in this particular cultural atmosphere? First, we must listen to marginalized voices. Then, we must do what is right and morally ethical to care for others and bring about equity. Gather with a group and formulate prayerful plans to right historical wrongs in your own community. Get involved in your local school system, your city politics, or local sports leagues. Join a mentoring program. Start or join a local Be the Bridge group or take a training course in the BTB academy, the organization I started to heal racial wounds and improve racial literacy. Above all, do not rewrite, ignore, or gaslight those who've experienced racial injustice, particularly systemic injustice. And if you're prone to dismiss racial injustice as something from the distant past, ask yourself why. Get curious about what and who you've allowed to drive the narrative around racism and reconciliation.

Finally, remember that education and empathy are our way forward. We cannot limit education as a method of controlling and oppressing. We can't ban books with racial themes because they make us

uncomfortable. Education is key to breaking stereotypes and prejudices, fostering cultural understanding and compassion. Education allows us to understand the experiences of others, particularly BIPOC
people, better equipping us to examine policies and legal frameworks
that address racial bias and injustice. So do your part in advocating for
education about racial injustice. This country desperately needs it.

As you close this book, commit to the work, understanding that if
we create a society that celebrates and harnesses the potential of every
individual, we'll live in a more just, prosperous, and peaceful world.
We'll live in a richer cultural environment, one with more cognitive
diversity, innovation, and creativity. As our spaces shift and we lead
with the *whole* of who we are as a country, we will see economic advantages, enhanced market opportunities, and global competitiveness.

Our strength lies in one another. Together we are strong.

In Brown faces, white spaces, a tale unfolds,
Where stories of resilience and strength are told.
A world of contrast, where colors collide,
A canvas of diversity, side by side.

In these once-white spaces, let justice flourish,
Embracing the richness that differences nourish
For Brown faces bring hues of vibrant grace,
Enchanting the spaces where they find their place.

Each face, a chapter, a narrative to share,
A tapestry of cultures, woven with care.
From every corner, a unique voice rings,
Enchanting the hearts as harmony sings.

In these once-white spaces, let prejudice cease,
As understanding and empathy increase.

For Brown faces hold wisdom and insight,
Illuminating paths with our radiant light.

Let bridges be built, connecting our souls,
Transcending boundaries, making us whole.
In the clasp of diversity's embrace,
We find strength, compassion, and boundless space.

So let us celebrate the beauty we see,
In Brown faces gracing all spaces with glee.
For when we connect, embracing our races,
World-changing love reigns in all of these places.

—Latasha Morrison

Afterword

They that shall be of thee shall build the old waste places: thou shalt raise up the foundations of many generations; and thou shalt be called, the repairer of the breach, the restorer of paths to dwell in. (Isaiah 58:12, KJV)

In the summer of my eighteenth year, a very handsome young man came to my parents' house to pick me up for a date. A very handsome young *white* man. As we backed out of the driveway, I noticed my grandmother, who lived with us at the time, watching from her bedroom window. I didn't think much of it then, since I was quite focused on my crush. However, when I returned home later that night, I was greeted by an unexpected sight: My grandmother was sitting on the edge of my bed, rocking back and forth, praying fervently.

"Nana?" I asked, reaching for her hand. Struggling against her arthritic knees, she stood up and stared intensely at my face, as if she needed to believe it was really me. Tears were streaming down her cheeks.

"Oh, thank you, Jesus!" she exclaimed. "Thank you, Jesus! Thank you, Jesus! Thank you—"

I interrupted her. "Nana, what's wrong?" I will never forget her answer.

"I saw you leave the house with that white boy. I was scared someone would see y'all and grab you up and lynch you." Then she walked out of my room, still giving praise for my safety.

I stood still for a very long time. It was a transformative moment. My view of history was forever changed.

FROM YEARS TO GENERATIONS

My parents made sure that I knew African American history, but until that night, the horrors of lynching in the Jim Crow South—and the American institution of slavery that birthed it—felt far away from my middle-class childhood in a largely white New Jersey suburb.

It wasn't.

I went on that date in 1992, but my grandmother's trauma had easily transported us to 1922. As I stood there reflecting on her pain, I recalled that we had wished Nana a happy eighty-fifth on her last birthday. I calculated her birth year: 1907.

I began assembling what I knew about American life in the early 1900s—and that's when it hit me: Harriet Tubman, the founder of the Underground Railroad, died in 1913. My grandmother was born in 1907. That night, for the first time, I realized that Harriet Tubman and Nana were alive *at the same time.* Harriet's story, and the story of every enslaved person she rescued, was not in the past. Their stories were all in my bedroom that night. The hundreds of years that converged in that moment represented just a few generations.

We equate history with the past. Something that is over. Something that is done with. But the proximity of history must be determined by the impact it's having on the present. Measuring history in years creates a false sense of distance. Because significant events have lasting consequences, history cannot truly be measured in years; *history must be measured in generations.*

THE SPIRITUAL SIGNIFICANCE OF GENERATIONAL WORK

The wisdom of Scripture affirms the power of using a generation as our unit of measurement. Throughout Scripture, history is measured by generations. From the creation of Adam to the birth of Christ, the story is told in generations. Until the resurrection of Christ, generations had the power to transmit curses. They still transmit blessings. And perhaps most powerfully, generations transmit stories.

There's one type of story I want us to all commit to writing and passing along: stories of praise. Psalm 145:3–4, 7 says,

Great is the LORD, and greatly to be praised; and his greatness is unsearchable.
One generation shall praise thy works to another, and shall declare thy mighty acts. . . .
They shall abundantly utter the memory of thy great goodness, and shall sing of thy righteousness. (KJV)

Generational praise should be both our inheritance and our legacy, so it's critical for us to recognize that generational trauma is the enemy of generational praise.

Generational trauma was exemplified in Nana's prayers in my room that night, but it's more than that. Generational trauma also manifests through the persistence of systemic racism and its consequences. But together, fueled by love, we can change the story that is being written. In fact, we have a mandate to do exactly that. Isaiah 58:12 says,

They that shall be of thee shall build the old waste places: thou shalt raise up the foundations of many generations; and thou shalt be called, the repairer of the breach, the restorer of paths to dwell in. (KJV)

So I say to you, dear reader: It's time to get to work! The work of generational repair and restoration is at hand. It belongs to us all, and in this book, Latasha Morrison has given us a road map for that work.

CHOOSE YOUR WORK

The legacy of generational trauma has been challenging the legacy of praise for long enough. In painstaking detail, through the lens of research and rooted in a heart full of love, Latasha has mapped ten areas laid waste by racism and systemic injustice:

- Education
- Healthcare
- The Justice System
- The Marketplace
- The Military
- Property Ownership
- Entertainment
- Sports
- The Church

I challenge you to choose. Which area most moves your heart? Find purpose there and begin doing your part. Today. You have been made *ready*. The course is *set*. Let's *go*.

—Dr. Anita Phillips, trauma therapist and
New York Times bestselling author
of *The Garden Within*

Acknowledgments

I am incredibly grateful for the support and encouragement I received throughout this journey of writing *Brown Faces, White Spaces*. It would not have been possible without the help and contribution of so many wonderful and inspiring individuals.

First and foremost, I want to express my deepest appreciation to my family and friends. Your unwavering belief in me and your continuous support kept me motivated during the challenging times. Thank you for being my pillar of strength and for understanding my countless hours spent immersed in writing. Thank you to all who shared your stories with grace. It has been an honor to be a steward of your words.

I would like to extend my heartfelt gratitude to my editor, Laura Barker, and amazing writing coach, Seth Haines, whose keen eye and insightful feedback transformed my manuscript into a polished piece of work. Your guidance and expertise were invaluable, and I am immensely grateful for your dedication to making this book the best it can be. Seth, your way with words brings hearts alive.

I am indebted to my literary agent, Mike Salisbury, for his belief in my vision and for tirelessly championing my book. Your guidance, negotiation skills, and unwavering support have been instrumental in bringing this book to fruition.

I am deeply thankful to the publishing team at WaterBrook for their trust and commitment to my book. Your professionalism and attention to detail have made this publishing journey a truly remarkable experience.

To the Fedd Agency: Thank you for dreaming with me and speaking words of life to my vision. I look forward to the next phase of the journey. And thank you for pulling up a chair to the uncomfortable tension—all for the glory of God.

My gratitude also goes out to my brilliant team of researchers and experts, who generously shared their knowledge and expertise. To my creative team, who spent the day with me dreaming of this book, your input carried me in every phase of this project. Your valuable insights enriched the content of my book and added depth to its message.

I am grateful to my Be the Bridge team and staff, who provided guidance and encouragement throughout this writing process. Your wisdom and advice have been invaluable, and I am honored to lead such an incredibly gifted community.

Lastly, I express my deep appreciation to all the readers who will embark on this literary journey with me. Your interest in racial literacy and support means the world to me, and I hope my book brings you healing, hope, inspiration, new perspectives, and, most of all, liberation.

To everyone who played a part, big or small, in the creation and publication of this book, thank you from the bottom of my heart. Your contributions have made this book a reality, and I am forever grateful for your presence in my life and your investment in every word of this book.

Notes

CHAPTER 1: OUR JOURNEY TOWARD TRUE EMANCIPATION

1. "Liberation Theology," JesuitResource.org, Xavier University, accessed March 20, 2023, www.xavier.edu/jesuitresource/jesuit-a-z/terms-l/liberation-theology.
2. Declaration of Independence, July 4, 1776, in "Declaration of Independence: A Transcription," National Archives, updated January 31, 2023, www.archives.gov/founding-docs/declaration-transcript.
3. Constitution of the United States, preamble, in "The Heritage Guide to the Constitution," Heritage Foundation, accessed May 20, 2023, www.heritage.org/constitution.

CHAPTER 2: LEARNING OUR LESSONS

1. Constitution of the United States, article 1, section 2.
2. Louisiana Railway Accommodations Act, Pub. L., 153–54, Stat. 111 (1890), in "Railroads and the Making of Modern America: A

Digital History Project," University of Nebraska–Lincoln, accessed May 17, 2023, https://railroads.unl.edu/documents/view_document.php?id=rail.gen.0060.

3. Henry Louis Gates, Jr. "'Plessy v. Ferguson': Who was Plessy?" PBS, accessed July 12, 2023, www.pbs.org/wnet/african-americans-many-rivers-to-cross/history/plessy-v-ferguson-who-was-plessy.

4. Plessy v. Ferguson, 163 U.S. 537, 541 (1896), https://supreme.justia.com/cases/federal/us/163/537.

5. *Encyclopaedia Britannica Online,* s.v. "Jim Crow Laws," by Melvin I. Urofsky, updated March 28, 2023, www.britannica.com/event/Jim-Crow-law#ref1225464.

6. *Encyclopaedia Britannica Online,* s.v. "Jim Crow Laws."

7. *Plessy,* 163 U.S. at 544.

8. *Plessy,* 163 U.S. at 551.

9. *Plessy,* 163 U.S. at 552, 559.

10. Terry Gross, "A 'Forgotten History' of How the U.S. Government Segregated America," NPR, May 3, 2017, www.npr.org/2017/05/03/526655831/a-forgotten-history-of-how-the-u-s-government-segregated-america.

11. Missouri ex rel. Gaines v. Canada, 305 U.S. 337 (1938), https://supreme.justia.com/cases/federal/us/305/337.

12. "1946: Mendez v. Westminster," in "A Latinx Resource Guide: Civil Rights Cases and Events in the United States," Library of Congress, accessed May 23, 2023, https://guides.loc.gov/latinx-civil-rights/mendez-v-westminster; "Mendez v. Westminster: The Mexican-American Fight for School Integration and Social Equality Pre-Brown v. Board of Education," Federal Bar Association (blog), June 16, 2021. See also the appeal case, Westminster School Dist. of Orange County v. Mendez, 161 F.2nd 774 (9th Cir. 1947), https://law.justia.com/cases/federal/appellate-courts/F2/161/774/1566460.

13. "Brown v. Board of Education," National Archives, last reviewed

June 3, 2021, www.archives.gov/education/lessons/brown-v-board #background.

14. Brown v. Board of Education of Topeka, 349 U.S. 294 (1955). This decision, given a year after the original *Brown* ruling of 1954, is often referred to as *Brown II*. See "Brown v. Board of Education (1954)," National Archives, last reviewed November 22, 2021, www.archives.gov/milestone-documents/brown-v-board-of -education.

15. "Civil Rights: The Little Rock School Integration Crisis," Dwight D. Eisenhower Presidential Library, Museum & Boyhood Home, ac- cessed May 23, 2023, www.eisenhowerlibrary.gov/research/online -documents/civil-rights-little-rock-school-integration-crisis.

16. Lonnie Bunch, "The Little Rock Nine," National Museum of Afri- can American History and Culture, Smithsonian, accessed May 23, 2023, https://nmaahc.si.edu/explore/stories/little-rock-nine.

17. "The Southern Manifesto of 1956," United States House of Repre- sentatives' Office of History, Art & Archives, accessed May 23, 2023, https://history.house.gov/Historical-Highlights/1951-2000/ The-Southern-Manifesto-of-1956.

18. 102 Cong. Rec. 4515–16 (1956), reprinted in "Southern Declara- tion on Integration (1956)," accessed March 21, 2023, https:// wwnorton.com/college/history/archive/resources/documents/ch33 _03.htm. See also "The 'Southern Manifesto,'" accessed May 23, 2023, https://content.csbs.utah.edu/~dlevin/federalism/southern _manifesto.html.

19. "Massive Resistance," Virginia Museum of History & Culture, accessed May 23, 2023, https://virginiahistory.org/learn/historical -book/chapter/massive-resistance.

20. Bob Vay, "Virginia Pupil Placement Board," Desegregation of Virginia Education (Dove), July 24, 2018, https://dove.gmu.edu/ index.php/2018/07/24/virginia-pupil-placement-board.

21. "The Closing of Prince Edward County's Schools," Virginia Museum of History & Culture, accessed May 23, 2023, https://

virginiahistory.org/learn/historical-book/chapter/closing-prince
-edward-countys-schools.

22. Griffin v. Bd. of Supervisors of Prince Edward, 322 F.2d (4th Cir.
1963), https://casetext.com/case/griffin-v-bd-of-supervisors-of
-prince-edward-2.

23. *Griffin v. School Board,* 377 U.S. 218 (1964), https://supreme.justia
.com/cases/federal/us/377/218.

24. Debra Michals, "Ruby Bridges," National Women's History
Museum, 2015, www.womenshistory.org/education-resources/
biographies/ruby-bridges.

25. Jimmie E. Gates, "What Is at Stake? The Cleveland Desegregation
Fight," *Clarion Ledger,* June 4, 2016, www.clarionledger.com/story/
news/local/2016/06/04/cleveland-mississippi-school-desegregation
-fight/85205994.

26. "QuickFacts: Cleveland City, Mississippi," United States Census
Bureau, July 1, 2022, www.census.gov/quickfacts/cleveland
citymississippi.

27. Sharon Lerner, "A School District That Was Never Desegregated,"
Atlantic, February 5, 2015, www.theatlantic.com/education/
archive/2015/02/a-school-district-that-was-never-desegregated/
385184.

28. Lerner, "School District."

29. Madeline Will, "'Brown v. Board' Decimated the Black Educator
Pipeline. A Scholar Explains How," *Education Week,* May 16, 2022,
www.edweek.org/teaching-learning/brown-v-board-decimated-the
-black-educator-pipeline-a-scholar-explains-how/2022/05.

30. Madeline Will, "65 Years After 'Brown v. Board,' Where Are All the
Black Educators?" *Education Week,* May 14, 2019, www.edweek.org/
policy-politics/65-years-after-brown-v-board-where-are-all-the
-black-educators/2019/05.

31. Will, "65 Years After 'Brown v. Board.'"

32. Will, "65 Years After 'Brown v. Board.'"

33. "Race and Ethnicity of Public School Teachers and Their

Students," National Center for Education Statistics, Data Point (Washington, D.C.: US Department of Education, September 2020), https://nces.ed.gov/pubs2020/2020103/index.asp.

34. Jerry Falwell, "Segregation or Integration: Which?" (Lynchburg, VA: Thomas Road Baptist Church, 1958), quoted in Max Blumenthal, "Agent of Intolerance," Nation, May 16, 2007, www.thenation.com/article/archive/agent-intolerance.

35. Jerry Falwell, *Strength for the Journey* (New York: Simon & Schuster, 1984), 294.

36. Edwin Rios, "US Schools Remain Highly Segregated by Race and Class, Analysis Shows," *Guardian* (US), July 15, 2022, www.theguardian.com/education/2022/jul/15/us-schools-segregated-race-class-analysis. Rios cites the United States Government Accountability Office, *"K–12 Education: Student Population Has Significantly Diversified, but Many Schools Remain Divided Along Racial, Ethnic, and Economic Lines,"* report to the chairman, Committee on Education and Labor, House of Representatives (Washington, D.C.: GAO, June 2022), www.gao.gov/products/gao-22-104737.

37. Rios, "Schools Remain Highly Segregated."

38. Madeline Will, "Study: Black Students More Likely to Graduate If They Have One Black Teacher," Education Week, April 6, 2017, www.edweek.org/leadership/study-black-students-more-likely-to-graduate-if-they-have-one-black-teacher/2017/04.

39. Rebecca Klein, "Black Students Are Less Likely to Get Suspended When They Have Black Teachers," HuffPost, November 1, 2016, www.huffpost.com/entry/black-students-suspension-study_n_581788e0e4b064e1b4b4070a.

40. Will, "65 Years After 'Brown v. Board.'"

41. Hope Allchin, "Hundreds of Schools Are Still Using Native Americans as Team Mascots," *FiveThirtyEight*, October 12, 2020, https://fivethirtyeight.com/features/hundreds-of-schools-are-still-using-native-americans-as-team-mascots.

42. Patrick Caleb Smith, "The Rebel Made Me Do It: Mascots, Race,

and the Lost Cause" (dissertation, University of Southern Mississippi, May 2019), 36, https://aquila.usm.edu/cgi/viewcontent.cgi
?article=2725&context=dissertations. Smith cites research from
Harold E. Gulley, "Southern Nationalism on the Landscape:
County Names in Former Confederate States," *Names: A Journal of
Onomastics* 38, no. 3 (September 1990), https://doi.org/10.1179/
nam.1990.38.3.231.

43. Smith, "Rebel Made Me," 36–37, citing Gulley, "Southern Nationalism."

44. Smith, "Rebel Made Me," 164.

45. Tiffany Cusaac-Smith, "US Students Are Becoming More Diverse.
So Why Does Segregation Persist?" *USA Today*, August 31, 2022,
www.usatoday.com/story/news/2022/08/31/racial-segregation
-school-students-integration/10339801002.

46. Luke Pruitt, "To a Town Divided: The History of the Southside
Rebel," Talk Business & Politics, July 23, 2015, https://talkbusiness
.net/2015/07/to-a-town-divided-the-history-of-the-southside
-rebel.

47. "About Our School," Northside High School (website), accessed
May 23, 2023, www.fortsmithschools.org/domain/223.

48. "History of Southside High School," Southside High School
(website), accessed May 23, 2023, www.fortsmithschools.org/
domain/211.

49. Pruitt, "To a Town Divided."

50. Dave Hughes, "Rebel Mascot, 'Dixie' Ousted by Fort Smith
School Board," *Arkansas Democrat-Gazette,* July 28, 2015, www
.arkansasonline.com/news/2015/jul/28/rebel-mascot-dixie-ousted
-fort-smith-school-board.

51. Aubry Killion, "Southside High Principal 'Blindsided' by Committee's Decision to Ban 'Dixie' and Mascot," 5News KFSM, June 24,
2015, www.5newsonline.com/article/news/local/outreach/back-to
-school/southside-high-principal-blindsided-by-committees

-decision-to-ban-dixie-and-mascot/527-cfd76394-f14a-460a-afb4
-39b4b78c2120.

52. Jacob Kauffman, "The Battle Over the Rebel at Fort Smith Schools
Winds Down," KUAR, May 30, 2016, www.ualrpublicradio.org/
2016-05-30/the-battle-over-the-rebel-at-fort-smith-schools-winds
-down.

53. Benny L. Gooden to Board of Education, Fort Smith, June 25,
2015, in "Regular School Board Meeting" (minutes of the Fort
Smith Board of Education, Fort Smith, AR, June 22, 2015), www
.fortsmithschools.org/cms/lib/AR02203514/Centricity/Domain/
137/minutesJUNE22and232015.pdf.

Chapter 3: An Inequitable Prescription

1. Christopher Klein, "Last Hired, First Fired: How the Great Depression Affected African Americans," History, updated August 31,
2018, www.history.com/news/last-hired-first-fired-how-the-great
-depression-affected-african-americans.

2. Gabriel R. Sanchez, Jillian Medeiros, and Kimberly R. Huyser,
"The Great Recession: Implications for Minority and Immigrant
Communities," *Recession Trends,* accessed May 24, 2023, https://
web.stanford.edu/group/recessiontrends-dev/cgi-bin/web/
resources/research-project/great-recession-implications-minority
-and-immigrant-communities.

3. Maritza Vasquez Reyes, "The Disproportional Impact of COVID-19
on African Americans," *Health and Human Rights Journal* 22, no. 2
(December 2020): 299–307, www.ncbi.nlm.nih.gov/pmc/articles/
PMC7762908.

4. Akilah Johnson and Dan Keating, "Whites Now More Likely to Die
from Covid Than Blacks: Why the Pandemic Shifted," *Washington
Post,* October 19, 2022, www.washingtonpost.com/health/2022/10/
19/covid-deaths-us-race.

5. Reyes, "Disproportional Impact of COVID-19."

6. "Kansas Population 2023," World Population Review, accessed May 24, 2023, https://worldpopulationreview.com/states/kansas -population.

7. Reyes, "Disproportional Impact of COVID-19."

8. Riis L. Williams, "Native American Deaths from COVID-19 Highest Among Racial Groups," Princeton School of Public and International Affairs, December 2, 2021, https://spia.princeton.edu/ news/native-american-deaths-covid-19-highest-among-racial -groups. Williams cites data from Katherine Leggat-Barr, Fumiya Uchikoshi, and Noreen Goldman, "COVID-19 Risk Factors and Mortality Among Native Americans," *Demographic Research* 45, no. 39 (November 2021): 1185–218, https://doi.org/10.4054/ DemRes.2021.45.39.

9. Williams, "Native American Deaths from COVID-19."

10. Amy Maxmen, "The Fight to Manufacture COVID Vaccines in Lower-Income Countries," *Nature* 597 (September 2021): 455–57, https://doi.org/10.1038/d41586-021-02383-z.

11. Monica Cronin, "Anarcha, Betsey, Lucy, and the Women Whose Names Were Not Recorded: The Legacy of J Marion Sims," *Anaesthesia and Intensive Care* 48, no. 3 (November 2020), https://doi .org/10.1177/0310057X20966606.

12. Cronin, "Anarcha, Betsey, Lucy."

13. Barron H. Lerner, "Scholars Argue Over Legacy of Surgeon Who Was Lionized, Then Vilified," *New York Times,* October 28, 2003, www.nytimes.com/2003/10/28/health/scholars-argue-over-legacy -of-surgeon-who-was-lionized-then-vilified.html.

14. W. Gill Wylie, *Memorial Sketch of the Life of J. Marion Sims, M. D.* (New York: New York Medical Journal, 1884; repr., New York: D. Appleton and Company, 1884), 6–7, https://archive.org/details/ 101310238.nlm.nih.gov/page/n7/mode/2up.

15. Cronin, "Anarcha, Betsey, Lucy."

16. Cronin, "Anarcha, Betsey, Lucy." Cronin quotes from James Marion Sims, *The Story of My Life* (New York: D. Appleton *and* Company, 1888), 227, www.google.com/books/edition/The_Story_of _My_Life/oya_9k2196UC?hl=en&gbpv=1&bsq=was%20so %20impacted%20in%20the%20pelvis.

17. Mari A. Schaefer, "The Controversial Legacy of Jefferson University-Educated 'Father of Gynecology,'" *The Philadelphia Inquirer,* August 30, 2017, www.inquirer.com/philly/health/the -controversial-legacy-of-a-thomas-jefferson-university-alum -marion-j-sims-20170830.html.

18. Cicely Harris and Andrew Lassalle, "Resolution Regarding Removal of James Marion Sims Statue from Central Park" (City of New York, Manhattan Community Board 10, New York, December 6, 2017), https://www1.nyc.gov/html/mancb10/downloads/pdf/ full_board_resolutions/2017/removal_of_james_marion_sims _statue_resolution.pdf.

19. Cronin, "Anarcha, Betsey, Lucy."

20. Sims, *Story of My Life,* 319–21.

21. Sims, *Story of My Life,* 236.

22. Deirdre Cooper Owens, *Medical Bondage: Race, Gender, and the Origins of American Gynecology* (Athens, Ga.: University of Georgia Press, 2017), 108.

23. Cooper Owens, *Medical Bondage,* 108.

24. DeNeen L. Brown, "A Surgeon from SC Experimented on Slave Women Without Anesthesia. Now His Statues Are Under Attack," *Herald,* March 30, 2023, www.heraldonline.com/latest-news/ article170155337.html.

25. Harris and Lassalle, "Resolution Regarding Removal."

26. Eric C. Schneider et al., *Mirror, Mirror 2021: Reflecting Poorly: Health Care in the U.S. Compared to Other High-Income Countries* (New York: Commonwealth Fund, August 2021), https://doi.org/ 10.26099/01dv-h208.

27. Robert Pearl, "Why Health Care Is Different If You're Black, Latino or Poor," *Forbes*, March 5, 2015, www.forbes.com/sites/robertpearl/2015/03/05/healthcare-black-latino-poor/?sh=798aa8f77869.

28. Pearl, "Health Care Is Different."

29. Khiara M. Bridges, "Implicit Bias and Racial Disparities in Health Care," *Human Rights Magazine* 43, no. 3, accessed September 14, 2023, www.americanbar.org/groups/crsj/publications/human_rights_magazine_home/the-state-of-healthcare-in-the-united-states/racial-disparities-in-health-care.

30. Latoya Hill, Nambi Ndugga, and Samantha Artiga, "Key Data on Health and Health Care by Race and Ethnicity," KFF, March 15, 2023, www.kff.org/report-section/key-facts-on-health-and-health-care-by-race-and-ethnicity-health-status-outcomes-and-behaviors.

31. "Infant Mortality," Centers for Disease Control and Prevention, updated September 13, 2023, www.cdc.gov/reproductivehealth/maternalinfanthealth/infantmortality.htm.

32. "Black Women and Breast Cancer: Why Disparities Persist and How to End Them," Breast Cancer Research Foundation, January 25, 2023, www.bcrf.org/blog/black-women-and-breast-cancer-why-disparities-persist-and-how-end-them.

33. Jonathan Zimmerman, "The GOP Is Reviving the Old History of Blaming Outsiders for Disease," *Washington Post*, August 15, 2021, www.washingtonpost.com/outlook/2021/08/15/gop-is-reviving-old-history-blaming-outsiders-disease.

34. Kate Raphael, "Racial Bias in Medicine," Harvard Global Health Institute, February 5, 2020, https://globalhealth.harvard.edu/racial-bias-in-medicine.

35. Andrew DePietro, "Poorest Counties in Every U.S. State 2021," *Forbes*, September 1, 2021, www.forbes.com/sites/andrewdepietro/2021/09/01/poorest-counties-in-every-us-state-2021/?sh=6502f187312a.

36. "QuickFacts: Lumberton City, North Carolina," United States

Census Bureau, July 1, 2022, www.census.gov/quickfacts/
lumbertoncitynorthcarolina.

37. "QuickFacts: Robeson County, North Carolina," United States
Census Bureau, July 1, 2022, www.census.gov/quickfacts/
robesoncountynorthcarolina.

38. Lizzie Presser, "The Black American Amputation Epidemic," Pro-
Publica, May 19, 2020, https://features.propublica.org/diabetes
-amputations/black-american-amputation-epidemic.

39. Presser, "Black American Amputation Epidemic."

40. Olamide Alabi et al., "Addressing Amputation Disparities," *Endo-
vascular Today*, May 2021, https://evtoday.com/articles/2021-may/
addressing-amputation-disparities.

41. Presser, "Black American Amputation Epidemic."

42. Presser, "Black American Amputation Epidemic."

43. Presser, "Black American Amputation Epidemic."

44. Lizzie Presser, "This Doctor Is Saving Limbs in Black Patients with
Diabetes," *The Healthy, Reader's Digest,* October 11, 2022, www
.thehealthy.com/diabetes/black-people-diabetes.

45. "Status of State Medicaid Expansion Decisions: Interactive Map,"
KFF, July 27, 2023, www.kff.org/medicaid/issue-brief/status-of
-state-medicaid-expansion-decisions-interactive-map.

Chapter 4: Liberty and Justice for Some?

1. Lesley Kennedy, "How the Immigration Act of 1965 Changed the
Face of America," History, August 12, 2019, www.history.com/
news/immigration-act-1965-changes.

2. Brenda Goodman, "Police Kill Woman, 92, in Shootout at Her
Home," *New York Times,* November 23, 2006, www.nytimes.com/
2006/11/23/us/23atlanta.html; Associated Press, "2 Plead Guilty in
Atlanta Police Shooting Death," NBC News, April 26, 2007, www
.nbcnews.com/id/wbna18328267.

3. Gracie Bonds Staples, "Remembering Kathryn Johnston 10 Years

After Deadly Atlanta Police Raid," *Atlanta Journal-Constitution*, October 27, 2016, www.ajc.com/news/crime—law/remembering -kathryn-johnston-years-after-deadly-atlanta-police-raid/ pXPW8i7zQakltq76YXc27N.

4. "Atlanta Policemen Imprisoned for Killing Woman, 92," Reuters, February 24, 2009, www.reuters.com/article/us-usa-police-killing/ atlanta-policemen-imprisoned-for-killing-woman-92 -idUSTRE51N6PP20090224.

5. Shaila Dewan and Brenda Goodman, "Prosecutors Say Corruption in Atlanta Police Dept. Is Widespread," *New York Times*, April 27, 2007, www.nytimes.com/2007/04/27/us/27atlanta.html.

6. "Cop Convicted of Lying About Shootout," CBS News, May 20, 2008, www.cbsnews.com/news/cop-convicted-of-lying-about -shootout.

7. Office of Public Affairs, "Three Former Atlanta Police Officers Sentenced to Prison in Fatal Shooting of Elderly Atlanta Woman," United States Department of Justice, February 24, 2009, www .justice.gov/opa/pr/three-former-atlanta-police-officers-sentenced -prison-fatal-shooting-elderly-atlanta-woman.

8. Ernie Suggs, "City to Pay Slain Woman's Family $4.9 Million," *Atlanta Journal-Constitution*, August 16, 2010, www.ajc.com/news/ local/city-pay-slain-woman-family-million/ GWqsgDArzmOhvpb7iPY6FI.

9. Matt Bruce, "Study: Blacks in One Georgia County Were 97 Times More Likely Than Whites to Be Arrested on Marijuana Charges," Atlanta Black Star, April 1, 2021, https://atlantablackstar.com/ 2021/04/01/study-blacks-in-one-georgia-county-were-97 -times-more-likely-than-whites-to-be-arrested-on-marijuana -charges.

10. Magnus Lofstrom et al., *Racial Disparities in Law Enforcement Stops* (San Francisco, Calif.: Public Policy Institute of California, October 2021), 3, www.ppic.org/publication/racial-disparities-in-law -enforcement-stops.

11. Olivia B. Waxman, "How the U.S. Got Its Police Force," *Time*, May 18, 2017, https://time.com/4779112/police-history-origins.

12. Waxman, "U.S. Got Its Police Force."

13. U.S. Const. amend. XIII, § 1, quoted in "13th Amendment to the U.S. Constitution: Abolition of Slavery (1865)," National Archives, updated May 10, 2022, www.archives.gov/milestone-documents/13th-amendment.

14. "Convict Leasing," Equal Justice Initiative, November 1, 2013, https://eji.org/news/history-racial-injustice-convict-leasing; Kathy Roberts Forde, "Peonage Explained: The System of Convict Labor Was Slavery by Another Name," *Milwaukee Independent,* July 3, 2020, www.milwaukeeindependent.com/syndicated/peonage-explained-system-convict-labor-slavery-another-name.

15. Douglas A. Blackmon, *Slavery by Another Name: The Re-Enslavement of Black Americans from the Civil War to World War II* (New York: Doubleday, 2008), 8.

16. "Enabling an Era of Lynching: Retreat, Resistance, and Refuge," *Lynching in America: Confronting the Legacy of Racial Terror*, 3rd ed. (Montgomery, Ala.: Equal Justice Initiative, 2017), https://lynchinginamerica.eji.org/report.

17. Avis Thomas-Lester, "A History Scarred by Lynchings," *Washington Post,* July 7, 2005, www.washingtonpost.com/archive/local/2005/07/07/a-history-scarred-by-lynchings/271bbec3-21f3-40dd-8650-31ffbd59d7cb.

18. Margot Adler, "Before Rosa Parks, There Was Claudette Colvin," *Up First,* NPR, March 15, 2009, www.npr.org/2009/03/15/101719889/before-rosa-parks-there-was-claudette-colvin.

19. "Montgomery Bus Boycott," History, updated January 10, 2023, www.history.com/topics/black-history/montgomery-bus-boycott.

20. "Freedom Riders," History, updated January 20, 2022, www.history.com/topics/black-history/freedom-rides.

21. Martin Luther King, Jr., "I Have a Dream," (speech, March on Washington, Washington, D.C., August 28, 1963), transcript ac-

cessed in "Read Martin Luther King Jr.'s 'I Have a Dream' Speech in Its Entirety," *NPR*, updated January 16, 2023, www.npr.org/2010/01/18/122701268/i-have-a-dream-speech-in-its-entirety.

22. "Baptist Street Church Bombing," Federal Bureau of Investigation, accessed May 26, 2023, www.fbi.gov/history/famous-cases/baptist-street-church-bombing.

23. Mark D. McCoy (@m_d_mccoy), Twitter, June 1, 2020, 12:07 a.m., https://twitter.com/m_d_mccoy/status/1267503074018578438?lang=en.

24. FBI Counterterrorism Division, (U) *White Supremacist Infiltration of Law Enforcement,* intelligence assessment (Washington, D.C.: Federal Bureau of Investigation, October 17, 2006), 4, www.justsecurity.org/wp-content/uploads/2021/06/Jan-6-Clearinghouse-FBI-Intelligence-Assessment-White-Supremacist-Infiltration-of-Law-Enforcement-Oct-17-2006-UNREDACTED.pdf.

25. FBI Counterterrorism Division, *White Supremacist Infiltration,* 5.

26. Kenya Downs, "FBI Warned of White Supremacists in Law Enforcement 10 Years Ago. Has Anything Changed?" *PBS* NewsHour, October 21, 2016, www.pbs.org/newshour/nation/fbi-white-supremacists-in-law-enforcement.

27. Downs, "FBI Warned of White Supremacists."

28. Downs, "FBI Warned of White Supremacists."

29. Andrew Knapp, "Police Officer Fired for Confederate Flag Underwear Settles Lawsuit Against City for $55,000," *Post and Courier,* October 27, 2017, www.postandcourier.com/news/police-officer-fired-for-confederate-flag-underwear-settles-lawsuit-against-city-for-55-000/article_03a2cb4c-bb43-11e7-b1e6-0f236c2bd1e2.html.

30. Shawn Maclauchlan, "Charleston, SC Officer Fired after Posting Picture of Self in Confederate Underwear," *NBC12,* June 26, 2015, www.nbc12.com/story/29415336/charleston-sc-officer-fired-after-posting-picture-of-self-in-confederate-underwear.

31. Tim Elfrink, "'We Are Just Gonna Go Out and Start Slaughtering Them': Three Cops Fired After Racist Talk of Killing Black Resi-

dents," *Washington Post,* June 25, 2020, www.washingtonpost.com/nation/2020/06/25/wilmington-racist-police-recording.

32. Juliana Kim, Emma Bowman, "After a Police Officer Sent a Racist Text, a Town Dissolved Its Police Department," NPR, August 8, 2022, www.npr.org/2022/08/07/1116221784/vincent-alabama-racist-text-police.

33. National Association for the Advancement of Colored People, "Two Public Appointees," *Crisis,* March 1917, 231, https://books.google.com/books?id=BloEAAAAMBAJ.

34. Erika Bryan, "Georgia Ann Hill Robinson (1879–1961)," Black-Past, March 19, 2016, www.blackpast.org/african-american-history/robinson-georgia-ann-hill-1879-1961; Cecilia Rasmussen, "Policewoman's Battle to Serve and Protect," *Los Angeles Times,* June 19, 1997, www.latimes.com/archives/la-xpm-1997-06-09-me-1608-story.html.

35. Bryan, "Georgia Ann Hill Robinson."

36. "Georgia Ann Robinson, a Pioneer African American Police Officer," Los Angeles Almanac, accessed May 27, 2023, www.laalmanac.com/crime/cr73c.php.

37. "Georgia Ann Robinson," National Law Enforcement Officers Memorial Fund, https://nleomf.org/georgia-ann-robinson.

38. *NBC Nightly News,* "In Plain Sight: Camden, America's Poorest City, Fights Crime, Poverty," hosted by Brian Williams, produced by Soshana Guy, edited by Justin Cece, aired March 8, 2013, on NBC News, 2:07, www.nbcnews.com/video/camden-americas-poorest-city-fights-crime-poverty-21203523820.

39. Katherine Landergan, "The City That Really Did Abolish the Police," *Politico,* June 12, 2020, www.politico.com/news/magazine/2020/06/12/camden-policing-reforms-313750.

40. Landergan, "City That Really Did."

41. "Unity Policing Model," Camden County Police Department, November 30, 2021, https://camdencountypd.org/unity-policing-model.

42. "Camden Crediting Community Policing Behind City's Lowest Crime Rate in Nearly 50 Years," CBS News Philadelphia, June 10, 2021, www.cbsnews.com/philadelphia/news/camden-county-police -department-community-policing.

43. Camden County Police Department, "Our Youth," https:// camdencountypd.org/resource/youth.

44. Noah Zucker, "Camden Cops Carry Out Community Policing Through Basketball," Tap Into Camden, July 31, 2021, www .tapinto.net/towns/camden/sections/police-and-fire/articles/ camden-cops-carry-out-community-policing-through-basketball.

45. WBFF Staff, Dan Lampariello, "In Camden, N.J., Crime Plum- meted After Police Was 'Disbanded,'" Fox 45 News, June 15, 2020, https://foxbaltimore.com/news/local/a-nj-citys-police-reform -methods-could-be-a-model-for-cities-like-baltimore.

46. Douglas Clark, "Rep. Norcross Touts Community Policing Funding Allocation," *Homeland Preparedness News,* November 11, 2022, https://homelandprepnews.com/stories/79057-rep-norcross-touts -community-policing-funding-allocation.

47. Troy McDuffie, conversation with the author, 2022.

48. Shawn Henderson, conversation with the author, 2022.

CHAPTER 5: THE BLACK MARKET

1. Brené Brown, *Braving the Wilderness: The Quest for True Belonging and the Courage to Stand Alone* (New York: Random House, 2017), 6–7.

2. Sam Roberts, "New Life in U.S. No Longer Means New Name," *New York Times,* August 25, 2010, www.nytimes.com/2010/08/26/ nyregion/26names.html.

3. Kirsten Fermaglich, "Why Are Some Americans Changing Their Names?" *MSUToday,* November 19, 2018, https://msutoday.msu .edu/news/2018/why-are-some-americans-changing-their-names.

4. Marianne Bertrand and Sendhil Mullainathan, "Are Emily and

Greg More Employable Than Lakisha and Jamal? A Field Experiment on Labor Market Discrimination," *American Economic Review* 94, no. 4 (September 2004): 991–1013, https://doi.org/10.1257/0002828042002561.

5. Patrick Kline, Evan K. Rose, and Christopher R. Walters, "Systemic Discrimination Among Large U.S. Employers," *Quarterly Journal of Economics* 137, no. 4 (November 2022): 1963–2036, https://doi.org/10.1093/qje/qjac024.

6. Payne Lubbers, "Job Applicants With 'Black Names' Still Less Likely to Get Interviews," *Bloomberg,* July 29, 2021, www.bloomberg.com/news/articles/2021-07-29/job-applicants-with-black-names-still-less-likely-to-get-the-interview.

7. Dina Gerdeman, "Minorities Who 'Whiten' Job Resumes Get More Interviews," Harvard Business School, May 17, 2017, https://hbswk.hbs.edu/item/minorities-who-whiten-job-resumes-get-more-interviews.

8. William Edward Burghardt Du Bois, *The Souls of Black Folk: Essays and Sketches,* 5th ed. (Chicago: A. C. McClurg, 1904), 3–4, www.google.com/books/edition/The_Souls_of_Black_Folk/JPv4-U5q5BEC?hl=en&gbpv=0.

9. "About," CROWN Act, accessed May 28, 2023, www.thecrownact.com/about.

10. JOY Collective, *The CROWN Research Study,* Dove research (London: Unilever PLC/Unilever N.V., 2019), 4–5, https://static1.squarespace.com/static/5edc69fd622c36173f56651f/t/5edeaa2fe5ddef345e087361/1591650865168/Dove_research_brochure2020_FINAL3.pdf.

11. H.R. 2116: Creating a Respectful and Open World for Natural Hair Act of 2022, 117th Cong. (2022), H.R. Rep. No. 117–252 (2021), www.congress.gov/bill/117th-congress/house-bill/2116/text.

12. "About," CROWN Act.

13. Margot Roosevelt and Russ Mitchell, "Black Tesla Employees Describe a Culture of Racism: 'I Was at My Breaking Point,'" *Los An-*

geles Times, March 25, 2022, www.latimes.com/business/story/2022 -03-25/black-tesla-employees-fremont-plant-racism-california -lawsuit.

14. Roosevelt and Mitchell, "Black Tesla Employees."

15. Roosevelt and Mitchell, "Black Tesla Employees."

16. Kari Paul, "Black Workers Accused Tesla of Racism for Years. Now California Is Stepping In," *Guardian* (US), February 19, 2022, www.theguardian.com/technology/2022/feb/18/tesla-california -racial-harassment-discrimination-lawsuit. Paul quotes from *Department of Fair Employment and Housing v. Tesla, Inc.: Civil Rights Complaint for Injunctive and Monetary Relief and Damages,* Superior Court of California County of Alameda (2002) (demand for jury trial filed by Siri Thanasombat, attorney for the DFEH), 12, https://calcivilrights.ca.gov/wp-content/uploads/sites/32/2022/02/ DFEH-vs-Tesla.pdf.

17. Joe Hernandez, "Tesla Must Pay $137 Million to a Black Employee Who Sued for Racial Discrimination," NPR, October 5, 2021, www .npr.org/2021/10/05/1043336212/tesla-racial-discrimination -lawsuit.

18. Jonathan Stempel and Daniel Wiessner, "Judge Finds Tesla Liable to Black Former Worker Who Alleged Bias, but Slashes Payout," Reuters, April 13, 2022, www.reuters.com/technology/us-judge -cuts-verdict-tesla-race-bias-case-15-mln-137-mln-2022-04-14; Rina Torchinsky, "Judge Cuts the Payout in a Black Former Tesla Contractor's Racial Discrimination Suit," April 14, 2022, NPR, www.npr.org/2022/04/14/1092804493/telsa-racial-discrimination -lawsuit-15-million.

19. Bernadette Giacomazzo, "The Fortune 500 List Has a 'Record Number' of Black CEOs—But There's Still Only 6 of Them," *AfroTech,* May 30, 2022, https://afrotech.com/fortune-500-black -ceos.

20. Daniel Kurt, "Corporate Leadership by Race," *Investopedia,* December 19, 2022, www.investopedia.com/corporate-leadership-by-race

-5114494. Kurt cites data from Crist|Kolder Associates, *Volatility Report 2021*, 38, https://static1.squarespace.com/static/62164a05607c3e5978f251ec/t/621f54d5be12b2210476bf79/1646220507917/volatility-report-2021-americas-leading-companies.pdf.

21. Rep. Joyce Beatty, "Statistics Don't Lie: Corporate America Lacks Minorities, Women," *The Hill*, October 29, 2018, https://thehill.com/blogs/congress-blog/politics/467809-a-wake-up-call-for-corporate-america-statistics-dont-lie.

22. Bryan Hancock et al., "Race in the Workplace: The Black Experience in the US Private Sector," McKinsey & Company, February 21, 2021, www.mckinsey.com/featured-insights/diversity-and-inclusion/race-in-the-workplace-the-black-experience-in-the-us-private-sector.

23. "EEOC Releases Fiscal Year 2020 Enforcement and Litigation Data," U.S. Equal Employment Opportunity Commission, February 26, 2021, www.eeoc.gov/newsroom/eeoc-releases-fiscal-year-2020-enforcement-and-litigation-data.

24. Rachel Siegel, "'They Can't Be Here for Us': Black Men Arrested at Starbucks Tell Their Story for the First Time," *Washington Post*, April 19, 2018, www.washingtonpost.com/news/business/wp/2018/04/19/they-cant-be-here-for-us-black-men-arrested-at-starbucks-tell-their-story-for-the-first-time.

25. Jacey Fortin, "2 Black Men Settle with Starbucks and Philadelphia over Arrest," *New York Times*, May 2, 2018, www.nytimes.com/2018/05/02/us/starbucks-arrest-philadelphia-settlement.html.

26. Claire Sasko, "Starbucks Will Close All 8,000 U.S. Stores for a Day of Racial-Bias Training," *Philadelphia*, April 17, 2018, www.phillymag.com/news/2018/04/17/starbucks-racial-bias-training.

27. Clementine Fletcher, "Starbucks' Training Shutdown Could Cost It Just $16.7 Million," Bloomberg, April 17, 2018, www.bloomberg.com/news/articles/2018-04-17/starbucks-training-shutdown-could-cost-them-just-16-7-million#xj4y7vzkg.

28. Sasko, "Starbucks Will Close."

29. "'The Story of Access' Explores the History of People of Color in Public Places," Starbucks, February 4, 2019, https://stories .starbucks.com/stories/2019/the-story-of-access.

30. "The Story of Access: Stanley Nelson Film for Starbucks," video shared by FirelightMediaNYC, June 5, 2018, on YouTube, 7:07, www.youtube.com/watch?v=lghpTEp_VpI&ab_channel= FirelightMediaNYC.

31. Marco Quiroz-Gutierrez, "The Top 20 Fortune 500 Companies on Diversity and Inclusion," *Fortune,* June 2, 2021, https://fortune .com/2021/06/02/fortune-500-companies-diversity-inclusion -numbers-refinitiv-measure-up.

32. Marguerite Ward, "Microsoft Tops the List of Most Transparent Companies for Diversity Data. Here's How Far the Top 5 Have Come—and How They Can Still Improve," Insider, June 7, 2021, www.businessinsider.com/top-fortune-500-companies-addressing -diversity-and-inclusion-2021-6.

33. Ward, "Microsoft Tops the List of Most Transparent Companies for Diversity Data."

34. "The Story of Access: Stanley Nelson Film for Starbucks."

CHAPTER 6: THE CODE OF SILENCE

1. Executive Order No. 9981 (1948), quoted in "Executive Order 9981: Desegregation of the Armed Forces (1948)," National Archives, updated February 8, 2022, www.archives.gov/milestone -documents/executive-order-9981.

2. Erica Thompson, "Serving Without 'Equal Opportunity': Vietnam Veterans Faced Racism at Home and Abroad," *Columbus Dispatch,* updated December 9, 2020, www.dispatch.com/in-depth/news/ 2020/12/03/black-vietnam-veterans-systemic-racism-military/ 3627846001.

3. Richard A. Kulka et al., *Contractual Report of Findings from the National Vietnam Veterans Readjustment Study,* vol. 1 (Research Triangle Park, N.C.: Research Triangle Institute, 1988), 3, www.ptsd.va.gov/professional/articles/article-pdf/nvvrs_vol1.pdf.

4. Andrew R. Chow and Josiah Bates, "As *Da 5 Bloods* Hits Netflix, Black Vietnam Veterans Recall the Real Injustices They Faced During and After the War," *Time,* June 12, 2020, https://time.com/5852476/da-5-bloods-black-vietnam-veterans.

5. James M. Fendrich, "The Returning Black Vietnam-Era Veteran," *Social Science Review* 46, no. 1 (March 1972): 60–75, www.jstor.org/stable/30021869.

6. Danielle DeSimone, "A History of Military Service: Native Americans in the U.S. Military Yesterday and Today" *USO,* November 8, 2021, www.uso.org/stories/2914-a-history-of-military-service-native-americans-in-the-u-s-military-yesterday-and-today.

7. Elizabeth M. Collins, "Black Soldiers in the Revolutionary War," U.S. Army, March 4, 2013, www.army.mil/article/97705/black_soldiers_in_the_revolutionary_war.

8. Farrell Evans, "America's First Black Regiment Gained Their Freedom by Fighting Against the British," History, February 3, 2021, www.history.com/news/first-black-regiment-american-revolution-first-rhode-island.

9. Evans, "America's First Black Regiment."

10. Elliot Partin, "1st Rhode Island Regiment," BlackPast, November 17, 2010, www.blackpast.org/african-american-history/first-rhode-island-regiment.

11. Slave Enlistment Act (1778), transcribed in "Act Creating the 1st Rhode Island Regiment, Also Known as the 'Black Regiment,' 1778," Rhode Island State Archives, accessed May 29, 2023, https://docs.sos.ri.gov/documents/civicsandeducation/teacherresources/Black-Regiment.pdf.

12. Cameron Boutin, "The 1st Rhode Island Regiment and Revolution-

ary America's Lost Opportunity," *Journal of the American Revolution, January 17, 2018,* https://allthingsliberty.com/2018/01/1st-rhode-island-regiment-revolutionary-americas-lost-opportunity.

13. Catherine Clinton, "The Legacy of Harriet Tubman: Freedom Fighter and Spy," HistoryNet, December 14, 2016, www.historynet.com/the-legacy-of-harriet-tubman-freedom-fighter-and-spy.

14. Helen Leichner, "Combahee River Raid (June 2, 1863)," BlackPast, December 21, 2012, www.blackpast.org/african-american-history/combahee-river-raid-june-2-1863.

15. Clinton, "Legacy of Harriet Tubman."

16. Erick Trickey, "One Hundred Years Ago, the Harlem Hellfighters Bravely Led the U.S. into WWI," *Smithsonian,* May 14, 2018, www.smithsonianmag.com/history/one-hundred-years-ago-harlem-hellfighters-bravely-led-us-wwi-180968977.

17. Michael Hancock, "'We Remember Our Heroes': Henry Johnson," Rediscovering Black History, National Archives, April 16, 2020, https://rediscovering-black-history.blogs.archives.gov/2020/04/16/we-remember-our-heroes-henry-johnson.

18. Gilbert King, "Remembering Henry Johnson, the Soldier Called 'Black Death,'" *Smithsonian,* October 25, 2011, www.smithsonianmag.com/history/remembering-henry-johnson-the-soldier-called-black-death-117386701.

19. Phil Reyburn, "WWI Unit Became Known as 'the Fighting Black Devils,'" Historical Society of Quincy and Adams County, December 3, 2017, www.hsqac.org/wwi-unit-became-known-as-the-fighting-black-devils.

20. Edwin Schupman, "Code Talking: Intelligence and Bravery," chap. 4 in *Native Words, Native Warriors* (Washington, D.C.: National Museum of the American Indian, 2020), https://americanindian.si.edu/nk360/code-talkers/code-talking.

21. Schupman, "Native Languages: Living the Culture," chap. 2 in *Native Words, Native Warriors,* https://americanindian.si.edu/nk360/code-talkers/native-languages.

22. Schupman, "Native Languages."

23. Ruth Quinn, "Charles Chibitty: Comanche Code-Talker," U.S. Army, November 1, 2012, www.army.mil/article/90294/charles _chibitty_comanche_code_talker.

24. Schupman, "Code Talking."

25. Quinn, "Charles Chibitty."

26. "Charles Chibitty," Oklahoma History Center, accessed May 29, 2023, www.okhistory.org/historycenter/militaryhof/inductee.php ?id=122.

27. Women of the 6888th Central Postal Directory Battalion (website), accessed May 29, 2023, www.womenofthe6888th.org.

28. Anthony Eley, "Charity Adams Earley," National Museum of the United States Army, accessed May 29, 2023, www.thenmusa.org/ biographies/charity-adams-earley.

29. Charity Adams Earley, *One Woman's Army: A Black Officer Remembers the WAC* (College Station, Tex.: Texas A&M University Press, 1989), 126.

30. Kathleen Fargey, "6888th Central Postal Directory Battalion," Women of the 6888th, February 14, 2014, www .womenofthe6888th.org/the-6888th.

31. Fargey, "Postal Directory Battalion."

32. Christina Brown Fisher, "The Black Female Battalion That Stood Up to a White Male Army," *New York Times*, updated September 2, 2020, www.nytimes.com/2020/06/17/magazine/6888th-battalion -charity-adams.html.

33. Faith Karimi, "She Knew Little About Her Mother's Military Service in Europe During World War II. Then She Did a Google Search and Got a Surprise," CNN, February 23, 2023, www.cnn .com/2023/02/23/us/6888th-battalion-world-war-2-cec/index.html; Wikipedia, s.v. "6888th Central Postal Directory Battalion," updated May 26, 2023, https://en.wikipedia.org/wiki/6888th_Central _Postal_Directory_Battalion.

34. Erin Blakemore, "How the GI Bill's Promise Was Denied to a Mil-

lion Black WWII Veterans," *History,* updated June 21, 2023, www
.history.com/news/gi-bill-black-wwii-veterans-benefits.

35. Walt Napier, "A Short History of Integration in the US Armed
Forces," United States Air Force, July 1, 2021, www.af.mil/News/
Commentaries/Display/Article/2676311/a-short-history-of
-integration-in-the-us-armed-forces. Napier quotes Exec. Order
No. 9981 (1948).

36. Napier, "Short History of Integration."

37. David Martin, "Race in the Ranks: Investigating Racial Bias in the
U.S. Military," *60 Minutes, CBS News,* August 22, 2021, www
.cbsnews.com/news/us-military-racism-60-minutes-2021-08-22.

38. Major Daniel Walker, "An F-22 Pilot on Why He Felt Discriminated
Against in the Air Force," interview by David Martin, in *60 Minutes,*
video shared March 21, 2021, on YouTube, www.youtube.com/
watch?v=b7wEYTa2ACU.

39. Walker, "F-22 Pilot."

40. Samantha Daniel et al., *2017 Workplace and Equal Opportunity Survey of Active Duty Members,* Department of Defense executive report (Alexandria, Va.: Office of People Analytics, August 2019),
14, https://taskandpurpose.com/uploads/2021/01/27/2017
-Workplace-and-Equal-Opportunity-Survey-Report.pdf.

41. Daniel et al., *Workplace and Equal Opportunity Survey,* 20.

42. Daniel et al., *Workplace and Equal Opportunity Survey,* 16.

43. Kat Stafford et al., "Deep-Rooted Racism, Discrimination Perme-
ate US Military," *AP News,* May 27, 2021, https://apnews.com/
article/us-military-racism-discrimination
-4e840e0acc7ef07fd635a312d9375413.

44. Martin, "Race in the Ranks."

45. Lolita C. Baldor, "For the First Time, Army Bases Would Be
Named After Black Soldiers and Women," *Greensboro News &
Record,* May 24, 2022, https://greensboro.com/news/state-and
-regional/for-the-first-time-army-bases-would-be-named-after
-black-soldiers-and-women/article_98005572-dba8-11ec-8883

-eb54271c8d97.html; W. J. Hennigan, "At Last, the U.S. Military Won't Have Bases Named After Confederates," *Time,* May 24, 2022, https://time.com/6180832/military-bases-remove -confederate-names-history.

46. "Tuskegee Airmen Congressional Gold Medal Ceremony," White House, accessed May 29, 2023, https://georgewbush-whitehouse .archives.gov/infocus/veterans/tuskegee/04.html.

47. Megan Brown, "Be the Bridge: How We Can Move Forward To- gether Toward Racial Healing," accessed May 29, 2023, www .militaryspouse.com/military-life/be-the-bridge-racial-healing.

CHAPTER 7: LAND OF BROKEN PROMISES

1. Don't Mess with Texas (website), accessed June 7, 2023, www .dontmesswithtexas.org.

2. Kate Whitehurst, "Explore Texas by Historical Eras: Spanish Colo- nial," Texas Our Texas, accessed May 29, 2023, https:// texasourtexas.texaspbs.org/the-eras-of-texas/spanish-colonial.

3. *Encyclopaedia Britannica Online,* s.v. "San Antonio," updated April 7, 2023, www.britannica.com/place/San-Antonio-Texas; Mary Ann Noonan Guerra, *The San Antonio River* (San Antonio: The Alamo Press, 1987), excerpted in "The First Civil Settlement in Texas—Journal of San Antonio," University of the Incarnate World, accessed June 7, 2023, www.uiw.edu/sanantonio/ FirstCivilSettlementinTexas.html.

4. Harriett Denise Joseph and Donald E. Chipman, "Spanish Texas," *Handbook of Texas,* Texas State Historical Association, February 1, 1996, updated May 4, 2022, www.tshaonline.org/handbook/ entries/spanish-texas.

5. David B. Gracy, "Austin, Moses (1761–1821)," *Handbook of Texas,* Texas State Historical Association, 1952, updated November 20, 2019, www.tshaonline.org/handbook/entries/austin-moses.

6. Christopher Long, "Old Three Hundred," *Handbook of Texas,* Texas

State Historical Association, 1952, updated April 24, 2019, www
.tshaonline.org/handbook/entries/old-three-hundred.

7. *Encyclopaedia Britannica Online,* s.v. "Stephen Austin," updated
    June 6, 2023, www.britannica.com/biography/Stephen-Austin.

8. Long, "Old Three Hundred."

9. "Decree Abolishing Slavery in Mexico in 1829," Newton Gresham
    Library, Sam Houston State University, accessed May 29, 2023,
    https://digital.library.shsu.edu/digital/collection/p243coll3/id/
    2243.

10. "Colonial Capital of Texas," Texas Historical Commission, ac-
    cessed May 29, 2023, www.thc.texas.gov/historic-sites/san-felipe
    -de-austin-state-historic-site/history/colonial-capital-texas.

11. "Texas Declares Independence," History, updated March 1, 2021,
    www.history.com/this-day-in-history/texas-declares-independence.

12. "The Rise and Fall of the Comanche 'Empire,'" *Fresh Air,* NPR,
    May 20, 2011, www.npr.org/2011/05/20/136438816/the-rise-and
    -fall-of-the-comanche-empire; "Cherokee War," *Handbook of Texas,*
    Texas State Historical Association, 1952, updated October 19,
    2020, www.tshaonline.org/handbook/entries/cherokee-war.

13. Becky Little, "Why Mexican Americans Say 'The Border Crossed
    Us,'" History, updated May 31, 2023, www.history.com/news/texas
    -mexico-border-history-laws.

14. "Texas Enters the Union," History, updated December 21, 2020,
    www.history.com/this-day-in-history/texas-enters-the-union.

15. Carmen Herrera Lawrence, "*Los Diablos Tejanos*: An Honest Look
    at the Texas Rangers," *Common Reader,* January 31, 2022, https://
    commonreader.wustl.edu/c/los-diablos-tejanos-an-honest-look-at
    -the-texas-rangers.

16. Little, "'The Border Crossed Us.'"

17. Roberto R. Calderón, "Tejano Politics," *Handbook of Texas,* Texas
    State Historical Association, February 1, 1996, updated Febru-
    ary 15, 2020, www.tshaonline.org/handbook/entries/tejano
    -politics.

18. "Demographic Patterns," section 2 of *Central Texas Assessment of Fair Housing,* draft report (Denver, Colo.: Root Policy Research, March 4, 2019), 2, shared by the city of Austin, www.austintexas .gov/sites/default/files/files/Housing/DRAFT_Central_TX_AI _March_2019_Section_Two_A.pdf.

19. "Demographic Patterns," 2.

20. "Demographic Patterns," 2.

21. Luke Winkie, "Austin Was Built to Be Segregated," *Vice,* June 16, 2014, www.vice.com/en/article/nnqdk7/austin-was-built-to-be -segregated.

22. Luz Moreno-Lozano, "As Austin's Black Community Shrinks, Moves to Suburbs, Community Leaders Push for Change, *Austin American-Statesman,* May 30, 2021, www.statesman.com/story/ news/2021/05/30/austins-black-community-shrinking-community -leaders-push-change/6547090002.

23. Alexa Ura, "Texas Cities Again Lead Population Growth, and Austin Is Now Country's 10th Largest," *Texas Tribune,* May 18, 2023, www.texastribune.org/2023/05/18/texas-cities-census-growth.

24. Hansi Lo Wang, "Broken Promises on Display at Native American Treaties Exhibit," *Code Switch,* NPR, January 18, 2015, www.npr .org/sections/codeswitch/2015/01/18/368559990/broken-promises -on-display-at-native-american-treaties-exhibit.

25. Treaty with the Six Nations, November 11, 1794, T.S. RIT 21, transcribed in "Treaty Between the United States and the Six Nations Signed at Konondaigua, New York, with the Instrument of Ratification Signed by President George Washington and Secretary of State Edmund Randolph on January 21, 1795," National Archives Catalog, accessed May 29, 2023, quoted in Wang, "Broken Promises on Display."

26. Maria Diaz-Gonzalez, "The Complicated History of the Kinzua Dam and How It Changed Life for the Seneca People," Environmental Health News, January 30, 2020, www.ehn.org/seneca -nation-kinzua-dam-2644943791.html.

27. Autumn Whitefield-Madrano, "Treaty of Canandaigua Remains a Powerful Symbol of Native Sovereignty," *ICT*, July 22, 2011, updated September 13, 2018, https://indiancountrytoday.com/archive/treaty-of-canandaigua-remains-a-powerful-symbol-of-native-sovereignty.

28. Wang, "Broken Promises on Display."

29. Dennis Zotigh, "A Brief Balance of Power—The 1778 Treaty with the Delaware Nation," *Smithsonian,* May 21, 2018, www.smithsonianmag.com/blogs/national-museum-american-indian/2018/05/22/1778-delaware-treaty.

30. Treaty with the Delawares, September 17, 1778, transcribed in Charles J. Kappler, ed., *Indian Affairs: Laws and Treaties,* vol. 2 (Washington, D.C.: Government Printing Office, 1904), 3, https://americanindian.si.edu/static/nationtonation/pdf/Treaty-with-the-Delawares-1778.pdf, quoted in Zotigh, "Brief Balance of Power."

31. Treaty with the Delawares, quoted in Zotigh, "Brief Balance of Power."

32. "Gnadenhütten Massacre," History, November 9, 2009, updated July 11, 2023, www.history.com/topics/early-us/gnadenhutten-massacre.

33. Zotigh, "Brief Balance of Power."

34. "The Treaty of New Echota and the Trail of Tears," North Carolina Department of Natural and Cultural Resources, December 29, 2016, www.ncdcr.gov/blog/2016/12/29/treaty-new-echota-and-trail-tears.

35. "Frequently Asked Questions," Trail of Tears, National Park Service, accessed May 29, 2023, www.nps.gov/trte/faqs.htm.

36. Jess Kung and Shereen Marisol Meraji, "A Treacherous Choice and a Treaty Right," *Code Switch*, NPR, April 8, 2020, www.npr.org/2020/03/31/824647676/a-treacherous-choice-and-a-treaty-right.

37. National Geographic Education, "The Indian Removal Act and the Trail of Tears," https://education.nationalgeographic.org/resource/indian-removal-act-and-trail-tears.

38. Eli Rosenberg, "Andrew Jackson Was Called 'Indian Killer.' Trump Honored Navajos in Front of His Portrait," *Washington Post*, June 8, 2023, www.washingtonpost.com/news/retropolis/wp/2017/11/28/andrew-jackson-was-called-indian-killer-trump-honored-navajos-in-front-of-his-portrait.

39. Mariko Chang et al., *Lifting as We Climb: Women of Color, Wealth, and America's Future* (Oakland, Calif: Insight Center for Community Economic Development, Spring 2010), https://static1.squarespace.com/static/5c50b84131d4df5265e7392d/t/5c5c7801ec212d4fd499ba39/1549563907681/Lifting_As_We_Climb_InsightCCED_2010.pdf.

40. New Georgia Encyclopedia, s.v. "Sherman's Field Order No. 15," by Barton Myers, updated September 30, 2020, www.georgiaencyclopedia.org/articles/history-archaeology/shermans-field-order-no-15.

41. Henry Louis Gates, Jr., "The Truth Behind '40 Acres and a Mule,'" PBS, www.pbs.org/wnet/african-americans-many-rivers-to-cross/history/the-truth-behind-40-acres-and-a-mule. Gates cites the *New York Daily Tribune*, February 13, 1865, https://chroniclingamerica.loc.gov/lccn/sn83030213/1865-02-13/ed-1.

42. Gates, "Truth Behind '40 Acres and a Mule.'"

43. Kim Kozlowski, "Wall Built to Separate Whites, Blacks in Detroit 'An Important Story to Tell,'" *Detroit News*, updated July 10, 2019, www.detroitnews.com/story/news/local/detroit-city/2019/07/10/wall-built-separate-whites-blacks-detroit-an-important-story/1551503001.

44. Drew Desilver and Kristen Bialik, "Blacks and Hispanics Face Extra Challenges in Getting Home Loans," Pew Research Center, January 10, 2017, www.pewresearch.org/fact-tank/2017/01/10/blacks-and-hispanics-face-extra-challenges-in-getting-home-loans.

45. Nyamekye Daniel, "'Taking the American Dream from Us': Detroit Overtaxed Majority Black Homeowners $600M. They're Still Wait-

ing to be Repaid Years Later," Yahoo!, April 21, 2022, www.yahoo
.com/video/taking-american-dream-us-detroit-164000271.html.

46. Steve Neavling, "Detroit Illegally Overtaxed Homeowners $600M.
They're Still Waiting to Be Compensated," *Detroit Metro Times*,
April 14, 2022, www.metrotimes.com/news/detroit-illegally
-overtaxed-homeowners-600m-theyre-still-waiting-to-be
-compensated-29800877.

47. Nolan Cool, "Leaving Home Behind: The Fates of Japanese American Houses During Incarceration," National Museum of American
History, August 3, 2017, https://americanhistory.si.edu/blog/
japanese-american-houses.

48. PR Newswire, "Truist Donates $40 Million to Launch Innovative
Nonprofit Fund Supporting Ethnically, Racially Diverse and
Women-Owned Small Businesses," Truist, September 23, 2020,
https://media.truist.com/2020-09-23-Truist-Donates-40-Million-to
-Launch-Innovative-Nonprofit-Fund-Supporting-Ethnically
-Racially-Diverse-and-Women-Owned-Small-Businesses, quoted in
Shelby R. King, "The Post-Protest Pledges: Banks' Racial Equity
Initiatives," *Shelterforce*, February 22, 2022, https://shelterforce
.org/2022/02/22/the-post-protest-pledges-banks-racial-equity
-initiatives.

49. King, "Post-Protest Pledges."

50. Kevin Cohee and Teri Williams, "Why Us?" OneUnited Bank,
accessed January 31, 2023, www.oneunited.com/about-us.

51. "Why Did OneUnited Bank Support the #TakeAKnee Movement?"
OneUnited Bank, accessed June 8, 2023, https://community
.oneunited.com/s/article/Why-does-OneUnited-Bank-support-the
-TakeAKnee-Movement.

52. William Yardley, "Bob Fletcher Dies at 101; Helped Japanese-
Americans," *New York Times*, June 6, 2013, www.nytimes.com/
2013/06/07/us/bob-fletcher-dies-at-101-saved-farms-of-interned
-japanese-americans.html.

Chapter 8: Appreciation Versus Appropriation

1.   "About," National Museum of African American Music, accessed May 29, 2023, www.nmaam.org/about.

2.   Encyclopedia of Alabama, s.v. "Willie Mae 'Big Mama' Thornton," accessed June 9, 2023, https://encyclopediaofalabama.org/article/willie-mae-big-mama-thornton.

3.   Samuel Z. Hamilton, "Willie Mae 'Big Mama' Thornton (1926–1984)," BlackPast, March 28, 2011, www.blackpast.org/african-american-history/thornton-willie-mae-big-mama-1926-1984.

4.   Encyclopedia of Alabama, s.v. "'Big Mama' Thornton."

5.   Arun Starkey, "The Mother of Rock and Roll: The Extraordinary Life of Big Mama Thornton," Far Out, December 11, 2021, https://faroutmagazine.co.uk/the-extraordinary-life-of-big-mama-thornton.

6.   "1952: 'Hound Dog' Is Recorded for the First Time by Big Mama Thornton," History, April 1, 2010, updated August 16, 2023, www.history.com/this-day-in-history/hound-dog-is-recorded-for-the-first-time-by-big-mama-thornton.

7.   Starkey, "Mother of Rock and Roll."

8.   Cynthia Shearer, "The Thinning of Big Mama," *Oxford American*, February 15, 2017, https://oxfordamerican.org/magazine/issue-95-winter-2016/the-thinning-of-big-mama.

9.   Harry Thompson, "Elvis 'Stole' Style from Little-Known Black Musician Who Sounds Identical," *Mirror,* November 3, 2021, www.mirror.co.uk/3am/celebrity-news/elvis-stole-style-little-known-25362045.

10.   "Tuti Frutti by Little Richard," Songfacts, accessed June 9, 2023, www.songfacts.com/facts/little-richard/tutti-frutti.

11.   Chris Jancelewicz, "The 'Whitewashing' of Black Music: A Dark Chapter in Rock History," *Global News,* July 30, 2019, https://

globalnews.ca/news/4321150/black-music-whitewashing-classic
-rock.

12. "Enlightenment, Freedom, and Slavery," Monticello, accessed
May 29, 2023, www.monticello.org/slavery/paradox-of-liberty/
thomas-jefferson-liberty-slavery/a-society-dependent-on-slavery/
enlightenment-freedom-and-slavery.

13. William Shakespeare, *A Midsummer Night's Dream*, Ben Greet
Shakespeare for Young Readers and Amateur Players ed. (New
York: Doubleday, 1912). 2.2.53, www.google.com/books/edition/A
_Midsummer_Night_s_Dream/BB0lAAAAMAAJ?hl=en&gbpv=0.
References are to act, scene, and page.

14. Shakespeare, *Midsummer Night's Dream*, 3.2.99.

15. Farah Karim-Cooper, "Anti-Racist Shakespeare," Shakespeare's
Globe, May 26, 2020, www.shakespearesglobe.com/discover/blogs
-and-features/2020/05/26/anti-racist-shakespeare/#0.

16. "Blackface: The Birth of an American Stereotype," National Museum of African American History and Culture, Smithsonian,
accessed June 9, 2023, https://nmaahc.si.edu/explore/stories/
blackface-birth-american-stereotype; Dr. David Pilgrim, "Who Was
Jim Crow?" Jim Crow Museum, September 2000, updated 2023,
https://jimcrowmuseum.ferris.edu/who/index.htm.

17. *Encyclopaedia Britannica Online*, s.v. "Thomas Dartmouth Rice,"
updated September 15, 2023, www.britannica.com/biography/
Thomas-Dartmouth-Rice.

18. *Encyclopaedia Britannica Online*, s.v. "Minstrel Show," updated September 2, 2020, www.britannica.com/art/minstrel-show.

19. James Wintle, "Stephen Collins Foster: A Guide to Resources,"
ed. Robin Rausch, Library of Congress, March 20, 2020, https://
guides.loc.gov/stephen-foster. Wintle cites Harold Vincent Milli-
gan, *Stephen Collins Foster: A Biography of America's Folk-Song Com-
poser* (New York: G. Schirmer, 1920), www.google.com/books/
edition/Stephen_Collins_Foster/UOIuAAAAIAAJ?hl=en&gbpv=0.

20. Allyson Hobbs, "A Hundred Years Later, 'The Birth of a Nation'

Hasn't Gone Away," *New Yorker,* December 13, 2015, www
.newyorker.com/culture/culture-desk/hundred-years-later-birth
-nation-hasnt-gone-away.

21. *Encyclopaedia Britannica Online,* s.v. "The Birth of a Nation," by
Dick Lehr and Lee Pfeiffer, updated May 18, 2023, www.britannica
.com/topic/The-Birth-of-a-Nation#ref1216929.

22. *The Birth of a Nation,* directed by D. W. Griffith (Los Angeles,
Calif.: Epoch, 1915), full movie shared by Khalbrae, in "The Birth
of a Nation—Full Movie—(1915) HD—The Masterpiece of Racist
Cinema," August 1, 2015, on YouTube, 1:32:30, www.youtube
.com/watch?v=ebtiJH3EOHo. It's worth noting that, while the
film's wording deviated slightly from the true quote, Wilson did
write and publish this sentiment in his five-volume *A History of the
American People*: "The white men of the South were aroused by the
mere instinct of self-preservation . . . until at last there had sprung
into existence a great *Ku Klux Klan,* an 'Invisible Empire of the
South,' bound together in loose organization to protect the southern country." Woodrow Wilson, *A History of the American People,*
vol. 5 (New York: Harper & Brothers, 1902), 58, 60, www.google
.com/books/edition/A_History_of_the_American_People/
KaUQ2j1xRocC?hl=en&gbpv=0.

23. Wilson, *History of the American People,* vol. 5, 60. See also Becky
Little, "How Woodrow Wilson Tried to Reverse Black American
Progress," History, July 14, 2020, updated September 11, 2023,
www.history.com/news/woodrow-wilson-racial-segregation-jim
-crow-ku-klux-klan.

24. Ed Rampell, "'The Birth of a Nation': The Most Racist Movie Ever
Made," *Washington Post,* March 3, 2015, www.washingtonpost
.com/posteverything/wp/2015/03/03/the-birth-of-a-nation.

25. *Encyclopaedia Britannica Online,* s.v. "Ku Klux Klan," updated September 15, 2023, www.britannica.com/topic/Ku-Klux-Klan.

26. Dorian Lynskey, "'A Public Menace': How the Fight to Ban *The
Birth of a Nation* Shaped the Nascent Civil Rights Movement,"

March 31, 2015, https://slate.com/culture/2015/03/the-birth-of-a
-nation-how-the-fight-to-censor-d-w-griffiths-film-shaped
-american-history.html.

27. Nicholas Sammond, "From Blackface to Blackfishing," interview
by Gene Demby, February 13, 2019, in *Code Switch*, NPR, produced
by Leah Donnella and Kumari Devarajan, podcast, MP3 audio,
4:15, www.npr.org/2019/02/13/694149912/from-blackface-to
-blackfishing.

28. Nicholas Sammond, *Birth of an Industry: Blackface Minstrelsy and
the Rise of American Animation* (Durham, N.C.: Duke University
Press, 2015), 5.

29. "Disney Updates Content Warning for Racism in Classic Films,"
BBC News, October 16, 2020, www.bbc.com/news/world-us
-canada-54566087.

30. Ben Kesslen, "Aunt Jemima Brand to Change Name, Remove Image
That Quaker Says Is 'Based on a Racial Stereotype,'" NBC News,
June, 17, 2020, www.nbcnews.com/news/us-news/aunt-jemima
-brand-will-change-name-remove-image-quaker-says-n1231260.

31. Some of McDaniel's mammy characters appear in the following
films: *Judge Priest* (directed by John Ford, 1934); *The Little Colonel*
(directed by David Butler, 1935); *Alice Adams* (directed by George
Stevens, 1935); *Music Is Magic* (directed by George Marshall,
1935); *Saratoga* (directed by Jack Conway, 1937); and *The Mad
Miss Manton* (directed by Leigh Jason, 1938).

32. *The Amos 'n' Andy Show,* "Sapphire's Easter Outfit," featuring Free-
man Gosden, Ernestine Wade, and Charles Correll, aired April 9,
1950, on CBS, recording shared by The Classic Archives Old Time
Radio Channel, "Amos 'n' Andy, Old Time Radio, 500409 Sapphire's Easter Outfit," March 11, 2017, on YouTube, https://youtu
.be/qa3kv-5uCtE.

33. "The Sapphire Caricature," Jim Crow Museum, accessed May 29,
2023, https://jimcrowmuseum.ferris.edu/antiblack/sapphire.htm.

34. "Sapphire Caricature."

35. *Encyclopaedia Britannica Online,* s.v. "Bruce Lee," by Adam Augustyn, updated April 24, 2023, www.britannica.com/biography/Bruce-Lee.

36. "Bruce Lee's Journey from Street Tough to Cinema Legend," *Newsweek,* December 12, 2017, www.newsweek.com/street-fighter-bruce-lees-tough-childhood-lead-fame-743061.

37. *Encyclopaedia Britannica Online,* s.v. "Bruce Lee."

38. "Jeet Kune Do," Bruce Lee Foundation, accessed June 10, 2023, https://bruceleefoundation.org/jeetkunedo.

39. *Encyclopaedia Britannica Online,* s.v. "Bruce Lee."

40. "The Kato Show: Bruce Lee as the Green Hornet's Sidekick," *Newsweek,* November 20, 2015, www.newsweek.com/bruce-lee-king-fu-martial-arts-390811.

41. Melanie McFarland, "'Warrior' Brings Bruce Lee's TV Vision to Life, Vividly and Violently," *Salon,* April 5, 2019, www.salon.com/2019/04/05/warrior-brings-bruce-lees-tv-vision-to-life-vividly-and-violently. See also Douglas Parkes, "Bruce Lee's Unfinished Film and TV Projects Revealed, from HBO Max's Warrior to the Controversial Game of Death—But Did Warner Bros. Really Steal Kung Fu from the Martial Arts Legend?" November 26, 2021, www.scmp.com/magazines/style/celebrity/article/3157371/bruce-lees-unfinished-film-and-tv-projects-revealed-hbo.

42. Kat Moon, "How a New *Kung Fu* TV Series Is Reclaiming Much More Than Just the Martial Arts," *Time,* April 7, 2021, https://time.com/5953090/kung-fu-cw-asian-representation.

43. *Encyclopaedia Britannica Online,* s.v. "Bruce Lee."

44. Kimmy Yam, "How Bruce Lee Became a Symbol of Solidarity with the Black Community," NBC News, June 11, 2020, www.nbcnews.com/news/asian-america/how-bruce-lee-became-symbol-solidarity-black-community-n1230136.

45. Sean Tirman, "Ranked: The 5 Best Bruce Lee Movies of All Time," Hiconsumption, March 11, 2021, https://hiconsumption.com/best-bruce-lee-movies-ranked.

46. Michael Cieply, "For Movie Stars, the Big Money Is Now Deferred," *New York Times,* March 3, 2010, www.nytimes.com/2010/03/04/movies/04stars.html.

47. Lee Vann, "Mo'Nique Explains Taking $50K for Her Oscar-Winning 'Precious' Role," Urban Daily, April 18, 2015, https://theurbandaily.com/2999917/monique-explains-50k-for-precious.

48. "Writers & Authors," Data USA, accessed May 29, 2023, https://datausa.io/profile/soc/writers-authors.

49. "Black History Month: Top African American Television Characters (Part Two!)," BET, accessed June 10, 2023, www.bet.com/photo-gallery/cufy1u/black-history-month-top-african-american-television-characters-part-two/a23b5s.

50. Marwa Eltagouri, "Chance the Rapper Hands Out Money for Arts Programs at 20 CPS Schools," *Chicago Tribune,* September 1, 2017, www.chicagotribune.com/news/breaking/ct-chance-the-rapper-back-to-school-0902-20170901-story.html.

51. Luchina Fisher, "How Chance the Rapper Earned BET's Humanitarian Award," ABC News, June 26, 2017, https://abcnews.go.com/Entertainment/chance-rapper-earned-bets-humanitarian-award/story?id=48281901#.

52. Gil Kaufman, "Anita Baker Thanks Chance the Rapper for Helping Her Regain Ownership of Her Masters," *Billboard,* May 31, 2022, www.billboard.com/music/rb-hip-hop/anita-baker-thanks-chance-the-rapper-helping-regain-ownership-masters-1235078950.

CHAPTER 9: SHUT UP AND DRIBBLE

1. "Looking Back: LeBron James' 10 Trips to the Finals," NBA, accessed June 10, 2023, www.nba.com/lebron-james-past-finals-trips-history.

2. "LeBron James Contributes $2.5 Million to the National Museum of African American History and Culture's Muhammad Ali Display," National Museum of African History and Culture, Smithson-

ian, November 17, 2016, https://nmaahc.si.edu/about/news/lebron
-james-contributes-25-million-national-museum-african-american
-history-and.

3. "Making a Difference with the LeBron James I Promise School,"
Schwinn, accessed February 2, 2023, www.schwinnbikes.com/
blogs/compass/making-a-difference-with-the-lebron-james-i
-promise-school.

4. LeBron James, "Kevin Durant x LeBron x Cari Champion | Rolling
with the Champion," interview by Cari Champion, January 14,
2018, on *Rolling with the Champion,* video shared by Uninterrupted,
February 15, 2018, on YouTube, 7:30, www.youtube.com/watch?v
=HtNWc1AIU20&t=2s.

5. Laura Ingraham, *The Ingraham Angle,* aired February 15, 2018, on
Fox News, video shared by Sports Illustrated (@SInow), February 16, 2018, 7:50 a.m., on Twitter, https://twitter.com/SInow/
status/964512313175871488. See also Emily Sullivan, "Laura Ingraham Told LeBron James to Shut Up and Dribble; He Went to
the Hoop," Two Way (blog), NPR, February 19, 2018, www.npr
.org/sections/thetwo-way/2018/02/19/587097707/laura-ingraham
-told-lebron-james-to-shutup-and-dribble-he-went-to-the
-hoop.

6. Uninterrupted (@uninterrupted), "We will never just 'shut up and
dribble,'" Twitter video, June 4, 2020, 5:19 p.m., https://twitter
.com/uninterrupted/status/1268683925737488385.

7. Merlisa Lawrence Corbett, "Why Are There So Few Black Team
Owners in US Professional Sports?" *Guardian* (US), March 14,
2023, www.theguardian.com/business/2023/mar/14/us-black
-owners-professional-sports-teams.

8. "Exclusion of Jews," The Nazi Olympics Berlin 1936, United States
Holocaust Memorial Museum, accessed June 6, 2023, www.ushmm
.org/exhibition/olympics/?content=sports_chronology&lang=en.

9. "Persecution of Athletes," The Nazi Olympics Berlin 1936, United
States Holocaust Memorial Museum, accessed June 6, 2023, www

.ushmm.org/exhibition/olympics/?content=persecution_athletes&
lang=en.

10. "Daniel Prenn," International Jewish Sports Hall of Fame, accessed June 6, 2023, http://www.jewishsports.net/BioPages/Daniel
Prenn.htm.

11. United States Holocaust Memorial Museum, "The Nazi Olympics
Berlin 1936," Holocaust Encyclopedia, July 28, 2021, https://
encyclopedia.ushmm.org/content/en/article/the-nazi-olympics
-berlin-1936.

12. *Encyclopaedia Britannica Online,* s.v. "Jesse Owens," updated September 8, 2023, www.britannica.com/biography/Jesse-Owens.

13. Marijke Everts, "Athlete Jesse Owens: Battling Poverty and Racial
Bigotry with Sporting Success," Europeana (blog), February 3,
2021, www.europeana.eu/en/blog/jesse-owens-an-athletes-struggle
-against-poverty-and-racial-bigotry-despite.

14. Avery Brundage, quoted in Everts, "Athlete Jesse Owens."

15. Sarah Fling, "'Running Against the World': Jesse Owens and the
1936 Berlin Olympics," White House Historical Association, June 28,
2021, www.whitehousehistory.org/running-against-the-world.

16. "A True American Hero—Jesse Owens," Black History Month
(website), January 2, 2017, www.blackhistorymonth.org.uk/
article/section/sporting-heroes/jesse-owens.

17. United States Holocaust Memorial Museum, "Albert Speer," Holocaust Encyclopedia, November 28, 2005, https://encyclopedia
.ushmm.org/content/en/article/albert-speer.

18. Albert Speer, *Inside the Third Reich: Memoirs* (New York: Simon and
Schuster, 1970), 73.

19. "Ruth Owens; Widow of Legendary Olympian," *Los Angeles Times,*
June 30, 2001, www.latimes.com/archives/la-xpm-2001-jun-30-me
-17013-story.html.

20. John Ashdown, "50 Stunning Olympic Moments No6: Jesse
Owens's Four Gold Medals, 1936," *Guardian* (US), December 21,

2011, www.theguardian.com/sport/london-2012-olympics-blog/2011/dec/21/jesse-owens-four-gold-medals.

21. "Jesse Owens Charges Roosevelt Snubbed," *Jefferson City Post-Tribune,* October 16, 1936, quoted in Fling, "'Running Against the World.'"

22. Geraint Hughes and Tejas Kotecha, "Iconic 1968 Olympic Protest: The Inside Story of the Protest by Tommie Smith and John Carlos at the Mexico Olympics," Sky Sports, accessed June 10, 2023, www.skysports.com/olympics/story-telling/15234/12242508/1968-iconic-olympics-protest-john-carlos-explains-what-happened-on-the-stand-and-why-its-still-relevant-today.

23. A Dimond, "Iconic Olympic Moments: The Black Power Salute," Bleacher Report, July 24, 2008, https://bleacherreport.com/articles/40675-iconic-olympic-moments-the-black-power-salute.

24. John Carlos and Dave Zirin, *The John Carlos Story: The Sports Moment That Changed the World* (Chicago: Haymarket Books, 2011), 120, quoted in DeNeen L. Brown, "'A Cry for Freedom': The Black Power Salute That Rocked the World 50 Years Ago," *Washington Post,* October 16, 2018, www.washingtonpost.com/history/2018/10/16/a-cry-freedom-black-power-salute-that-rocked-world-years-ago.

25. Carlos and Zirin, *John Carlos Story,* 121, quoted in DeNeen L. Brown, "They Didn't #TakeTheKnee: The Black Power Protest Salute That Shook the World in 1968," *Washington Post,* September 23, 2017, www.washingtonpost.com/news/retropolis/wp/2017/09/24/they-didnt-takeaknee-the-black-power-protest-salute-that-shook-the-world-in-1968.

26. Nadra Kareem Nittle, "Why Black American Athletes Raised Their Fists at the 1968 Olympics," History, updated September 12, 2023, www.history.com/news/black-athletes-raise-fists-1968-olympics.

27. Ted Widmer, "Why Two Black Athletes Raised Their Fists During the Anthem," *New York Times,* October 16, 2018, www.nytimes.com/2018/10/16/opinion/why-smith-and-carlos-raised-their-fists

.html. Widmer cites Tommie Smith and David Steele, *Silent Gesture* (Philadelphia, Pa.: Temple University Press, 2007). However, other sources list this same quote as having come from Smith's comments to the press after making his Black Power salute. See Fred Jeter, "Olympic 'Black Power Salute' Rises 50 Years Later," *Richmond Free Press,* November 1, 2018, https://richmondfreepress .com/news/2018/nov/01/olympic-black-power-salute-rises-50-years -later.

28. Catherine E. Shoichet and Jill Martin, "Off-Duty Cops Walk Out Over WNBA players' Black Lives Matter Shirts," CNN, updated July 12, 2016, www.cnn.com/2016/07/12/us/wnba-minnesota-lynx -black-lives-matter-shirts/index.html.

29. Shoichet and Martin, "Off-Duty Cops Walk Out." Shoichet and Martin cite the Minneapolis *Star Tribune,* but the original article is no longer available online.

30. Matt Ellentuck, "4 Minneapolis Cops Leave Minnesota Lynx Security Posts After Players Call for Justice and Peace," SBNation, July 12, 2016, www.sbnation.com/2016/7/12/12160566/ minneapolis-police-minnesota-lynx-wnba-protest. Ellentuck cites the *Star Tribune.*

31. Betsy Hodges, "Bob Kroll's remarks about the Lynx are jackass remarks," Facebook, July 12, 2016, www.facebook.com/betsy.hodges .7/posts/10208437502789800?pnref=story, quoted in Ellentuck, "4 Minneapolis Cops Leave."

32. Jordan J. Wilson, "Indiana Fever Speak Out After WNBA Fines Team, Players for Black Lives Matters Shirts," *Indianapolis Star,* July 21, 2016, www.indystar.com/story/sports/basketball/wnba/ 2016/07/21/indiana-fever-among-those-fined-wnba-shirts-wake -shootings/87395098.

33. Chris Bumbaca, "Timeline: The WNBA Has Been on Forefront of Racial Justice Movement for Years," *USA Today,* August 6, 2020, www.usatoday.com/story/sports/wnba/2020/08/06/wnba -players-protest-racial-justice-years-timeline-kelly-loeffler/

3304129001. Bumbaca cites an Instagram post from Tina Charles (@tina31charles), but the original post is no longer available online.

34. Kurt Streeter, "Jonathan Irons, Helped by W.N.B.A. Star Maya Moore, Freed from Prison," *New York Times,* July 1, 2020, updated September 16, 2020, www.nytimes.com/2020/07/01/sports/ basketball/maya-moore-jonathan-irons-freed.html.

35. Rashawn Ray, "Five Things John Lewis Taught Us About Getting in 'Good Trouble,'" Brookings Institution, July 23, 2020, www .brookings.edu/blog/how-we-rise/2020/07/23/five-things-john -lewis-taught-us-about-getting-in-good-trouble.

36. John Branch, "The Awakening of Colin Kaepernick," *New York Times,* September 7, 2017, www.nytimes.com/2017/09/07/sports/ colin-kaepernick-nfl-protests.html.

37. Branch, "Awakening of Colin Kaepernick."

38. Ameer Hasan Loggins, "Guest Column: The True Colin Kaepernick . . . from Someone Who Has Been There and Calls Him a Friend," *Athletic,* August 26, 2017, https://theathletic.com/ 89431/2017/08/26/guest-column-the-true-colin-kaepernick-from -someone-who-has-been-there-and-calls-him-a-friend.

39. Giles Fraser, "Like the Prophets of Old, Colin Kaepernick Uses Prayer as Protest," *Guardian* (US), September 28, 2017, www .theguardian.com/commentisfree/belief/2017/sep/28/like-the -prophets-of-old-colin-kaepernick-uses-prayer-as-protest; Angela Denker, "Colin Kaepernick and the Powerful Religious Act of Kneeling," *Washington Post,* September 24, 2017, www .washingtonpost.com/news/acts-of-faith/wp/2017/09/24/colin -kaepernick-and-the-powerful-religious-act-of-kneeling.

40. Charles Curtis, "Colin Kaepernick: I Won't Stand 'to Show Pride in a Flag for a Country That Oppresses Black People,'" For the Win, August 27, 2016, https://ftw.usatoday.com/2016/08/colin -kaepernick-49ers-national-anthem-sit-explains. Curtis cites Steve Wyche, whose original NFL story, "Colin Kaepernick Explains

Why He Sat During the National Anthem," is no longer available online.

41. Juliet Macur, "Colin Kaepernick's Anthem Protest Leaves the N.F.L. Necessarily Uneasy," *New York Times,* September 7, 2016, www.nytimes.com/2016/09/08/sports/football/colin-kaepernick -anthem-protest-nfl-roger-goodell.html. Macur cites the Associated Press for the interview quotes with NFL commissioner Roger Goodell, but the original article is no longer available online.

42. John Breech, "Poll: Majority of Americans Disagree with Colin Kaepernick's Protest," CBS Sports, September 15, 2016, www .cbssports.com/nfl/news/poll-majority-of-americans-disagree-with -colin-kaepernicks-protest.

43. Julie Hirschfeld Davis, "Trump Calls for Boycott if N.F.L. Doesn't Crack Down on Anthem Protests," *New York Times,* September 24, 2017, www.nytimes.com/2017/09/24/us/politics/trump-calls-for -boycott-if-nfl-doesnt-crack-down-on-anthem-protests.html.

44. Bryan Armen Graham, "Donald Trump Blasts NFL Anthem Protesters: 'Get That Son of a Bitch off the Field,'" *Guardian* (US), September 23, 2017, www.theguardian.com/sport/2017/sep/22/ donald-trump-nfl-national-anthem-protests.

45. Guardian Sport, "Nike's 'Dream Crazy' Advert Starring Colin Kaepernick Wins Emmy," *Guardian* (US), September 16, 2019, www .theguardian.com/sport/2019/sep/16/nikes-dream-crazy-advert -starring-colin-kaepernick-wins-emmy.

46. Roger Goodell on behalf of the National Football League (@NFL), "We, the NFL, condemn racism and the systematic oppression of Black People," Twitter video, June 5, 2020, 4:31 p.m., https:// twitter.com/NFL/status/1269034074552721408. See also Ethan Cadeaux, "Roger Goodell Releases Statement Condemning Racism, Admits NFL Was Wrong Not Listening to Players," NBC Sports, June 5, 2020, www.nbcsports.com/washington/redskins/ roger-goodell-releases-statement-condemning-racism-admits-nfl -was-wrong-not-listening.

47. Dana Kennedy, "Most Americans Now Agree with Colin Kaepernick's Anthem Protest: Poll," *New York Post*, June 13, 2020, https://nypost.com/2020/06/13/most-americans-now-agree-with-colin-kaepernicks-protest-poll. Kennedy cites Jay Busbee, "Yahoo News / YouGov Poll: Majority of Americans Now Support NFL Players' Right to Protest," Yahoo! Sports, June 11, 2020, https://sports.yahoo.com/poll-majority-of-americans-now-support-nfl-players-right-to-protest-151212603.html.

48. Judy Battista, "NFL Commits $250M over 10-Year Period to Combat Systemic Racism," NFL, June 11, 2020, www.nfl.com/news/nfl-commits-250m-over-10-year-period-to-combat-systemic-racism.

49. Rob Maaddi, "NFL Returns Social Justice Helmet Decals, End Zone Stencils," AP News, September 2, 2021, https://apnews.com/article/sports-nfl-c10867c92924cc9a59c99e220c8ee84e.

50. Michael Levenson, "N.F.L. Will Allow Six Social Justice Messages on Players' Helmets," *New York Times*, September 5, 2021, www.nytimes.com/2021/09/05/sports/nfl-social-justice.html.

51. Scott Polacek, "Roger Goodell Says He Won't Discipline NFL Players for Kneeling During Anthem," Bleacher Report, August 24, 2020, https://bleacherreport.com/articles/2906106-roger-goodell-says-he-wont-discipline-nfl-players-for-kneeling-during-anthem.

52. Levenson, "N.F.L. Will Allow."

53. "Share of Players in the NFL in 2022, by Ethnicity," Statista, 2023, www.statista.com/statistics/1167935/racial-diversity-nfl-players.

54. Fred Jeter, "NFL Black Coaches Now Total 3; Flores Hired as Assistant Coach in Pittsburgh," *Richmond Free Press*, March 3, 2022, https://richmondfreepress.com/news/2022/mar/03/nfl-black-coaches-now-total-3-flores-hired-assista.

55. Justin Holiday, "Athletes and Activism," interview by Latasha Morrison, in *Be the Bridge*, produced by Travon Potts, podcast, 32:49, https://bethebridge.com/episode-13-athletes-and-activism-with-justin-holiday.

Chapter 10: One Body, One Spirit, One Hope

1. Chip Reid, "What Was Heard Inside the Freddie Gray Van," CBS News, April 30, 2015, www.cbsnews.com/news/what-was-heard -inside-the-freddie-gray-van.

2. "Spine Nearly Severed in Police Custody, but Few Explanations," CBS News, April 20, 2015, www.cbsnews.com/news/freddie-gray -nearly-severed-spine-police-custody-few-explanations.

3. Mike Cummings, "Yale Sociologist Phil Gorski on the Threat of White Christian Nationalism," *Yale News,* March 15, 2022, https:// news.yale.edu/2022/03/15/yale-sociologist-phil-gorski-threat-white -christian-nationalism.

4. David M. Goldenberg, *The Curse of Ham: Race and Slavery in Early Judaism, Christianity, and Islam* (Princeton, N.J.: Princeton University Press, 2003), 141.

5. Jeannie Ortega Law, "'Slave Bible' on Display at Museum of the Bible; Edition Removes Chapters to Uphold Slavery," *Christian Post,* April 26, 2019, www.christianpost.com/news/slave-bible-on -display-at-museum-of-the-bible-edition-removes-chapters-to -uphold-slavery.html.

6. Michel Martin, "Slave Bible from the 1800s Omitted Key Passages That Could Incite Rebellion," *All Things Considered,* NPR, December 9, 2018, www.npr.org/2018/12/09/674995075/slave-bible-from -the-1800s-omitted-key-passages-that-could-incite-rebellion.

7. Jerry Falwell, "Segregation or Integration: Which?" (Lynchburg, Va.: Thomas Road Baptist Church, 1958), quoted in Michelle Goldberg, "Of Course the Christian Right Supports Trump," *New York Times,* January 26, 2018, www.nytimes.com/2018/01/26/ opinion/trump-christian-right-values.html.

8. Cummings, "Yale Sociologist Phil Gorski."

9. Ruth Graham, "A Pastor and His Congregation Part Ways," *New York Times,* May 10, 2022, www.nytimes.com/interactive/2022/05/ 10/us/evangelical-pastor-politics.html.

About the Author

Latasha Morrison is a distinguished author renowned for her transformative work in fostering racial reconciliation and unity.

As the *New York Times* bestselling author of the influential book *Be the Bridge,* she captured the hearts and minds of readers worldwide with her powerful words and insightful perspectives. *Be the Bridge* has become a beacon of hope, guiding individuals and communities toward a future free from racial division.

Beyond her literary achievements, Morrison's insight and expertise have been featured in outlets such as *Oprah Daily* and *USA Today,* in which she inspires readers to engage in meaningful conversations about race, justice, and equality, further solidifying her as a leading voice in the fight against racial injustice.

In recognition of her outstanding efforts, Morrison was honored with the Christian Book of the Year Award by the Evangelical Christian Publishers Association. This esteemed accolade highlights her exceptional literary contributions and the profound impact she has had on the lives of countless individuals seeking to build bridges of understanding and compassion.

Through her work as the founder of the nonprofit Be the Bridge, Morrison continues to ignite conversations, challenge societal norms, and empower others to take action toward a more inclusive and equitable world. Her commitment to fostering unity and dismantling racial barriers makes her a beacon of hope and an inspiration to all who aspire to create lasting change.

Additional Resources

Access additional resources, including Be the Bridge Academy; Better-mode, the platform of Be the Bridge groups; links to my first book, *Be the Bridge: Pursuing God's Heart for Racial Reconciliation*; guides and curriculum; and Be the Bridge social media pages, by scanning the QR code below.

To scan the QR code, open the camera app on your phone and point it at the QR code below. A notification will then pop up, alerting you to the source page. Click on the link to take you to a landing page with all the available resources.

https://bethebridge.com/brown-faces-white-spaces

Bring the Reconciliation Power
of the Gospel to the Racial Divide

Firmly rooted in the biblical principle of
reconciliation, *Be the Bridge* is a power-packed
guide that inspires and equips Christians to
dismantle barriers and pursue racial healing.

Learn more at BeTheBridge.com